KEEP OFF THE GRASS

KEEP
OFF
THE
GRASS

Gabriel G. Nahas, M.D., Ph.D., D.Sc.

Foreword by
Jacques Yves Cousteau

PAUL S. ERIKSSON, *PUBLISHER*
Middlebury, Vermont 05753

First edition published 1976 by Reader's Digest Press
Second edition published 1978 by Pergamon Press
Third edition published 1982 by Futura
Fourth edition published 1985 by Paul S. Eriksson
Printed in the United States of America
10 9 8 7 6

Library of Congress Cataloging-in-Publication Data

Nahas, Gabriel G., 1920–
    Keep off the grass / by Gabriel G. Nahas. – 5th ed.
       p.   cm.
    Includes bibliographical references.
    Includes index.
    ISBN 0-8397-4384-X : $10.95
    1. Marihuana–Toxicology. 2. Marihuana–Pharmacology.
3. Marihuana–Pathology–Research. I. Title.
    [DNLM: 1. Cannabis. 2. Substance Abuse.   WM 276 N153k]
RA1242.C17N33 1990
615′.7827–dc20
DNLM/DLC
for Library of Congress   90–3658
                                                  CIP

To Marilyn, to our children and grandchildren.
To the parents of America
and to Peggy Mann, the valiant champion of
their cause.

Contents

Foreword

Some ants are among the few social animals known to use "drugs." Their custom is to drag live plant lice deep into their nests, to ingest some of the juice excreted by their captives, and thus, apparently, to find in the resulting intoxication relief from the pressure of their working day. But these ants pay a price for their intoxication because the "drug" also reduces their awareness and their aggressiveness. They are then unable to compose an adequate defense should their colony be attacked by another "nation" of ants.

Marijuana, like most drugs ingested by *man,* gives the user the impression that his senses are enhanced, when in fact they have been distorted and impaired. Those who explore beneath the surface of the sea know this problem. Diving on air, deeper than one hundred feet, they are subjected to what is often called "rapture of the deep" or "nitrogen narcosis," which I understand, is subjectively very similar to the feeling experienced when smoking a "joint." "Stoned" by "rapture of the deep," a diver is seriously endangered because he loses his instinct for self-preservation. But on land, car drivers "stoned" by marijuana become a hazard not only to themselves but also to all the other users of the road!

One of the oldest intoxicants known to humankind, marijuana is now widely spread throughout the Western world, where two decades ago it was practically unused. But little has been known about the *scientific* effects of the drug. In this timely and important book, Dr. Gabriel Nahas describes, as a result of careful scientific studies, the damaging biological effects associated with the marijuana habit. They are of the most serious nature. They impair the formation of basic chemicals essential for the orderly division of our cells, for the normal transmission of heredity, and for the preservation of memory. If we remain ignorant of these effects, we too may lose our instinct for self-preservation!

If we are concerned about the external pollutants that threaten our environment, we should be equally concerned about internal pollutants—like marijuana products. For sheer survival, we must defend ourselves against both kinds of pollution. Furthermore, I believe that we need to keep all our senses constantly at their maximum keenness if we are to enjoy and to take full advantage of our short participation in the miracle of life.

Jacques Yves Cousteau

Preface

It is with both pleasure and a sense of the need to urge caution that I introduce this crusading effort of my friend and colleague Dr. Gabriel Nahas. The pleasure derives from Dr. Nahas' accomplishment in this book. To it he has brought the same enthusiasm and zeal that have marked everything he has done throughout an extraordinarily active life. During World War II, Dr. Nahas, then an adolescent, helped many downed British and American airmen to pass through occupied France to the safety of Switzerland or Spain. His efficiency and courage in the face of the risks involved in running this underground operation became legendary. In his subsequent career as a scientist, Dr. Nahas has not been one to shirk the unpopular problem, nor to do it less than full scientific justice, as his efforts in relation to the subject of this book testify.

He is one among a growing number of physicians who believe that, besides providing for the physical, as well as the mental, well-being of the individual, medicine must become increasingly aware of, and responsive to, the demands of the community.

Thanks to the work of Dr. Nahas and others who have conducted well-controlled investigations, some of the physiological effects of chronic exposure to marijuana of known potency are now being defined. There is no question in my mind that the chronic use of marijuana in these concentrations is hazardous, both to the user and also to the society that is exposed to the consequences of the user's judgment during his "high." But I believe that one must go beyond the superficial and obvious to ask: what is the relationship between drug use, pandemic in many sectors of American society, and socioeconomic status? What is there in American education that might facilitate habituation/addiction to the use of psychoactive materials? How does the problem of drug use relate to the all-important question of ethics in the developing society, and to the dignity of man? I believe this constellation of questions is linked with the marijuana problem. Let the reader bear them in mind while going through Dr. Nahas's fascinating account.

André F. Cournand, M.D.
Winner of the Nobel Prize
in Medicine and Physiology

Introduction

Dr. Gabriel Nahas is one of the most knowledgeable scientists in the world on the medical and biological effects of marijuana, which he has studied for twenty years. He is also PRIDE's Man of the Decade. His first book for the lay public "Keep Off The Grass" has become a household word in America, and it has also been translated into 5 languages. I am most pleased to urge everyone to read the revised fifth edition of this important book, which reports the latest evidence of the damaging effects of marijuana on man. "Keep Off The Grass" should be required reading for anyone who wishes to know the facts about marijuana, and the steps which have to be taken in order to stop the spread of this destructive weed which has already done such harm to our country.

Dr. Thomas Gleaton
President, PRIDE

Author's Introduction
to the Fifth Edition

This title, first published in 1976, was written to illustrate the damaging effects of marijuana on the brain and body, at a time when the *Columbia University Encyclopedia* of 1975 stated: "Most evidence indicates that marijuana does not induce mental or physical deterioration." Such a statement reflected, at that time, the general opinion of many intellectuals in and out of Academia which was amplified by a complacent media extolling the pleasant properties of this "mild intoxicant." And yet a careful analysis of the biological properties of marijuana in experimental animals and in man, reported in the 1975 Helsinki Symposium, pointed out the probable long-term damaging effects of the drug on brain, learning and behavior, immunity system, reproductive functions and fetal development (pp. 168–173). At the same meeting, it was pointed out that "the human pathology of marijuana smoking could only be written after several decades, when long-term studies of the marijuana-smoking population will have been completed." Fifteen years later, the damaging effects of marijuana on some of the most vital functions of man have been scientifically documented: Brain, fetal growth, and immunity system are impaired by this drug.

DAMAGING EFFECTS OF MARIJUANA ON BRAIN AND
BEHAVIOR

The acute impairment of mental performance by marijuana
is well recognized. A stoned individual is incapable of thinking straight. Professor M.I. Soueif, from Cairo University,
reported in the fifties that this impairment was present well
beyond the period of acute intoxication; but many American
psychologists refused to acknowledge the carefully documented measurements performed by Soueif on several hundred chronic hashish users (p. 80–81). These psychologists
referred to a Costa Rican study by Professor Fletcher of
Miami University, who had reported in 1973 that heavy
marijuana users scored as well as non-smokers on several
test of learning and memory. In a 1984 follow-up study,
Fletcher and his colleagues performed a new battery of
psychological tests on the same cohort of Latin American
marijuana users and of non-smoking controls. Selective cannabis impairment of short-term memory skills and attention
was recorded, contradicting the results obtained ten years
before. In 1988, a study by V.K. Varma also reported short-
term memory impairment in heavy marijuana smokers
studied in India. Finally, in 1989, Dr. Richard Schwartz of
Georgetown University reported the results of an exceptionally well-controlled study of persistent short-term memory impairment in a group of primarily white, American,
middle-class adolescents. Their median age was sixteen, and
they had at least eight years of education. Their performance was compared with that of a group of controls
matched for age and I.Q. Schwartz began this study after he
noticed that cannabis-dependent adolescents who have just
entered a rehabilitation program experienced difficulties in
recalling newly learned rules as well as remembering con-
versations and exchanges in their group-therapy sessions.
These adolescents report that such memory deficits persist
for at least three to four weeks after their last use of cannabis.

When initially tested, the cannabis-dependent boys and

girls did much worse on short-term memory tests than the control group, and after six weeks of supervised abstention from intoxicants, they still presented short-term memory deficits. "Marijuana mangles memory," says Schwartz, "and memory loss poses one of the main problems with kids who smoke pot. They think they are losing their minds for good!" Marijuana use hits hardest those teenagers who do poorly in school. For them, remedial teaching without concurrent abstention from marijuana is ineffective. While the brightest might compensate for a while, the average hardly get by, and those with low I.Q.'s are devastated by it.

The Schwartz study proves the specific property of marijuana to impair in a lasting fashion memory storage, a function of the brain which is an essential part of the learning process and of psychomotor performance. Such impairment has now been observed on subjects from North and Central America, India and Egypt. All of the effects of marijuana on man might have been predicted from studies on animals reported in the previous editions of *Keep Off The Grass* (p. 225–26). Confirming these earlier studies, Dr. Merle G. Paule and his colleagues from the National Center for Toxicological Research in Jefferson, Arkansas, reported in 1989 the disruptive effects of chronic marijuana-smoke exposure on the complex behavior of rhesus monkeys. The animals were exposed daily or twice a week for one year to the smoke of one marijuana cigarette. Both exposures resulted in impairment of their response to standard tests of acquired or conditioned behavior, which were adequately performed by control animals exposed to smoke without THC. The data conclude, the authors indicate, that chronic marijuana exposure, whether daily or on weekends only, produces deficits in complex behavior.

Such observations of animal and man illustrate the lasting damaging effects of marijuana on the brain's biochemical mechanisms involved in memory storage. Their integrity is essential for adequate performance of all tasks which require rapid coordination and recall of past events. The lingering effects of marijuana on memory storage result

from basic neurochemical alterations which have been identified in certain parts of the brain. Many studies, since those
reported by Joseph Moreau in 1846, have indicated that
acute exposure to cannabis produces in humans the loosen-
ing of associations, fragmentation of thought and confusion
in attempting to remember recent events. As Dr. Loren L.
Miller from Research Triangle Park concluded in 1984, the
most consistent effect of delta-9-THC on performance of human volunteers is the disruption of selective aspects of
short-term memory tasks, similar to that found on monkeys
and patients with brain damage presenting memory disorders. These memory deficits caused by disease, trauma or
THC have been traced, by Loren Miller and others, to impairment of a part of the brain, the *hippocampus,* which is
the central relay which gets information during memory
consolidation, and codes spatial and temporal relations
among stimuli and responses. And Dr. Miles Herkenham
from the National Institute of Mental Health, reported in
1990 that THC binds to the hippocampus of rat, dog, monkey and man. Herkenham's observations, made with most
refined techniques, confirm studies performed on the brains
of monkeys twenty years earlier by Professor McIsaac and
associates from the University of Texas. Little is known
about the biochemical steps which are associated with memory or information processing in the brain. Decreases in
mental performance due to marijuana have been related to
an impairment of the turnover of a major neurotransmitter,
acetylcholine, but many other mechanisms are also involved. In order to pinpoint these mechanisms, studies on
animals and man, using the newest imaging techniques
(nuclear magnetic resonance, NMR, and positron emission
tomography, PET) will have to be performed with specific
biochemical markers. Dr. Nora Volkow and colleagues from
Brookhaven National Laboratory have undertaken such
studies. Another important part of the brain, the cere-
bellum, which controls coordination and equilibrium, was
also shown to be the prime target of THC. As scientists
accumulated new knowledge about how THC impairs brain

mechanisms controlling memory, the residual consequences of marijuana-smoking on the performance of complex tasks was becoming all too apparent in our technological society.

The most striking evidence of the lingering effects of marijuana on memory and coordination was reported in 1985 by Dr. Jerome Yesavage and colleagues of Stanford University. The investigators recruited ten experienced private pilots with a mean age of twenty-nine years and a mean of 303 hours of flying experience. They had all smoked marijuana before, but none was a daily user, and they agreed to abstain from drug use for the test period. The subjects were trained eight hours on a computerized flight simulator, to perform a simple piloting task. They were told to take the test as if they were on an examination flight, and to perform to the maximum of their abilities. The test started one morning with a control "flight" for baseline measurements, after which each subject smoked a marijuana cigarette containing nineteen milligrams of THC, a good "social dose." The simulated landing was repeated one, four and twenty-four hours later. The worst performance, compared with the baseline flight, occurred one hour after THC inhalation. But twenty-four hours later, the pilots still experienced significant difficulty in aligning the computerized landing simulator and landing it at the center of the runway. There were marked deviations from the proper angle of descent in the last 6,000 feet of the approach to landing, and one of the pilots landed off the runway. "In actual flight, where there is wind and turbulence, such errors can easily lead to crashes," concludes Yesavage. The pilots, however, reported no awareness of any marijuana aftereffects on their performance, mood or alertness.

It is not known exactly how long beyond twenty-four hours a single marijuana cigarette will disrupt the fine brain mechanisms controlling memory banks. Their integrity is essential for the piloting of a plane. But it is known that traces of THC are still present in the brain after twenty-four hours. The present-day widespread use of the drug suggests that pilot performance should be more closely studied, adds

Yesavage. More down-to-earth tasks, such as operating complicated heavy equipment or railway trains, may also be susceptible to "day-after" marijuana effect.

THC-positive urine screens have been found among railroad crews responsible for train accidents, notes Yesavage, and the pilot in a 1983 commercial air crash at Newark, New Jersey, Airport, which involved landing misjudgment, was found to have smoked marijuana twenty-four hours before the accident. The results of this study were widely publicized by the media, but did not convince everyone of the risks inherent in marijuana smoking. Dr. David Greenblatt, chief of the Division of Clinical Pharmacology at New England Medical Center in Boston, claimed that Yesavage's study was incomplete, since it was not performed under "double blind" conditions. In such studies, the effects of an active medication must be compared with those of an inactive one or "placebo," and both investigators and study participants must be unaware (blind) of the nature of the medication administered. Greenblatt fails to recognize that when a subject takes a drug which changes brain chemistry and induces euphoria, he cannot help but "peek through the double blind." Anyone can recognize the difference between the effects of a glass of champagne and of sweetened carbonated water, even if the test is given in a double-blind fashion.

MARIJUANA AND PSYCHOMOTOR PERFORMANCE

Several major railroad accidents have dramatized the impairing effects of marijuana on the performance of complex tasks. In January 1987, a freight train rammed at full speed into the Metroliner traveling from Washington to New York. Sixteen dead and forty-eight injured were recovered from the remains of the passenger train. The conductor of the train had ignored three red signals before the crash. Cannabinoids were detected in his body fluids. The liability settlement of Amtrak to the victims of the crash totaled 68 million dollars, a very high price for a joint of marijuana. A year later, marijuana was detected in the system of a thirty-year-old switchman who had fled his post in a control tower after a train derailment in Chester, Pennsylvania. The switchman had failed to take an incoming train off a stretch of track undergoing maintenance, and where a work vehicle was stationed. In the ensuing crash, twenty-five people were injured. A few months later, in May of 1988, tests on five employees involved in the fatal crash of a commuter train in Mt. Vernon, near New York City, showed traces of drugs after the accident. The seventeen-year-old engineer who died in the accident had marijuana traces in blood and urine. Samples of the body fluids of a tower operator contained marijuana; those of two other tower operators showed amphetamines; and the dispatcher's had traces of codeine and morphine. After the Mt. Vernon accident, John Riley of the Federal Railroad Administration stated that over the previous sixteen months there had been on the average one major rail accident every ten days, with more than 375 people killed or injured. In the previous two years, added Riley, drug-positive results had been found in one of every five railroad accidents where drug detection tests were performed, and 65% of the fatalities occurred in accidents where one or more trainmen tested positive for alcohol or drugs. And Riley called for random testing of train personnel.

A study issued in February of 1990 by the National Transportation safety board offered the most extensive evidence linking fatal accidents among truck drivers to illicit drugs. The study covered 182 accidents involving 86 trucks in which 210 people were killed. One-third of the victims whose bodies were examined had recently used alcohol or drugs. The highest percentage (12.8%) had used marijuana; next came alcohol (12.5%); then cocaine (8.5%), over-the-counter stimulants (7.9%), and amphetamines (7.3%). As these percentages indicate, many drivers used more than one substance. All of this massive evidence puts to rest earlier studies published in *Science* and *Scientific American* in the sixties, claiming that marijuana did not impair driving performance!

MARIJUANA AND SCHIZOPHRENIA

Since marijuana can impair in a lasting fashion the neurochemical mechanisms of memory, one might surmise that its long-term heavy use could also damage in a durable way other biochemical brain pathways, and lead to severe mental incapacity and plain madness (p. 253). Throughout recorded history of the past 2000 years, cannabis has been associated with mental disturbances ranging from distorted perceptions to hallucinations and dementia (schizophrenia). The acute state of mental confusion, or "acute psychotic episode" which may result from a *single* large does of hashish was masterfully described by the French psychiatrist Joseph Moreau 150 years ago, in his treatise "Hashish and mental illness' (p. 16, 194). He described the "temporal disorganization" or alterations in the order, sequence, and goal-orientation of mental processes, delusional ideas (feelings of grandiosity or persecution), panic reactions (feelings of impending death or of becoming insane), acute brain syndrome or toxic psychosis (delirium with confusion, prostration, disorientation and hallucinations). All of these temporary malfunctions of the brain recede spontaneously after a few days, and are not frequent enough in the United States to become a serious public health concern.

However, for some physicians like Professor J. Griffith-Edwards, from Maudsley Hospital in London, marijuana-induced "acute psychosis" should not be discarded as a minor consideration, but deserves scrutiny. "Will cannabis," asked Griffith-Edwards, "which can produce acute disabling mental disturbance, have any likelihood to produce long-term mental disorders, such as schizophrenia, especially if taken regularly in large amounts?"

This question, raised in 1975, was positively answered in 1981 by Professor Doris Milman from Downstate Medical Center in Brooklyn, and Professor José Carranza from the University of Texas, who reported prolonged psychotic episodes in young marijuana smokers. However, the possibility still remained that the use of marijuana had merely trig-

gered an underlying psychosis in "predisposed patients."
But now Professor Sven Andreasson, Peter Allebeck and Ulf
Rydberg from Karolinska University in Stockholm reported, in 1989, a fifteen-year study on 55,000 Swedish conscripts. The relative risk for developing schizophrenia
among those who were high consumers of cannabis (use on
more than fifty occasions) was six times greater than in nonusers.

The property of cannabis to induce long-lasting mental
disturbances in Western man has now been epidem-
iologically documented, which confirms older anecdotal reports from medieval Islam (1396), India (1878–1972), Egypt
(1843–1925), Brazil (1955), Bahamas (1970), and Jamaica
(1976). Cannabis-induced psychosis provides evidence that
the repetitive and pleasant disturbance of brain neurotransmission carries the most serious risk of impairing last-
ingly the basic biochemical neural mechanisms which control coherent behavior.

Marijuana A "Gateway" Drug

It appears that the biochemical changes induced by marijuana in the brain results in a drug-seeking, drug-taking
behavior, which in many instances will lead the user to
experiment with other pleasurable substances. The risk of
progressing from marijuana to cocaine or heroin is now well
documented.

Marijuana users are *sixty-six times* more likely to use
cocaine subsequently than subjects who have never consumed marijuana. This 1990 survey of PRIDE documents
further the fact that marijuana is a "gateway" drug to more
destructive dependency-producing drugs such as heroin or
cocaine. Such a most significant risk of escalation from
marijuana to cocaine was reported by Kandel and colleagues
in 1975 (*Science* 190 (1975): 912). Clayton and Voss (*U.S.
Journal of Drug and Alcohol Dependence,* Jan. 1982) confirmed Kandel's observation and reported that the risk for a
marijuana user to progress to cocaine consumption is *ten*

times greater than the risk of a heavy tobacco smoker to develop cancer of the lung. Dr. Herbert Kleber (*Journal of Clinical Psychiatry,* 1988, 48:3), reports that 75% of frequent users of marijuana have used cocaine at least once. It is a fact that the major epidemic of cocaine consumption besetting the country since the mid-eighties was preceded by the marijuana epidemic of the seventies.

DAMAGING EFFECTS OF MARIJUANA ON HUMAN FETAL
DEVELOPMENT

The unabated progression of the social acceptance of marijuana as a soft recreational drug in American society has harmed not only millions of bright young American brains. In addition, tens of thousands of unborn children whose mothers smoked marijuana during pregnancy have been impaired. Yet it was known since the early seventies that the "cannabinoids," or specific compounds contained in marijuana impaired the formation of chemicals like DNA and proteins which are essential for proper division of cells (pp. 120–121, 130–134, 153–156). I was one of several scientists who made this observation, and in reporting our finding issued the following warning (p. 141): "It is urgent to find out to what extent chronic marijuana use will impair the genetic equilibrium of dividing cells and possibly affect adversely the offspring of the marijuana user." For issuing this statement to the press, I was fiercely attacked by the marijuana lobby (p. 142), and criticized by many of my colleagues in the scientific community. Subsequent experiments performed in the seventies by a score of researchers, and among these Professor Harris Rosenkrantz from Clark University (p. 222–223) and Professor Ethel Sassenrath from University of California at Davis (pp. 181–187, 222–223), demonstrated that marijuana was toxic to fetal development in all species studied. These included fish, birds, rodents, hamsters, rabbits, dogs and monkeys. Sassenrath concluded her studies by stating: "The pattern of reproductive failure in female primates treated with THC indicates that this drug is toxic to the embryo and fetus." (p. 222) The experiments performed by Rosenkrantz on rodents (p. 222) supported this conclusion.

However, all of these experimental studies on animals did not impress the marijuana experts funded by the National Institute on Drug Abuse, to study the effects of marijuana on man. One of them, Professor of Psychiatry Reese Jones from The University of California at San Francisco, stated the following in a review on "Cannabis and Health" published in the Annual Reviews of Medicine in 1983, "Data are inadequate to document subtle functional impairment of the very low level of teratogenicity (due to cannabis) in the newborn (man)." Jones adds, "The clinical significance of most effects of cannabis is not known, and probably will only be determined by controlled studies of large human populations."

Jones was merely echoing the conclusion of the 1982 "Report on Marijuana and Health of the Institute of Medicine, National Academy of Science, which stated (p. 244), "Marijuana crosses the placental barrier, but there is no evidence as yet of deleterious effects on the human fetus." So in the name of scientific objectivity, a clear public warning against the use of marijuana during pregnancy was not issued in 1982 by the most prestigious scientific body in the nation. I failed to understand the disregard by my colleagues of the massive experimental evidence accumulated in the seventies, which demonstrated the damaging effects of cannabis on the psychomotor performance, the cell division and metabolism, and the fetal development of seven animal species. All mammals have in common very similar fundamental biological and physiological mechanisms when it comes to reproduction!

Two years after the noncommittal conclusion of the Institute of Medicine's report, Professor of Pediatrics Doris Milman reported, in 1984, abnormalities in newborn babies exposed to marijuana during their mothers' pregnancies, and Professor Ralph Hingson from Boston University also described deficits in babies born from marijuana-smoking mothers. They had smaller head circumferences and were of lighter weight (p. 252). These studies illustrating the damaging effects of cannabis on the growing human fetus were confirmed later by three independent groups of investigators—in 1986 by Professor Elizabeth Hatch from Yale University, in 1987 by Professor Melanie Dreher from the University of Miami, and in 1989 by Professor Barry Zuckerman from Boston University. Dreher used a new technique of high-speed computer voice analysis to assess the maturity of newborn infants. The cries of infants born to marijuana-smoking mothers in Jamaica showed a much higher percentage of voice anomalies than did cries of infants from non-smokers. According to this investigator, the results suggest possible impairment of fetal brain development by maternal marijuana smoking during pregnancy.

In 1989, Zuckerman and colleagues published a most convincing paper on the subject in the New England Journal of Medicine. It was a long-term study of 1226 mothers from Boston followed during their pregnancy. Marijuana use was documented by urinalysis in 16% of the prospective mothers (of the 202 women whose samples were positive for marijuana, fifty-three or more than a quarter, denied use). Infants born to marijuana-smoking mothers were shorter, weighed less and had a smaller head circumference. Zuckerman notes that "In addition to the fetal toxicity of cannabis itself, one must also consider the elevated carbon monoxide level in the blood produced by marijuana smoking." As reported in 1988 by Professor Donald Tashkin from the University of California, marijuana, compared with tobacco smoking, produces a threefold increase in the amount of tar inhaled, and a five-times increase in carbon monoxide which binds to blood hemoglobin. As a result, there will be a decrease in blood oxygenation with subsequent impairment of fetal growth.

The fetotoxicity of marijuana in the human has finally been scientifically proven, ten years after the effect in rodents and monkeys was firmly established by Rosenkrantz and Sassenrath, in 1979. In the meantime, tens of thousands of infants were born throughout the land with deficits which they might never overcome. Some progress has been made, however, in the scientific forecasting of drug-induced fetal damage, considering that it took seventy years to document "scientifically" the damaging effects of maternal tobacco smoking on the growing human fetus, and several centuries to link maternal alcohol consumption to fetal damage. The so called "fetal alcohol syndrome" was described for the first time in the 1960's.

DAMAGING EFFECTS OF MARIJUANA ON IMMUNITY

In the late sixties, when I became interested in studying the debilitating effects of marijuana, it occurred to me that this drug might impair the immunity system (p. 97). This intricate network of communicating white blood cells allows the organism to preserve its integrity and fight off the bacteria and viruses attacking the internal environment, as well as the abnormal cancer cells produced by our own organism. At the time of our original studies, there were only crude methods to assess the integrity of the major components of the immunity system, which consists of groups of specialized cells with specific functions: The macrophage are scavenger cells, the T lymphocyte cells recognize any substance foreign to the body and the B lymphocytes make antibodies to neutralize the invaders. We first reported that marijuana products impaired the function of T cells, sampled from "street marijuana-users," decreasing their ability to divide when stimulated by substances foreign to the body. We attributed this impairment of the division of T lymphocytes by marijuana to its property of preventing the formation of DNA, the chemical in the nucleus of the cell which carries the genetic code from one cell to its two daughter cells. Other investigators reported that the ability of the B lymphocytes to produce antibodies was impaired by marijuana, and so was the property of the macrophages to migrate to the site of an infection. Our general conclusion was that marijuana depressed the immunity systems of man, and probably ren-

dered him more vulnerable to infection. "Over periods of
prolonged usage of marijuana," we said (p. 158), "the [result-
ing] slow cellular erosion might well become clinically apparent if a serious disease [developed]." Our findings were
immediately attacked by the marijuana lobby (NORML) as
the "great Nahas red herring" (p. 142).

Some investigators were not able to duplicate our observations on T lymphocytes, while others did, and extended the
impairing properties of marijuana on immunity to the B
lymphocytes and to the migration of macrophages. A long
period of controversy ensued concerning the exact interaction of marijuana on the immunity system.

After attending, in December 1989, a meeting on Drugs of
Abuse and the Immunity System, organized by Professor
Herman Friedman of South Florida University in Tampa, I
believe that the damage marijuana does to this system is
now well documented. Friedman and his group, applying
the newer techniques used to study cells of the immunity
system, demonstrated that THC suppresses the natural activity of the human "killer cells" which destroy the foreign
substances present in the body. Friedman also reported that
cannabinoids interfere with the production of interleukins
and interferon, substances produced by white blood cells to
neutralize infectious agents. Professor Guy Cabral of the
University of Virginia reported that THC impairs the ability of the macrophage to destroy virus-infected and tumor
cells. In a patient with an immunity system compromised by
prolonged marijuana use, the macrophages may still attract
and incorporate the bacteria, but instead of killing them,
carry them around throughout the body. In addition, Cabral's group demonstrated that marijuana decreases the capacity of the body to resist genital herpes-virus infections,
and that even casual smoking of one or two marijuana
cigarettes will cause a much more severe intoxication: more
virus will be produced at the site of infection, and the infection will be much more severe, with more rapid onset, and
longer duration. These phenomena, first documented by
Cabral on experimental animals, were subsequently ob-

served in marijuana smokers, who developed severe herpetic lesions of the genitalia which had a high rate of recurrence. "There is an additive effect of THC on the infectivity of certain viruses," says Cabral. The immunodepression produced by marijuana will be compounded by that of the virus, and as a result infectivity of the latter will be specially severe. The property of cannabis to weaken immune defenses and increase infectivity of certain viruses most likely applies to the HIV virus of AIDS, though it has not yet been scientifically proven. Other investigators from Friedman's group reported that THC impaired the immune response to treponema, the infectious agent of syphilis. This observation might account for the report from Costa Rica (p. 176). A positive blood test for syphilis was observed among 25% of the marijuana smokers versus 9% for the control non-smoking group, a difference reported to be statistically significant.

What might possibly be the most dramatic consequence of the immunosuppression effect of marijuana smoking was presented at the Tampa meeting by Professor Paul Donald, Chairman of the Department of Head and Neck Surgery at the University of California at Davis. Donald reported eight cases of advanced head and neck cancers in young patients with an average age of twenty-six. One was nineteen. All had been daily marijuana or hashish smokers since high school or college, but did not smoke tobacco or use much alcohol. They all had fast-growing tumors of the tongue or jaw, which Donald had seen before only among subjects sixty years of age or older who had been heavy drinkers and tobacco smokers for decades. "Such cases do not prove scientifically a cause-effect relationship," says Donald, "but they are unprecedented in this young age group." Dr. James Endicott, Chairman of Head and Neck Surgery at South Florida University, reported similar observations in twenty young marijuana smokers, who had developed tumors of the mouth, larynx and upper jaw. Let's not forget that it took seventy years to link scientifically cancer of the lung to heavy tobacco-cigarette smoking. With the improvement of

diagnostic methods, one might surmise that it will take less
time, ten more years maybe, to establish an acceptable scientific link between marijuana smoking and cancer of the
mouth. Meanwhile, the observations of Donald (first reported in the medical literature in 1986, but ignored by the
media) and the more recent ones of Endicott, constitute
additional evidence of the health hazards of marijuana.

The pioneering observations of Dr. Donald, associating
marijuana use with cancer, was followed by other, similar
reports. Dr. Frank Taylor, a pathologist from the University
of South Florida, in Tampa, reported that among ten patients under age forty diagnosed with cancer of the respiratory tract, seven of them had a history of daily marijuana
use. Taylor concluded that "regular marijuana use appears
to be an additional significant risk factor for the development of cancer of the upper airways." Six months later, in
the Journal of the American Medical Association, Dr. Robert Ferguson and colleagues from the University of Connecticut School of Medicine, reported the case of a twenty-seven-
year-old man who died of metastic lung carcinoma. He had
smoked marijuana heavily and steadily since age eleven.
Both Taylor and Ferguson quote in their bibliography the
early observations made by Dr. Forest Tennant. Tennant
reported squamous metaplasia (precancerous lesions) in the
lung tissue of American soldiers stationed in Europe who
were daily hashish users (p. 124–125). Dr. Harris Rosenkrantz had also reported irreversible lesions of the lungs in
rats exposed to marijuana smoke for three to twelve months
(p. 217), and Drs. Rudolph and Cecile Leuchtenberger had
reported in 1972 (p. 132, 133, 149, 216) that lung tissue
exposed in vitro to marijuana smoke underwent abnormal
changes, including alterations in DNA content "disturbing
the genetic equilibrium of the cell population." (p. 150). The
"test tube" studies of the Leuchtenbergers led them to suggest that marijuana had "mutagenic" potential; it is able,
like X-rays, to change permanently the character of a gene
in a cell, which will be perpetuated in subsequent cell divisions. These chemically induced mutations are cancer pro-

ducing (see p. 282). Professor Arthur Zimmerman from the
University of Toronto conducted experiments reported at
the Reims Symposium (pp. 215, 216) that mice administered
the active ingredients of marijuana for one month, presented an increased incidence of abnormal sperm cells. Zimmerman interpreted his data as indicative of a mutagenic
potential for marijuana. Such warnings were given credibility by the study published in "Cancer" in 1989 and performed by Dr. Leslie Robinson from the University of Minnesota and colleagues from three other medical centers. All
of these investigators conducted a broad "multicentric" investigation to assess in utero and post-natal exposure to
different medications in children who had developed a
deadly form of leukemia (non-lymphoblastic) usually diagnosed in adults. Analyses were performed for reported maternal use of medications and drugs in the year preceding
and during pregnancy of the 204 case-control pairs of children. An elevenfold increase in risk was found for the development of leukemia in the offspring of mothers who had
smoked marijuana just before pregnancy, or during pregnancy. No other drug use during pregnancy (including tobacco, alcohol and painkillers) could be associated with such
a risk. This observation is probably the worst possible indictment of marijuana to date, since it predicts a marked
rise in childhood leukemia in the coming years in view of
the elevated incidence of marijuana use among pregnant
women. This incidence was reported to be 14.8%, by Dr. Ira
Chasnoff in a study published in the *New England Journal
of Medicine,* April 26, 1990. There is no way to stop this
disaster as long as women of child-bearing age smoke marijuana.

TOWARDS A MEDICAL AND NATIONAL CONSENSUS?

The first scientifically documented long-term damage to
man due to marijuana consumption is now part of the medical record. It might have been predicted fifteen years earlier
by many experimental studies on animals, which some med-

ical scientists elected to disregard in the name of scientific objectivity. But today it is hard to imagine that a scientist could declare "a verdict of no verdict" concerning the health hazards of marijuana, and that "marijuana can not be exonerated as harmless, neither can it be convicted of being as dangerous as some have claimed." This statement appeared in the *New England Journal of Medicine* in 1982 under the signature of its editor. And in 1986 Professor Leo Hollister, a veteran clinical pharmacologist from Stanford University, wrote a lead article for the prestigious "Pharmacological Reviews" on "health aspects of cannabis." His conclusion: "Compared with other licit drugs such as alcohol, tobacco and caffeine, marijuana does not pose greater risks." Hollister was expressing a viewpoint not uncommon among pharmacologists, and staff members of the National Institute on Drug Abuse (NIDA) which funded most of the studies on the biological effects of marijuana. One NIDA official declared to *Scientific American,* November 1988, "Never has so much money been spent trying to find something wrong with a drug and produced so few results." Such pronouncements were used by editors of widely circulated texts to describe the properties of marijuana in misleading, even erroneous terms. For instance, the 1989 edition of the *Columbia Encyclopedia* defines "marijuana" as a "relatively mild, non-addictive drug. . . . Adverse reactions are relatively rare, and most can be attributed to adulterants frequently found in marijuana preparations." The *Merck Manual* of diagnosis and therapy, 1987 edition, used by hundreds of thousands of physicians throughout America and the world says the following about marijuana: "Cannabis can be used on an episodic but continuous basis without evidence of social or psychic dysfunction. . . . There is little evidence of biologic damage even among relatively heavy users."

But the damaging effects of marijuana reported in animal studies during the seventies have now been observed in man. They should be further documented in the years ahead because of the widespread usage of this drug in the past and present decades. Such damaging effects on the health of present and future generations, should constitute the cornerstone of a new medical and national consensus, essential for the reinstatement of a social refusal of marijuana use.

Though medical scientists and physicians have always been considered the wardens of public health, they can not be held entirely accountable for either the social refusal or acceptance of drug abuse. Marijuana use in a society is not solely determined by the scientific merits of the case, but by society itself. In a democracy, society reflects the majority views of its citizens who, in the last analysis, define the society in which they wish to live, namely the values they believe in and are willing to defend and the battles they wish to fight.

By now the foundation for a national consensus on the refusal of recreational drug use is largely in place. The scientific evidence of widespread damage to the human body and mind is in, and it is irrefutable. Our society has undergone decades of suffering, and is paying for decades of error.

All together, Americans can choose to refuse marijuana and other enslaving drugs, preferring instead to rebuild an environment in a country that aims at health and freedom.

References

Andreasson, S.; Allebeck, P.; Engstrom, A., et al., "Cannabis and Schizophrenia; A Longitudinal Study of Swedish Conscripts." *The Lancet,* 2:1483–1485, 1987.

———; Allebeck, P.; Rydberg, U., "Schizophrenia In Users and Nonusers of Cannabis." *Acta Psychiatr. Scand.,* 79:505–510, 1989.

Cabral, G.A.; Mishkin, E.M.; Marciano-Cabral, F.; et al., "Effect of Delta-9-tetrahydrocannabinol on herpes simplex virus type 2 vaginal infection in the guinea pig." *Proc. Soc. Exp. Biol. Med.,* 182; 181, 1986.

Chasnoff, I.J.; Landress, H.J.; Barrett, M., "The Prevalence of Illicit-Drug or Alcohol Use During Pregnancy and Discrepancies in Mandatory Reporting in Pinellas County,

Florida." *New England Journal of Medicine*, 322:1202–1206, 1990.

Donald, P.J., "Marijuana Smoking–Possible Cause of Head and Neck Carcinoma in Young Patients." *Otolaryngology Head and Neck Surgery*, 94:517–521, 1986.

Ferguson, R.P.; Hasson, J.; Walker, S., "Metastic Lung Cancer In a Young Marijuana Smoker." *Journal of the American Medical Association*, 261(1):41–42, 1989.

Hatch, E.E.; Bracken, M.B., "Effect of Marijuana Use in Pregnancy on Fetal Growth." *American Journal of Epidemiology*, 124:986, 1986.

Herkenham, M.; Lynn, A.B.; Little, M.D.; et al. "Cannabinoid receptor localization in brain." *Proceedings Natl. Acad. Sci.*, 87:1932–1936, 1990.

Jones, R.T., "Cannabis and Health." *Annual Review of Medicine*, 34:247–58, 1983.

Lester, B.M.; Dreher, M.C., "Effects of Marijuana Smoking During Pregnancy on Newborn Cry Analysis." *Abstracts of Pediatric Research*, 1987.

Nahas, G.G. (with Paris, M.; Harvey, D.; Brill, H.), *Marihuana in Science and Medicine*. Raven Press, 1984.

Page, J.B.; Fletcher, J.; True, W.R., "Psychosociocultural Perspectives on Chronic Cannabis Use: The Costa Rican Follow-up." *Journal of Psychoactive Drugs*, 20:57–65, 1988.

Paule, M.G.; McMillan, D.E.; Bailey, J.R., et al., "The Effects of Chronic Marijuana Smoke Exposure on Complex Behavior in the Rhesus Monkeys." *The Pharmacologist*, A115, 1989.

Robison, L.L.; Buckley, J.D.; Daigle, A.E.; et al., "Maternal Drug Use and Risk of Childhood Nonlymphoblastic Leukemia Among Offspring." *Cancer*, 63:1904–1910, 1989.

Schwartz, R.H.; Gruenewald, P.J.; Klitzner, M; et al., "Short-Term Memory Impairment In Cannabis-Dependent Adolescents." *Am. J. Dis. Child*, 143:1214–19, 1989.

Soueif, M.I., "Differential Association Between Chronic Cannabis Use and Brain Function Deficits." *Annals of the NY Academy of Science*, 282:323–43, 1976.

Taylor, F.M., "Marijuana as a Potential Respiratory Tract Carcinogen: A Retrospective Analysis of a Community Hospital Population." *Southern Medicine Journal,* 81: 1213–1216, 1988.

Varma, V.K.; Malhotra, A.K.; Dang, R.; et al., "Cannabis and Cognitive Functions: A Prospective Study." *Drug and Alcohol Dependency,* 21:147–52, 1988.

Wu, Tzu-Chin; Tashkin, D.P.; Djahed, B., "Pulmonary Hazards of Smoking Marijuana as Compared With Tobacco." *New England Journal of Medicine,* 318:347–51, 1988.

Yesavage, J.A.; Leirer, V.O., Denari, M.; et al., "Carry-Over Effects of Marijuana Intoxication on Aircraft Pilot Performance: A Preliminary Report." *American Journal of Psychiatry,* 142:1325–29, 1985.

Zuckerman, B.; Frank, D.A.; Hingson, R.; et al., "Effects of Maternal Marijuana and Cocaine Use on Fetal Growth." *New England Journal of Medicine,* 762–768, 1989.

KEEP OFF THE GRASS

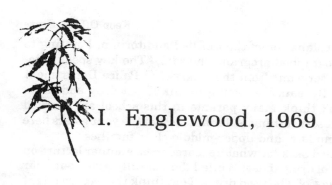

I. Englewood, 1969

Rush-hour traffic moved slowly as I drove from West Side Highway north toward the George Washington Bridge. After weeks of the dreariest kind of cold, rainy weather, New York was experiencing a springlike day in April.

As I headed toward my home in Englewood, New Jersey, I turned on the car radio just in time to catch the hourly news. The announcer made short mention of the fine weather and then launched into what had become a familiar litany of daily news events—the continuing war in Southeast Asia; the mounting wave of demonstrations and protests on college campuses; a major drug bust in Harlem.

I confess to listening only half-heartedly to the problems discussed in the news. It wasn't apathy so much as the fact that my life was taken up with other, more immediate, considerations; my work as a pharmacologist at the Columbia University Medical Center, where I was then engaged in research on the way drugs act on the body, and my wife and three children in our suburban community. That evening we were scheduled to attend a parents' meeting at the junior high school where our oldest daughter was enrolled.

When we arrived at the school, there was only a moderate turnout of parents. "Probably the weather," said my wife. "Not too many people want to sit in a stuffy school auditorium on a balmy night like this."

But a friend, sitting just behind us, leaned over with

1

another explanation of the unfilled auditorium. Pointing to the mimeographed program, she said, "The key speaker tonight is a sergeant from the Englewood Police Department Narcotics Bureau. He's going to talk about drug addiction, and I don't think many parents in this school are worried about that sort of thing. After all, most of the youngsters here are from middle- and upper-middle-class families."

We settled back for what appeared to be another lecture on the perils of drug abuse. While I did not fully agree with our friend's view of who used drugs, I did think the lecture might have been better directed at parents from less affluent neighborhoods. After all, weren't drugs the traditional outlet for the poor, the downtrodden, and the disenchanted?

The police officer, in his practiced delivery, covered ground very familiar to a pharmacologist. He described the various drugs favored by the current generation; he told about their effects on body and mind; and he even demonstrated the paraphernalia used in their preparation and administration.

"As far as marijuana is concerned," he said, "we don't know exactly how much is being used in the United States today, but there's no doubt that it has undergone a sharp increase in the last few years, particularly among young people. Surveys conducted on several college campuses indicate that a majority of the students have tried it at least once, and a significant percentage smoke it once a week or more."

Then came the evening's shocking statement. The sergeant leaned over the lectern and said, "I think you should know that the youngsters in this school are not exempt from this problem. In fact, there's good evidence that some of them are either experimenting with marijuana or using it regularly." He went on to say that for some youngsters in our community, marijuana had become a way of life, a situation comparable to the use of liquor by the chronic alcoholic.

These remarks caused quite a stir in the audience and the question-and-answer session that followed the sergeant's talk was lively. His answers, however, served only to heighten our concern. For one thing, we learned that this was not just an educated guess on his part. School authorities had already caught several children smoking marijuana in the bathrooms and had smelled the weed's distinctive odor on other occasions. For another, we were told that the drug probably was being distributed among our thirteen-, fourteen-, and fifteen-year-olds by their fellow students who, in turn, got it from older siblings. Then, as a final warning, the sergeant added:

"As a police officer I make no judgments about the rightness or wrongness of our present marijuana laws. My job is to apprehend lawbreakers, no matter what their age or background. But I must admit I do it with grave misgivings because I know what a serious effect arrest can have on the life of young persons. It may interrupt their education and shadow their future in many ways. In some states, for example, a single arrest is enough to prevent a teen-ager from obtaining a driver's license or working at jobs that are licensed by the state. Conviction, even without a sentence, may prevent youngsters from ever being licensed as a physician or a lawyer; and it can make it difficult for them to get responsible positions in business or industry. A police record may eliminate the possibility of ever getting a government job. And it may spotlight them for a long time as a troublemaker—even though they are, in fact, no more troublesome than most teen-agers."

Although no poll was conducted to find out how the other parents felt after the officer's speech, I'm sure many still believed that a certain affluence, education, and social position could protect their children from such perils. From the vantage point of the past seven turbulent years, during which time marijuana use has spread across every social and economic barrier and has achieved even some de facto legal acceptance, the reactions and responses from the adult audience that evening seemed naïve, even ludicrous. But in the early spring of 1969, the plague of drug use was not yet widely recognized, or at least not yet taken seriously by most Americans.

My own view of drug use has always been different. I know its dangers. I saw them first many years ago in Alexandria,

Egypt, where I was born and spent the early years of my life. My father was an engineer, and we lived a comfortable life with a constant influx of visiting relatives and friends. One of my uncles was a physician, the other a dentist, and the third a stockbroker, and they all lived with their families in our neighborhood.

Some mornings as we left the house for school, I would see a man sprawled on the sidewalk, apparently sleeping in the blazing sun. One day I asked my father, "Who is this man and what is he doing here?"

"The man is a *hashishat*," my father explained, "an unfortunate individual who is addicted to a drug called hashish. He is sleeping there because the drug has dulled his mind and sapped his energy."

To an impressionable eight-year-old, this was a startling revelation. I stared at the man for a moment and then asked, "But why does he take the drug if it is so bad?"

"Because he is poor and it is a way to forget his misery," came the reply. "But if you want to know more about hashish, ask your Uncle Selim."

The next time I saw my Uncle Selim, the physician, I brought up the subject. "Hashish is like a poison," he said. "You should never use it."

"Oh, no!" I exclaimed. I already knew that in Egyptian society (and this also holds true for most other Middle Eastern countries where hashish is used) there is an unwritten law that makes the drug taboo among the educated classes. On my frequent visits to the city I had seen many people in the same condition as the man in front of our house. They could be found everywhere, sleeping in the most unlikely places, begging for alms, or simply shuffling along the streets in a semistupefied way. And, judging by their clothes and bedraggled appearance, they were always the poor.

As a child, I didn't understand the "vicious-cycle" nature of drug use that helped to keep these people in a perpetual state of poverty. But it was easy to grasp the simple equation that "the prominent, well-educated people who visited our house never used hashish," while "the poor unfortunates in the street couldn't live without it."

These childhood impressions were the reason that I was stunned by the revelations of the police officer at my daughter's school that evening. I remained in my seat as the other parents filed out for the traditional post-meeting coffee and chatter. I needed time to think—time to try to understand what was happening in American society.

Back in the early 1950s, in order to help defray the expenses of earning my Ph.D. degree at the University of Minnesota, I served for two years as the counselor of one of the large dormitories on campus. In the course of living in close proximity to several hundred young men, I came to know their way of life. Then there was no drug problem of any kind; in fact, other than weekend beer drinking, there was not even a serious alcohol problem.

Now, only eighteen years later, we were talking about millions of youngsters at the elementary, junior high, senior high, and college levels experimenting with a wide range of drugs—and using marijuana almost freely. There was no doubt this was a huge departure from previous American habits.

When I joined the parents milling about in the lobby, I listened to bits and pieces of their conversation. Most expressed the same shock and concern I felt. But there were a few whose reaction frankly astounded me.

"At least it isn't addictive," commented one lady. "According to the medical reports I've read, it doesn't do any physical harm."

"In my day it was beer and homemade cider behind the barn," a man said with a laugh. "Today it's a fast puff on a 'joint'!"

"The thing that disturbs me," said another, "is the way they pull in kids who are caught smoking pot the same way as those caught using 'hard' drugs. Seems to me we should start thinking about legalizing marijuana so this can't happen."

I had very little to add to these discussions, but I was deeply concerned. I remember saying to my wife, "How can they even consider legalization of marijuana when they don't yet know what effect it has on the human body, let alone on youngsters who are still in the process of growth and development? Seems to me they're putting the cart way before the horse."

How far ahead the cart was might be realized best when I describe to what scrutiny other drugs must be subjected before they are released for public use. Enormous progress has been made in the field of pharmacology since my medical training before World War II, and the pharmaceutical industry has been able to develop new products that have had an extremely positive impact on health and life expectancy.

But what is less widely known is that the development of these new medicines has been accompanied by a corresponding increase in adverse effects, some of them obvious and some extremely subtle. The skin rash that some people get after taking penicillin, for example, is an almost immediate sign of an allergic reaction to this drug. On the other hand, the more than 5,000 women in eight nations who took the drug thalidomide during their pregnancy experienced no signs of a reaction. Routine blood tests taken during their term showed nothing that might alert the doctor to a possible side effect. Instead, the toxic substance in the drug worked only on the developing fetus. As we now know, months after these women took the drug many of their babies were born grossly deformed.

Still more striking for its long term adverse effect is the story of the synthetic hormone diethylstilbesterol, a drug used in the 1940's and 1950's to avert spontaneous abortions. At the time the drug was administered, it showed no apparent effect on the mother. When the babies were born, they showed no effect either. But when the female offspring of these women reached puberty, doctors detected a high incidence of vaginal cancer. Further research indicated that the diethylstilbestrol was responsible.

As a result of these reactions, the National Research Council of the National Academy of Sciences made recommendations to carry out in-depth research into the effect of drugs on the developing fetus. Said a spokesman: "The concerns of scientists with respect to contamination of the fetal and neonatal environments have an interesting analogy in the recent national interest in environmental pollution. Medical practitioners are convinced that the young are uniformly more susceptible than adults to the toxic effects of drugs or pollutants. It is apparent that drugs can affect the fetus at every stage of its development, from the crucial beginning of blastocyst when it consists of only a few hundred cells, to its birth."

A major function of research pharmacology is to make sure that drugs that will be commonly used will not induce permanent cellular damage. To do this, however, requires a major investment in fundamental and applied research. As a first step, the literature must be searched to find out if the compound under investigation or any similar chemical substance was ever used before and, if so, what effects it had on the human organism. It's amazing how many "new" ideas turned out to be variations on an older theme. Thus, we can save a lot of time and effort, and perhaps some lives, if we consider the results or effects achieved in the past.

If there is no precedent for a drug, then the next step is to see how the compound metabolizes—the way it is broken down, absorbed, or eliminated by the body. This requires marking, or tagging the drug under study with a radioactive atom, usually hydrogen or carbon. By tracing the atom it is then possible to detect very small amounts of the chemical or some of its by-products in body fluids, tissues and excretions. The radioactive substance is placed in a vial which goes into the "scintillation counter." This indispensable workhorse of the research pharmacologist is an instrument that counts radioactivity.

The next step is a critical and lengthy series of evaluations in laboratory animals. Since the thalidomide episode, a search for toxicity in at least two distinct animal species is required. As a rule, these animal investigations involve a trial group that receives the drug and a control group that is raised, fed, and housed in the same manner, but is given no chemical substance. If a toxic result should show up in the trial group, chances are the drug would be dropped. On the other hand, absence of a reaction in the first generation is still no assurance that the compound is safe. In fact, it may require up to four generations before the researchers are satisfied that the compound may be given to man.

The problem in animal testing is that there is no model truly similar to man. The closest is the rhesus monkey, but its use on the scale required for drug testing (at enormous expense) would lead rapidly to extinction of the species. Also, the tests used to measure toxicity in animals are rather crude—loss of weight, analysis of body fluid composition, and death. Beyond these more-or-less obvious criteria, there is no way to determine subtle effects that may not show up for many years.

If the chemical has met all criteria up to this point—that is, if it has passed laboratory and animal experimentation without producing any acute or observable adverse effects—then physicians are selected to administer the drug to patients who, in turn, are observed over an extended period of time. Generally, this observation requires the patients to come in regularly for blood tests and other medical evaluations.

The use of the new drug is then carefully followed for many more years by both the United States Food and Drug Administration and the World Health Organization in order to detect any delayed adverse effects. Sometimes the people who are most sensitive to a drug are not represented in the field trials. This happened in 1973 with an antidiarrhea medicine sold over the counter in several European nations. Although it had been tested extensively before being put on the market, neither pregnant women nor children under age ten were represented in the trials. As a result, when these people took the drug, they experienced severe neuritislike symptoms, symptoms that fortunately disappeared after the offending medicine was discontinued.

What has all of this to do with marijuana? Simply that I had just sat through two hours of a lecture and discussion about a widely used drug that, to my knowledge, had never been subjected to any series of rigorous evaluations and had no part in any official pharmacopoeia. It was, from a pharmacologist's point of view, a totally unknown substance.

Nevertheless—and this is the frightening thing—it was being ingested or inhaled regularly by millions of young Americans and was on the threshold of achieving a legal status.

On the way out to the parking lot of the school, we met a young pediatrician who had a son our daughter's age. "If I ever prescribed a medicine made from weeds in my backyard and mixed on the kitchen counter," he said, "you'd hear the screaming from here to Washington! I'd lose my license. Yet I heard people in there tonight making judgments about marijuana on the basis of nothing more than rumor and fifth-hand observation. They don't know what they are talking about!"

I agreed, and many disturbing questions came to mind as we drove home: Exactly how much do we know about marijuana and its effects on the human body? Exactly what was the composition of the pot the youngsters were smoking and did it contain harmful substances? Was there any historical precedent we could use to predict or evaluate the effects of the current drug epidemic? Was marijuana really nothing more than a mild intoxicant, with fewer after-effects than alcohol, or did it have the long-term destructive effects my father and Uncle Selim had attributed to this weed and that I suspected?

"It may take a long time to answer all these questions," said my wife. But I knew that before marijuana was legalized at a risk to society, scientists like myself must speak out, must further investigate this drug. I knew that night that marijuana would become a personal and professional concern of mine. The quest had begun.

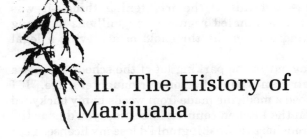

II. The History of Marijuana

During the following weeks I was preoccupied by my regular work in the laboratory and the preparation of a series of lectures I was to give at the University of Paris, where I had recently been elected adjunct professor and where I would spend my sabbatical from Columbia. But I could not forget the marijuana problem or my commitment to its resolution. Indeed, a week did not pass without the media reporting arrests of young people for smoking marijuana. At the same time, voices from the universities came to the defense of those arrested, claiming that marijuana was a "mild intoxicant, less dangerous than tobacco or alcohol, which should be legalized and made commercially available."

In my concern, I observed our oldest daughter closely for any signs of drug intoxication. Her behavior continued as before: She was involved in her busy school schedule; she walked the daily mile to school with her friends; she had a good appetite, studied regularly every evening, and did not even smoke tobacco. However, she was reluctant to discuss fully the drug problem with me because she did not want to inform on her friends. But I did learn that some of the other girls were experimenting with marijuana. Typically, a girl would arrive in school one day with a joint that she had gotten from an older brother or sister. The marijuana cigarette would be passed around during recess or lunch, with the implied challenge to neophytes that smoking one was a very sophisticated or "in" thing to do. My daughter was convinced that many of the girls who took up the challenge did so only because they were afraid of being thought "square." While most of the experimentation took place outside of school, there were some youngsters who smoked marijuana almost regularly in the girls' rest rooms.

I discussed the marijuana problem with my colleagues at Columbia, expressing my fears. A surgeon spoke for many of my colleagues: "All of this is just a youthful fad which will blow over. The worst thing we could do would be to dramatize it!"

In France, there was also concern about marijuana. For that reason, I decided to make the drug the subject of one of my lectures at the University of Paris.

During the next few months I started reading all of the documents on marijuana I could obtain from the medical libraries of Columbia University and the University of Paris. Most of the literature dealt with the historical and anecdotal aspects of marijuana rather than with documented scientific or pharmacological information.

First I learned that there were two main varieties of marijuana plant—or *Cannabis sativa,* the Latin name used by botanists—the fiber type and the drug type.

In Europe, the fiber type has been known under the name of "hemp" and used for rope-making since the tenth century. It was introduced to America by the early settlers. Cultivation of this hemp-type marijuana, which contains little intoxicating material in its flowering tops, was discontinued with the advent of synthetic fibers. In contrast to the fiber type, the drug type is a variant cultivated for the intoxicating substance in its flowering tops. The drug-type plant requires a warm dry climate and adequate moisture in the soil. Ideal areas of cultivation are located in the hills and mountains of semitropical areas: Mexico, Colombia, the Rif mountains of Morocco, Mount Lebanon, and the lower Himalayas.

The plant is considered by most botanists to be a single, nonstabilized species, with as many as 100 varieties. These many variations are due to a certain genetic plasticity, to environmental influences, and to human manipulation, not specifically to the country of origin. In Latin, *Cannabis* means hemp and denotes the genus of the hemp family of plants, *sativa* means planted or sown and denotes the species and the nature of the plant's growth. Other adjectives are added to denote the variety according to geographic location; for example, *Cannabis sativa indica* is the plant that grows in India.

In lay parlance, the wide geographical distribution of *Cannabis sativa* accounts for the different names given to the drug-type variety of the plant as well as to its intoxicating derivatives. The 1968 United Nations multilingual list of stupefying drugs under international control gives 267 names for *Cannabis sativa,* the plant, and for *cannabis* preparations, although usually the names for both are used interchangeably. While the term *Cannabis sativa* is most exact, it is used interchangeably with *cannabis* or *cannabis* products. In Morocco and on the North African Coast the term is kif; in the Middle East, Egypt and Iran it is known as hashish; in India, the drink made from brewing the leaves and tops of the plant is called bhang, whereas ganja refers to the resinous material that is smoked. This name is also used in Jamaica because the plant was introduced there by Indian workers. The name marijuana familiar in the United States and Canada is derived from Mexico; hashish is also used, but to describe a stronger preparation. Hashish is the term most commonly used in Europe.

Since the turn of the century, the derivatives of *Cannabis sativa,* as well as those from the poppy (source of opium, morphine, heroin), and from coca leaves (source of cocaine), have been considered by international agreement to be "stupefying drugs," dangerous to man and society, whose use should be strictly restricted to medical purposes.

The use of the drug type of marijuana began more than 4,000 years ago in China. It has been attributed to the Chinese emperor and pharmacist, Shen Nung, whose work on pharmacy advocated the use of the plant as a sedative and all-purpose medication. Although included in the Chinese pharmacopoeia for hundreds of years cannabis never really caught on, perhaps because the Chinese had more powerful psychoactive substances available to dull the pains of illness and mask the trials of everyday living.

The first indication that cannabis was being used by large numbers of people for its mind-altering effects rather than strictly as a medication is found in the Indian subcontinent. About 2000 B.C., cannabis was considered a holy plant to be used in religious rites. Priests cultivated the plant in temple gardens, harvesting the leaves, stems, and flowering tops for brewing into a highly potent liquid called bhang. This liquor was supposed to promote "closer union with God" when drunk before religious ceremonies. The Indians described bhang as a "joy-giver," "sky-flyer," "soother of grief"—adjectives that attest to its euphoric effects. A Persian poet of the time was prompted to write, "We drank bhang and the mystery that 'I am God' grew plain—so grand a result, so tiny a sin."

The formula for brewing bhang was carefully guarded by the priests so that it would be used only for religious purposes, like sacramental wine or holy water. But it did not take long for others to realize that the plant could be found growing wild in many places, and that bhang could be brewed at home as easily as in the temple. Moreover, it was discovered that the psychoactive effects of cannabis could be achieved more easily by smoking a chopped-up mixture of the plant tops as by drinking bhang. As a result, an orderly system for growing, preparing, and distributing cannabis extracts— and making a good profit—was soon worked out. Thus, from occasional medicine or religious elixir, cannabis became readily available and widely used as an inexpensive, mind-altering drug.

From India, cannabis spread to the Middle East. Once again, religion played a prominent role in its introduction to the populace. Since the Muslim faith specifically and strictly forbids the use of alcohol, there was an immediate and lively interest in a substitute that could produce a similar euphoric effect without burdening the user with a mortal sin.

The Arabic name for the cannabis extracts used in the Middle East is hashish, and translated into English, this means "grass." A monk, living in the mountains of Rama in A.D. 500, told his followers, "Almighty God has bestowed upon you by a special favor the virtues of this plant, which will dissipate the shadows that cloud your souls, and brighten your spirits." With such a holy dispensation, is it any wonder that so many soon were smoking hashish for its euphoric effects?

The Arab invasions of the ninth through the twelfth centuries introduced cannabis into North Africa, from Egypt to the east to Tunisia, Algeria, and Morocco in the west. First extolled by the intellectuals and poets of the time, the drug quickly found acceptance among the people. The only land conquered by the Arabs where cannabis usage did not become widespread was Spain. Although there is evidence that some people there smoked hashish, the majority of Spaniards avoided it. One can speculate that the availability of wine and the lack of religious strictures against alcohol shut off the popular market for cannabis.

In the Middle East, however, the ever-widening growth of cannabis usage was having its effects on the life and tempo of the times, some of the effects subtle, others quite dramatic. *The Tales of the Thousand and One Nights* (more popularly known as *Tales of the Arabian Nights*), for example, were written when the use of hashish and bhang was spreading throughout North Africa. Careful reading of the original versions of these works shows that the authors frequently referred to cannabis and its mind-altering properties. This may even explain the idea of a "flying carpet"!

The greatest effects of widespread cannabis usage, however, were felt in Egypt. According to the Arab historian Magrizy, hashish was first introduced in the thirteenth century at a time when Egypt was flourishing culturally, socially, and economically. First, the drug was accepted and used primarily by the wealthier classes as a form of self-indulgence. When the peasants adopted the habit, though, it was as a means of alleviating the dreariness of their daily life.

There is no way, of course, to measure accurately what effect the use of hashish had on the productivity and national strength of the Arab civilization. No studies were made at the time, and any observations of cause-and-effect came centuries later. Nevertheless, the appearance of cannabis products in the Middle East did coincide with a long period of decline during which Egypt fell from the status of a major power to the position of an agrarian slave state, exploited by a series of Circassian, Turkish, and European rulers.

As often happens, the very decline of the nation prompted the increased use of what may have hastened its fall. The hashish habit became so prevalent among the masses that some sultans and emirs made attempts to prohibit its use, knowing that they were going against a practice participated in by a large percentage of the population. In the fourteenth century, Emir Soudouni Schekhouni ordered that all cannabis plants be uprooted and destroyed, and that any users of the substance be condemned to have all their teeth extracted without benefit of anesthesia. Unfortunately, this painful prospect had little effect on the national hashish habit.

Napoleon, too, tried to curb the use of hashish. When the French conquered Egypt in 1800, one officer noted, "The mass of the male population is in a perpetual state of stupor." Hoping to breathe some life into the stagnant nation, but mostly wishing to protect his own soldiers, Napoleon decreed, "The use of the strong liquor made by some Moslems with a certain weed called hashish, as well as the smoking of the flowering tops of hemp, is forbidden in all of Egypt." Although he did manage to restrain his troops from using the drug, the mighty French emperor had little effect on cannabis abuse in the Moslem world.

Although there was a commercial and cultural interchange between the Arab world and the European nations lining the Mediterranean Sea during this period, the cannabis habit was never a part of this contract. This still held true when the major European powers, France and England, entered the colonial era of the eighteenth and nineteenth centuries. Although large numbers of military and civilian forces spent long periods of time in areas where cannabis intoxication was commonplace, there is no evidence that the Europeans were tempted by it. As one historian has written: "There seemed to be a cultural cleavage that prevented the Europeans from adopting this Oriental habit."

When the intoxicating substances of *Cannabis sativa* were introduced to Western man in the middle of the nineteenth century, it was for the purpose of scientific experiment rather than a desire to blot out reality. Jacques Joseph Moreau, who is regarded by many as the father of clinical psychopharmacology, deliberately ingested hashish in 1840 in order to experience and describe the mental effects of cannabis intoxication. Moreau experienced euphoria, hallucinations, and incoherence, accompanied by an extremely rapid flow of ideas. The process of intoxication, for him, was akin to mental illness. He also noted that the environmental and social settings, as well as the psychological and emotional condition of the user, profoundly influenced the effect.

Moreau's experimentation with hashish was performed in order to gain insight into mental disease. Without consideration of any possible permanent effects, he advised some of his pupils and friends to share in the extraordinary psychological and emotional experience of hashish intoxication. One earlier user was Theophile Gautier, a talented poet of the romantic era. He was so excited about the hallucinatory effects of cannabis that he organized a meeting of his literary friends and in their presence ingested a large amount of potent hashish extract. Here is how he described the ensuing experience:

"Hallucination, that strange guest, had set up its dwelling place in me. It seemed that my body had dissolved and become transparent. I saw inside me the hashish I had eaten in the form of an emerald which radiated millions of tiny sparks. All around me I heard the shattering and crumbling of multicolored jewels. I still saw my comrades at times but as disfigured half plants, half men. I writhed in my corner with laughter. One of the guests addressed me in Italian, which hashish in its omnipotence made me hear in Spanish."

The transposition of languages described so clearly by Gautier is considered a sign of profound mental disorganization. Another effect observed by Gautier was the waxing and waning of his hallucinations:

"For several minutes I found myself with all my composure and quite amazed at what had happened. Then I fell again under the power of hashish. Millions of butterflies, with wings beating like fans, continuously swarmed in a faintly luminous atmosphere. I heard the sounds of colors: green, red, blue and yellow sounds in successive waves. An overturned glass echoed through me like thunder. My voice appeared so powerful that I dared not speak for fear of breaking the walls and bursting like a bomb. I became entirely disengaged from myself, absent from my body, that odious witness which accompanies you wherever you are. I experienced the particular discontinuous effect of hashish which takes you and leaves you—you mount to heaven and you fall back to earth without transition, as insanity has its moments of lucidity."

Gautier's friends were so impressed by the experience they decided to call their group "The Club of the Hashish Eaters," and partake of this mind-expanding substance themselves. Charles Baudelaire, another member, wrote of his hashish experience:

"Sounds have colors and colors are musical. The eyes pierce infinity and the ears perceive the most imperceptible sound in the midst of the sharpest noises. . . . External objects take on monstrous appearances and reveal themselves in forms hitherto unknown."

Although these chemically induced hallucinations were soon abandoned by Gautier and his friends, Baudelaire went on from using hashish to opium in the same way that today some heavy marijuana smokers go on to use heroin. When he finally recognized the dangers of experimenting with these drugs, he wrote:

"Like all solitary pleasures, it makes the individual useless to men and the society superfluous to the individual. Hashish never reveals to the individual more than he is himself.

Moreover, there is a fatal danger in such habits. One who has recourse to poison in order to think will soon be unable to think without taking poison."

The French flirtation with the psychoactive effects of cannabis was short-lived. But it was a different story in England where the drug served other purposes altogether.

To understand why and how the English used cannabis, its colorful history as a medicament must be considered. In the beginning the legendary Chinese emperor-pharmacist Shen Nung was alleged to have prescribed cannabis for "female weakness, gout, rheumatism, malaria, beriberi, constipation, and absentmindedness," and one of his disciples, Hoa-tho, is said to have mixed it with wine and used the potent liquor as a surgical anesthetic and as an analgesic. About 2000 B.C., in India and in the Middle East, physicians prescribed hashish and bhang for various ills—without any real evidence that it did anything more than temporarily help the patient forget his pain.

Cannabis came into Western medicine via Sir William O'Shaughnessy Brooke, a physician serving in the Bengal Medical Service of Britain's East India Company. In 1839, after observing the use of the drug in India, he wrote a long article in a Calcutta medical journal reporting his successful use of cannabis in the treatment of rabies, rheumatism, epilepsy, and tetanus. He found it to be an effective analgesic, anticonvulsant, sedative, and muscle relaxant. "In hemp," he wrote, using the English name of the plant, "the profession has gained an anticonvulsant remedy of the greatest value."

In an era where patent medicines were numerous and scientific evaluation of the effects of a compound almost nonexistent, such claims were enough to skyrocket a drug into the category of a wonder substance. In England, cannabis extracts were prescribed for scores of different ills. Judging from the records, though, the dosages given were not even strong enough to produce a mild euphoria.

As for the curative powers of cannabis, it seems likely that some patients were, in fact, relieved of their symptoms. This was probably due more to the placebo effect of taking a pill than to the drug itself. One astute physician of the time, after trying cannabis on some of his patients, came to the conclusion that "it is hardly worthy of a place in our list of remedial agents." And when more specific medications such as aspirin, barbiturates, and anesthetic agents came along, cannabis was quickly dropped.

In the United States, the fiber type of cannabis plant was cultivated on our shores as early as 1720. The fibers in the stem were used in the manufacture of rope, twine, carpet, sailcloth, sacks, bags, and webbing. The seeds became the source of an oil for soap, paints, and similar products. Among the many colonial planters who cultivated a crop of hemp was George Washington.

Early American physicians copied the English in prescribing cannabis extracts for a variety of ills. The preparation they used was an olive-brown paste imported from India with the consistency of pitch and an aromatic odor. It was called Tilden's Extract of *Cannabis sativa indica*. Once again we can assume that it was more of a placebo or muscle relaxant than a healing agent.

Cannabis, fiber and drug type, was available in America for over one hundred years before the first report of its intoxicating properties appeared. This came in 1855 from Fitz Hugh Ludlow, a bright young scholar from Poughkeepsie, New York. Ludlow, it seems, was an amateur psychopharmacologist who spent much of his spare time examining and smelling the various substances in a friend's pharmacy. Sniffing chloroform, for example, he described the sensation as "careening on the wings of an exciting life." But it was cannabis intoxication that really triggered Ludlow's literary imagination.

At that time a very small dose of Tilden's Extract of *Cannabis sativa indica,* no more than one to six grains, was recommended by physicians for the relief of a variety of ailments ranging from epilepsy to rheumatism and menstrual cramps. When Ludlow helped himself from his friend's shelves to more than ten times this dose, he was quickly captured by the euphoria of hashish. He oscillated between deep beatitude and uncontrollable terror; he was transported to Venice, the Alps, and Paradise, then his heart began beating so loud and so fast that he sought the help of a doctor.

Ludlow repeated the hashish experience many times, always using Tilden's Extract. Almost without realizing it, he became dependent on the drug, using it daily to produce hallucinations that increasingly were of a religious nature. Finally, recognizing that he was addicted, he sought the help of a doctor and with a considerable amount of suffering, he rid himself of the habit.

Ludlow's chronicle pretty much stands alone in the early history of American cannabis use. It was not until 1910, in fact, that marijuana was imported into the United States from Mexico. The substance, smoked in cigarette form, was widely used among poor black and Mexican workers in Texas and Louisiana. When jazz became popular in New Orleans after World War I, the marijuana habit was adopted by many of the black musicians and the weed became associated with the mystique of the new rhythm. Some claimed that intoxication from "reefers" helped the musicians to sustain the faster beat. And as jazz and its proponents moved up the Mississippi River to the large northern cities, marijuana was introduced to a wider segment of the population.

In Louisiana, marijuana use was widespread enough to cause public concern, particularly after a series of "scare" articles appeared in the *New Orleans Morning Tribune*. The stories, which were highly racist in tone, implied that blacks "crazed" on marijuana were responsible for most of the heinous crimes committed in Louisiana. This was enough to trigger a wave of arrests and police brutality against large numbers of the black population in the area.

Outside of Louisiana, there were few Americans concerned about marijuana use, which, as one observer put it, was "a practice alien to the basic American way of life." Nevertheless, there were some people who saw in marijuana a potential threat that might cause harm to the individual and society. The most outspoken of these critics was Harry Anslinger, director of the Federal Bureau of Narcotics. At his prompting, Congress passed the Marijuana Tax Act of 1937 that prohibited cultivation, possession, and distribution of hemp plants. The only exemptions were for the cordage industry, which used the mature stalks to make rope and twine, and the birdseed industry, which purchased almost two million tons of cannabis seed each year for food mixes. To make sure that none of this seed slipped out for planting by marijuana dealers, the law required that all of the seed be sterilized before being distributed.

The Marijuana Tax Act, which for the first time brought cannabis under federal control, produced a small wave of criticism from some physicians and scientists. "The dangers of marijuana to the health and social structure of the United States have been exaggerated," said one scientist. "The 'killer weed' theory put forward by the Federal Bureau of Narcotics is designed only to frighten people, not to educate them. And without a supply of cannabis for experimental purposes, we'll never be able to find out if it is good or bad."

In truth, the United States was merely fulfilling its international obligations by passing the Marijuana Tax Act, not snuffing out a then nonexistent national problem. In 1925, Egypt had asked the International Opium Conference to place cannabis products in the same category as the opiates. This meant rigid control of the hashish that had plagued the Middle East for centuries. The United States, which was a member of the Conference, strongly supported the Egyptian proposal and agreed to pass stringent national laws prohibiting the cultivation and distribution of cannabis in any form.

The controversy was short-lived because in 1937 marijuana usage was far from a national threat. There was little enthusiasm about prolonging a debate that, as one congressman put it, "was of more concern to Arabs." And, in truth, there was no drug problem in the United States until after World War II.

The first indication of an impending "*Cannabis* problem" came from England where postwar recovery and an insatiable job market brought an influx of West Indian, Indian, and Turkish workers. These men arrived in Great Britain with a cannabis smoking habit many generations old. Hashish imported from Pakistan and Lebanon rapidly became the favored preparation, preferred to a mild marijuana of uncertain potency.

For reasons worthy of prolonged scientific investigation, the marijuana smoking habit of the workers was soon adopted by the new "swinging" generation of young men and women. From about 1950 to the present day, marijuana and even some hashish smoking grew apace with the appearance of rock music, popular singing groups, coffee houses, and the beatnik and hippie cultures. In May 1971, the English newspaper *Observer* noted, "Cannabis smoking is an established part of British university life, increasingly accepted by both academics and the police. But anxieties remain."

In the United States, the postwar generation, now in high school and college, was affluent, articulate, and eager to experiment. It was also disenchanted and rebellious. Church, country, and family were no longer values that interested or motivated a large number of young people, and they rebelled against these values as "irrelevant vestiges of the past." Freedom and liberation were the catchwords of the day. Anything that entailed regulation was considered to be repressive. There was outrage at the Vietnam War, the consumer society, and social inequities. Marijuana smoking became not only a pleasurable pastime, but also a sign of independent behavior, and an expression of rebellion against a rigid, uninspiring society. Marijuana smoking was acknowledged, even promoted, in some rock songs and sympathetically portrayed in movies like *Easy Rider* and *Superfly*. Newspapers, journals, radio and TV have repeatedly featured promarijuana spokesmen, and radical politics has also played a part in the spread of the marijuana epidemic through its underground press and its organizations.

Some members of the older generation also adopted a permissive attitude toward marijuana use and provided strong support to a growing demand for legalization of cannabis. In 1970, Dr. John Kaplan, a distinguished professor of international law at Stanford University, published a book entitled *Marihuana—the New Prohibition*. This study, which rapidly became a best seller, claimed that marijuana smoking was less dangerous than alcohol or tobacco, and that it should therefore be made commercially available. (But the medical evidence cited by Kaplan to indicate that marijuana was harmless was, from a scientist's viewpoint, fragmentary.)

In such an environment, and with evidence that an estimated 20,000,000 Americans were smoking marijuana either occasionally or regularly, it would seem sensible to at least consider a change of attitude toward the drug. After all, even such responsible organizations as the American Bar Association and the American Public Health Association were calling for legalization. Why punish young men and women for something that was being done openly, and with de facto legal approval, in many parts of the country? And why, in the first place, prohibit a substance that seemed fairly innocuous?

These questions, I want to stress, are not presented lightly. Concern about the many layers of legal interpretation that have been built up around marijuana is justified. A young man in one part of the country should not be arrested and jailed for marijuana possession when people in another section can smoke it openly with no fear of prosecution. It has never been my viewpoint that young users should be prosecuted and jailed for marijuana possession. In virtually all cases, they have yielded to marijuana experimentation only because of peer pressure, immaturity, or emotional difficulties.

However, licensing or legalizing a drug for mass use does not mean simply finding out who is in favor of legalizing it or even what behavioral results have been observed in those who have tried the substance. The most important factor to be considered in the formulation of any new legislation is: What effect does cannabis have on the human organism? This question could be answered only through competent and painstaking medical research. My recent perusal of the literature and my past observations convinced me that without research into the biological effects of marijuana smoking, legalizing marijuana would be a risk our country could ill afford—the possible impairment of the health of our children and grandchildren.

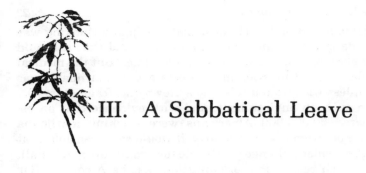

III. A Sabbatical Leave

My first public lecture on cannabis was at the medical school of the University of Paris. Then my subject was apparently not of enough interest to attract more than a few colleagues and a handful of medical students. The year was 1970 and at the time, my research into cannabis had consisted almost totally of library work. For this reason, my first talk was mainly a summary of material that had already appeared in books and journals. The only recent information I could offer had to do with two studies, one chemical and one psychological. In the first, a colleague, Dr. Raphael Mechoulam of the Hebrew University in Jerusalem, described the chemical components of *Cannabis sativa* that are called "cannabinoids." Included among these is the psychoactive chemical in cannabis, Delta-9-tetrahydrocannabinol, or THC as it is commonly known, which is responsible for its intoxicating effects. In the second study, Andrew Weil and Norman Zinberg, psychiatrists from Harvard University, described the immediate effects of smoking one marijuana cigarette. Aside from an increased rate of heartbeat in their selected student volunteers, the Harvard team could find few other kinds of changes either in mental or in motor performance. In conclusion, I told the audience that a great deal of new research was needed. "Pending further study, marijuana should remain, like all new drugs, guilty until proven innocent."

My talk was followed by the observations of Professor M. Mabileau, a noted pharmacologist who is consultant to the French government on dangerous drugs. He had returned from a trip to Africa where he had conducted experiments with certain tribes. He found that when large amounts of cannabis extracts were given to natives ready for war, they resembled savage beasts who had lost all sense of danger. In contrast, the lack of incentive and stagnation usually associated with hashish is caused by prolonged usage. He concluded by saying, "Every public health official in France is agreed that marijuana products are damaging to the health of the individual and should be banned just as opium and coca leaf derivatives are banned."

As I pressed forward to shake hands with Professor Mabileau, several of the people in the audience came up to me with less-than-friendly questions:

"What is wrong with your Food and Drug Administration?" a professor of toxicology asked.

Taken aback by the query, I replied defensively, "They seem to be doing a good job."

"An inconsistent one, you mean," said the man. "On the one hand, they take a very hard-line attitude and ban the use of pharmaceutical compounds which we Europeans consider to be perfectly safe. On the other, they seem to be ready to give marijuana a clean bill of health without benefit of clinical trials and even though most pharmacologists in the rest of the world are convinced it is harmful to health."

Before I could respond, another colleague added his criticism, this time a bit more tactfully. "You in the United States should be more careful about your handling of the marijuana problem. Your example is immediately flashed to the rest of the world. It is very contagious." I could only agree.

As I walked home with my two children in the damp rainy evening, it occurred to me that in France at least there was moral support for my position on cannabis. In the United States, my criticism of those who had spoken out in favor of legalization without full awareness of the biological effects involved had earned for me only harsh words. At least here there was encouragement from professionals who believed that much more pharmacological research was needed before any form of legalization was taken. Although French researchers had not made any more progress than scientists in the United States, they were well supported in their efforts to unlock the mysteries of cannabis.

A few months later a colleague and friend, Dr. Escoffier Lambiotte, medical editor of the French newspaper *Le Monde,* invited me to attend a drug conference in Paris. This gathering of sociologists, philosophers, scientists, psychiatrists, and lawmakers turned out to be a veritable talkfest on the pros and cons of psychoactive drugs. Those who advocated legalization of marijuana, for example, were mostly young sociologists who had studied in the United States. "The virtue of legalization," said one, "is that it allows young people to do their own thing, even if that 'thing' is experimentation with drugs such as marijuana."

The overwhelming majority of people at the conference, however, agreed that a general ban on all "stupefying drugs" should be enforced and maintained by society. The representatives from law enforcement agencies expressed a concern that laws should be used wisely. "This means," said one, "vigorous prosecution of the drug trafficker, but compassionate and understanding treatment of the occasional drug-user."

The conference focused attention once again on the need for more evidence. Over a dozen scientists had described experiments where varying amounts of cannabis had a definite impact on mental and motor skills. Others spoke of the lethargy and lack of initiative that has developed in persons who have used marijuana and hashish over a period of many generations. Still others told of finding physical effects that, if not serious or permanent by themselves, deserved much deeper medical investigation.

Following these meetings and lectures, I contributed to a general review of cannabis that assembled the old and new information about marijuana and its close relative, hashish. This review was published in *La Presse Medicale,* the leading French medical journal. Our conclusion was brief:

"The derivatives of *Cannabis* contain substances which impair thinking and behavior. They do not have any therapeutic application. Adolescents who use these compounds frequently tend to become apathetic, to lose individual ambition and social responsibility, without the benefit of solving their emotional problems. For certain adolescents, *Cannabis* intoxication is the first step towards the regular use of drugs."

It was evident from my discussions with various French medical authorities that marijuana had little chance of ever becoming legal in their country in the foreseeable future. "No matter what happens in the United States," a physician told me, "we'll fight to prevent its introduction here."

Of all the lessons learned during my sabbatical in Paris, however, none was more valuable than the one garnered from Professor Marcel Bessis in the laboratory of cellular pathology at the Paris Medical School. Marcel was an old friend; we had served together as battalion doctors with the First French Army during World War II. In the years after the war, he became one of the world's leading scientists in the study of blood cells.

Hearing of my interest in the white cells of blood—an interest now heightened by my new preoccupation with the biological effects of cannabis—he put his laboratory at my disposal and invited me to carry out basic research there. During the months of using these facilities, I learned a great deal about the structure and function of blood cells.

Blood cells are the only single cells that can be obtained easily and analyzed individually. To study these cells, blood is first drawn from an arm vein, then put in a test tube that is in turn spun very fast in a centrifuge. This is an instrument that resembles the inside tub of a washing machine. The spinning action causes the heavier red cells in the test tube to fall to the bottom while the white cells remain on top. To analyze these white cells, a drop of the top layer is removed with a pipette, a slim glass tube used like an eyedropper, and placed on a glass plate. This plate is then put under a special microscope with an attachment that projects the magnified image on a TV screen.

There are two main types of white blood cells: the lymphocytes, which are round-shaped, and the phagocytes, blob-
shaped cells that are always moving and changing their
configuration. The phagocytes captivated me and for hours I
watched their constant movement on the TV screen. At times
the cell medium was heated to see how temperature affected
their motion. At other times we added an acid or base substance. Staring at the screen, observing the cells under these
varying conditions, we discovered that phagocytes have
maximum speed at high temperatures in an acid solution.
Since heat and excess acidity are associated with infection,
we could see how these two conditions make the phagocytes
spring into action.

The lymphocytes, on the other hand, do not move of their
own volition. Instead they float indifferently around the
phagocytes in the medium on the glass plate. Nevertheless,
they are the most important of the white blood cells because,
like minicomputers, they store all the information concerning the chemical structure of our bodies. The lymphocytes are
able to recognize any substance or molecule foreign to our
body because it will not conform to the acceptable chemical
structure. If a foreign substance should invade our body, the
lymphocytes react by growing in size—they are, in effect,
"turned on"—and produce antibodies and other special factors designed to neutralize and eventually destroy the in-
vader. They send chemical messages to the phagocytes to
destroy foreign cells. All in all, it is a finely tuned system that
represents our first line of defense against sickness.

Two American scientists working in Dr. Bessis' lab—Dr.
William Manger, a friend from my early training at the Mayo
Clinic, and Dr. Marty Murphy—showed me how a lymphocyte looked when observed under the newly introduced scan-
ning microscope. This instrument shows a cell in three dimen-
sions. When viewed in 3-D, the nicely rounded lymphocyte
looks like a forbidding iceberg with a rough surface full of
crevices and small holes. When the lymphocyte is sectioned
and sliced with a precision-slicing machine called a micro-
tome, all sorts of complex structures appear. It occurred to

me that, for future reference, lymphocytes would make excellent models to test the action of drugs. If a way could be found to measure the normal "appetite" of these cells to take up the key chemicals (thymidine, uridine, and leucine) necessary for cell growth and division then the effect of different drugs on this appetite could be determined.

At the time, I was simply learning the rudiments of cell physiology. My interest in the subject was generated by research work in anesthesia and pharmacology. As for marijuana, it never dawned on me then that this knowledge would help me to demonstrate later how cannabis impairs the function of certain white blood cells.

During these busy months in France, I also worked on another problem—a plasma substitute, made with gelatin, that could be used in patients who were suffering from a moderate blood loss. I had studied such a substance twenty years earlier, and now, in collaboration with Dr. André Charra, we found a way of making this gelatin solution come very close—chemically, at least—to real plasma. We were given permission by the French authorities to run clinical trials on patients in several Paris hospitals when our exhaustive laboratory tests showed that our substitute neither interfered with the body's immune system nor effected blood coagulation. When the plasma substitute, called Plasmion, proved to be well tolerated by human subjects, I hoped to introduce it to the United States. This research work also expanded my knowledge of the immune system.

Although my first few months in France were spent almost entirely in laboratories and lecture halls, the summer of 1970 proved to be a little less strenuous. August was spent at the Oceanographic Institute of Monaco, directed by Captain Jacques Yves Cousteau, where, as in past years, I had worked on the effects of drugs on the nervous system of the sea slug, one of the first living creatures to appear in the salty waters of our planet.

My stay in Monaco, however, was marred somewhat by one of the other major problems of our age: While swimming in the blue waters of the Mediterranean, I contracted a severe bacterial infection attributable to sea water pollution. This gave Captain Cousteau the opportunity to express his deep concern about the various forms of environmental pollution that are rapidly destroying many of our most precious natural resources. From there the discussion turned to my concern: "internal pollution" by drugs. As Captain Cousteau spends a great deal of his time in the United States, he was well aware of the widening drug epidemic there. He did not foresee any easy solution to the problem. "We already have tobacco and alcohol," he said. "Why add a third plague on our house?"

Before returning to Paris, I detoured to Geneva for an appointment with Dr. Olaf Braenden, director of the Technical Laboratory of the United Nations Commission on Narcotics. Dr. Braenden, a heavyset man with the agility of an athlete, greeted me cordially. In the course of our conversation, we discovered that we both had been graduate students at the University of Minnesota in 1952. Yet, even though this was our first face-to-face encounter, we'd been following each other's work by means of scientific papers published in various professional journals.

"We are now engaged in analytical research on the many marijuana products," explained Dr. Braenden as he took me on a tour of his laboratory. "These workers use a variety of instruments to analyze samples of cannabis products that are shipped to us from different parts of the world. Dr. Shilov, our research chemist, will show you our supplies."

Dr. Yuri Shilov, a Soviet scientist, worked the combination lock on the heavy door to the small room where opium derivatives and cannabis products are neatly labeled and assembled on shelves that extend from the floor to the ceiling. The storage room contained samples of cannabis in just about every known form. There were plants in plastic bags; compressed bricks of prepared marijuana; slabs of dark cannabis resin that look like carpenters' glue; and more recently seized oily extracts of cannabis. Holding up a glass bottle filled with a thick, dark substance, Dr. Shilov said, "This vial contains seventy percent THC [using the familiar initials of delta-9-

tetrahydrocannabinol] which was seized in Norway." It was a red oil I had heard about. One drop placed on a tobacco cigarette is enough to produce almost immediate and prolonged intoxication!

I met other workers in the laboratory. They came from all over the world—Japan, Lebanon, England, the United States. They were helping to analyze cannabis and to devise more accurate methods of detection. Among the new techniques used in the lab was chromatography. This is a way of distinguishing molecules by the varying speeds at which they pass through layers of special material. In this way the different chemical compounds of a substance can be separated and analyzed. THC, for instance, was isolated from the other nonpsychoactive cannabinoids with this method.

After my laboratory tour, Dr. Braenden showed me his library and reference service. It is probably the most complete source of cannabis information in the world today. Despite the shelf upon shelf of books and articles, Dr. Braenden and I agreed that very little information was available on the medical effects of cannabis.

At lunch I met still another specialist in the field of drug control. He was Dr. Adolph Lande, a colleague from Columbia who is on the faculty of the School of Law. Dr. Lande is concerned with the legal aspects of international drug control. He had participated in the drafting of the 1961 Single Convention on Narcotic Drugs and probably knows more about the history of cannabis than any man. He asked if he could help me. Although my concern is mainly with the medical aspects of marijuana, the question of legalization is intertwined with it at every step of the way.

"There is a great deal of talk about legalization of marijuana," I began. "I know," he said, as if waiting for the question, "but it should be only for the right reasons. The direction of the change should wait upon the information that people like you can uncover in the laboratory."

When I reviewed the events of my day at the United Nations Commission on Narcotics in Geneva, three basic points stood out, and they have guided me ever since: The problem of

marijuana is one that cannot be solved with social surveys—
polls that inquire about the number, occupation, and age
group of smokers in a given country and are so favored by the
social scientists; the effects produced by the whole drug, not
only by THC, must be studied; and there is a possibility of
another biological effect more serious, more damaging than
the obvious mind-altering effects.

It was the last possibility that concerned me the most.
Here, truly, would be the crucial avenue of research to follow.

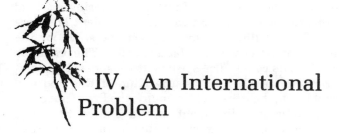

IV. An International Problem

Most Americans think that antimarijuana laws were created in recent years just to thwart use of the drug by younger people. Not true! They are actually the result of international agreements signed by the United States a half century ago in order to halt traffic in what was then considered to be a dangerous substance.

Aware of this fact, on my return to the United States in the autumn of 1970, I decided that the logical place for my own detailed research into that aspect of marijuana would be the Dag Hammarskjöld Library for International Scholars at the United Nations in New York. If the nations of the world had seen fit to meet on several occasions in order to control the distribution of cannabis derivatives, then they must have suspected or known of specific health hazards. The examination of these international documents might lead to some clues that would aid me in the direction of my own laboratory work.

My study soon revealed that at the turn of the century, with the development of intercontinental communications, it became apparent to the nations of the world that the control of substances dangerous to man's health and to society—mainly opium at that time—had to be controlled on a global basis. Representatives of sovereign nations held conferences to formulate regulations for the international control of opium and other dangerous drugs. The first such gathering was held in Shanghai in 1904 at the instigation of President Theodore Roosevelt. This preliminary meeting set the stage for the First Opium Conference at The Hague in 1912. The preamble to the text of this conference speels out its general goals:

"The Emperor of all Russias, the King of England and Emperor of India, the Kaiser of Germany, the President of the French Republic, the President of the United States of America . . . desirous of advancing a step further on the road opened by the International Commission of Shanghai of 1909; determined to bring about the gradual suppression of the abuse of opium, morphine and cocaine and also of the drugs prepared or derived from these substances which might give rise to similar abuses; taking into consideration the necessity and the mutual advantage of an international agreement on this point; convinced that in this humanitarian endeavor they will meet with the unanimous adherence of all States concerned; have decided to conclude a convention with this object."

Almost as an afterthought, an "Indian Hemp Resolution" was tacked on, calling for the "study [of] the question of Indian Hemp from the statistical and scientific point of view with the object of regulating its abuses, should the necessity be felt, by internal regulation or by international agreement."

By the time of the Second Opium Conference, held in Geneva in 1924, some scientists had agreed that the time for cannabis control was at hand. While opium was still the major consideration, Egypt's delegate, Dr. El Guindy, said, "There is, however, another product, which is at least as harmful as opium, if not more so, and which my government would be glad to see in the same category as the other narcotics already mentioned. I refer to hashish, the product of *Cannabis sativa*. This substance and its derivatives work such havoc that the Egyptian government has for a long time past prohibited their introduction into the country. I cannot emphasize sufficiently the importance of including this product in the list of narcotics, the use of which is to be regulated by this Conference."

In answer to questions from other delegates, Dr. El Guindy claimed that although the Egyptian government had banned the growing of cannabis, large amounts were still smuggled in from neighboring countries. "This illicit use of hashish," he told the Conference, "is the principal cause of insanity in Egypt, varying from thirty to sixty percent of the total number of cases reported. Taken occasionally and in small doses, hashish perhaps does not offer much danger, but there is always the risk that once a person begins to take it, he will continue. He acquires the habit and becomes addicted to the drug and once this happens it is very difficult to escape."

The greatest hazards of cannabis intoxication mentioned by Dr. El Guindy were "acute hashishism," marked by crises of delirium and insanity, and "chronic hashishism," marked by visible mental and physical deterioration. Because of pressure from the Egyptian and Turkish delegates, who would not sign a ban on opium unless cannabis was also included, after some debate all the delegates voted in favor of controlling "Indian Hemp" as defined by the "dried flowering or fruiting tops of the pistillate plant *Cannabis sativa* from which the resin has not been extracted, under whatever name they may be designated in commerce." Thus, cannabis was put on the forbidden list, not because of medical reasons, but for social ones.

After World War II, the United Nations inherited the duty of enforcing the highly complex international agreements on control of dangerous drugs, including the above cannabis control resolution. When the World Health Organization came into being in 1948, this responsibility was shifted to them in the form of an expert Committee on Drug Dependence that served as an advisory group to the United Nations Commission on Narcotics. The committee, made up of physicians and scientists, reviewed the cannabis situation and quickly came to the conclusion "that use of the drug was dangerous from every point of view, whether physical, mental or social." The ultimate result of this review was the 1961 Single Convention on Narcotic Drugs in which 500 delegates from seventy-four nations, including some of the best toxicologists and pharmacologists in the world, recommended that cannabis, in all its forms, be limited exclusively "to medical and scientific purposes." The primary reason for this strict regulation was that all the available expert advice from the World Health Organization indicated that cannabis did constitute a danger to health and a hazard to society, although, admittedly, not well-documented.

While the United States was a signatory member of both the Second Opium Conference and the United Nations agreements, the signing was done with the attitude that the inclusion of cannabis in an international drug ban was "more important to *them* than to *us*." Marijuana was not yet a problem in America, and there were only a farsighted few like the head of the American delegation, career diplomat Harry Anslinger, who recognized its dangers.

The Single Convention was hailed by most countries as a landmark for the control of dangerous drugs throughout the world. It was also hailed as a model of the kind of international cooperation the United Nations can achieve. The agreements reached by the Convention were unanimously ratified by the participating nations.

Ten years later, however, in the United States the climate of opinion had changed as the use of marijuana had become widespread. Now there were dissenters who objected to the inclusion of cannabis in the Single Convention. Thus, Harry Anslinger became the focal point of the attack of the new proponents of pot. One critic said, "The inclusion of cannabis into an international agreement mainly concerned with opiates and cocaine was due to the efforts of one determined man, Harry Anslinger." But anyone who has read the documents would realize that the agreement was the result of a historical movement to control or eliminate dangerous psychotropic drugs, including cannabis—as are virtually all the United States federal and state antimarijuana laws.

In any event, the United Nations Single Convention of 1961 was not the last one to be held on this subject. A new conference in Vienna in 1971 produced an international agreement to control many of the newer psychotropic drugs such as hallucinogens, barbiturates, and stimulants.

While my research at the Dag Hammarskjöld Library did not produce any major revelations, it did clarify certain points that I considered to be important to the evolution of my own work. Essentially, I became convinced that the present legal strictures against marijuana in the United States were not based on one man's perversity but were the result of international agreements that went back to the beginning of this century; cannabis was included in these international agreements because the majority of delegates to the conventions were aware of both mental and physical harm produced by the drug; and in the international community, at least, there was no doubt of the dangers to health inherent in marijuana.

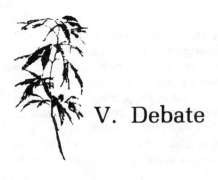

V. Debate

As for my own research projects in the laboratory at Columbia University, the trip abroad and subsequent research had now splintered my interests in new directions: Besides my regular anesthesia research and my work on Plasmion, the plasma substitute, I now wanted to investigate the pharmacological effects of marijuana on cells. It was a propitious time to launch such an effort because chemicals isolated from cannabis were now being made available to licensed researchers by the National Institutes of Mental Health.

At this time an article appeared in the *New York Times:* "Minister Urges Legal Marijuana." The article went on to say that Canon Walter D. Dennis, Jr., of the Cathedral of St. John the Divine in New York had urged in a sermon that marijuana smoking be legalized. Estimating that 20,000,000 people smoke it regularly, the twenty-eight-year-old minister told the congregation, "The pressing question for us is: How should the Church in the 1970s respond? Perhaps the task of Christians is not to condemn marijuana use but rather to find out what if any is the good use of marijuana. Then we might know the meaning of the text 'And God saw everything that he had made and behold, it was very good.'"

According to the article, Canon Dennis' opinions were supported by the Episcopal Bishop of New York and by many of the listeners in the congregation. He urged the church to take the lead in pressing for more equitable and realistic laws to replace the current irrational ones. The *Times* went on to say that Canon Dennis' sermon was praised by many of the young, among them an eighteen-year-old from New Jersey who was quoted as saying, "It's revolutionary, instead of hearing another sermon that is twenty years old, I'm hearing something that's today and tomorrow. It's great. That is what we need."

But what upset me most in the article was this statement: "Discussing his remarks later, Canon Dennis pointed that that the main factor that had crystalized his outrage about 'discriminatory' marijuana laws was the growing body of medical knowledge indicating that the drug was harmless."

In my searches no such knowledge had been found. I wrote to Canon Dennis asking for the source of his information. In reply, he referred me to an article in *Scientific American,* written by Harvard psychiatrist Dr. Lester Grinspoon, and to a book I knew, *Marijuana—the New Prohibition,* by Dr. John Kaplan, a professor of international law at Stanford.

When I read the article and reread the book, however, I could find no evidence whatever concerning the biological effects of marijuana. The studies were all concerned primarily with psychomotor reactions. That is, they described the reactions of marijuana smokers to various psychological and manual dexterity tests. But there was no reference to chemical investigations that might show what effect the drug has on body tissues and fluids. Moreover, for every study that the authors felt demonstrated the harmlessness of marijuana, I could cite data that came to the opposite conclusion.

A few days later, the *New York Times* ran a letter to the editor signed by Dr. Franz Winkler, who wrote:

"Although the existing laws clearly indicate that the majority of scientists are aware of the damage the drug causes to the physical, mental and genetic organism, years may pass before a sufficient number of case histories can be collected to offer irrefutable proof. Then it will be too late for millions. Unfortunately a group of well-meaning, but certainly misguided, individuals declare publicly that marijuana is harmless, without possessing either the training or the opportunity for a valid judgment on the matter."

Dr. Winkler added that on the basis of his observations in his practice as a family physician, he was convinced marijuana is a dangerous drug that leads to a gradual disintegration of the personality.

Here was someone who shared my views on the subject, so I quickly got in touch with him. In return Dr. Winkler sent me his pamphlet called "About Marihuana," along with some of his notes and observations.

I did not hear anything more from Dr. Winkler until a month later when a letter came from him inviting me to a debate, "The Pros and Cons of Marijuana," to be held in Darien, Connecticut. In support of the drug would be the Reverend Dennis. Taking the negative side would be Dr. Winkler, who asked me along to discuss the scientific aspect of marijuana use. I accepted immediately.

Undeterred by a raging snowstorm the night of the debate, Dr. Winkler, a graying gentleman in his late sixties, called for me at my laboratory in his car. Assuring me that he was used to such weather, "I was born in Austria," he said, "and we have very thick snow out there," he continued to fill me in on his background. He explained that his interest in marijuana was due to his training in both psychiatry and internal medicine that gave him the opportunity to study the interaction between mind and body. For the past twenty-five years he had been practicing family medicine in New York, a type of practice that is rapidly disappearing in favor of specialities. "This is one reason," he told me, "why some segments of the medical profession have been so slow to recognize the disastrous effects of marijuana. It takes a general practitioner, with intimate knowledge of a family's physical and emotional problems, to observe what happens when the drug is introduced."

By the time we reached Darien, over a foot of snow was on the ground. Our destination was "The Source," a small house on the old Boston Post Road that was headquarters for the group that had organized the debate. Our hosts were, for the most part, business executives and their wives. To our surprise and delight, the women had prepared a hot supper, which we shared with the Reverend Dennis.

The debate, broadcast on a local radio station, was held in the high school auditorium. Despite the weather there was a large audience divided evenly between conservatively dressed adults and jean-clad youngsters. The meeting opened with statements from each of the speakers, followed by questions from a panel of students and from the audience.

The main thrust of Reverent Dennis' speech was that marijuana should be legalized because Professor Grinspoon of Harvard had proven "scientifically" that it was less harmful than the tobacco and alcohol to which so many members of our society are addicted. Legalization, he contended, would provide a better way of controlling the substance. Among his other points: Marijuana laws, like the prohibition laws, are unpopular and therefore ignored; police officers don't want the job of enforcement; it's extreme to make criminals out of teen-agers who are caught smoking "a harmless joint"; an unenforceable law breeds dangerous contempt for the majesty of our judicial system.

There was vigorous applause after his speech, mostly from the youngsters in the audience. Then Dr. Winkler, speaking in a tired-sounding voice, rose to make his statement.

"No, Reverend Dennis is mistaken, as is Dr. Grinspoon. Marijuana is a very harmful substance, because it has subtle long-term effects which the family physician will detect over a period of several months or a year. An early effect of marijuana and hashish use is a progressive loss of willpower, already noticeable to the trained observer after only six weeks of moderate use. Soon all ability for real joy disappears to be replaced by a noisy pretense of fun."

There were giggles from the audience.

"Whereas healthy teen-agers will eagerly participate in sports and other activities, a marijuana user will show an increasing tendency to talk endlessly of lofty goals without doing anything about them. Instead of developing strong feelings towards others, the marijuana user is apt to wallow in sentimental emotion."

Then Dr. Winkler threw a direct challenge to the audience:

"I'm aware that pot smokers will refuse to accept such news. For this reason, I encourage you to conduct your own investigation. Pick from among your classmates one who has been taking marijuana for at least a year, one whom you knew well before he or she began smoking pot. Then compare his present personality with his former self. If you do not find that his personality has changed profoundly, and that the person is turning into a empty shell, then I'll make no further effort to convince you."

Dr. Winkler's closing remarks were devoted to the myth that marijuana is less dangerous than alcohol. Although he recognized that chronic alcoholism is a scourge, he had observed during a lifetime of patient care that while people can tolerate moderate, even daily, comsumption of alcohol, the same is not true of marijuana. "An illness does not become more attractive by a statement that another one is just as bad," he said.

Now came time for my remarks. I explained to the audience that no scientific evidence of biological damage or lack of it existed at the present time. Studies looking into the effects of marijuana on the human body had just begun. Until proven harmless, however, a drug is presumed dangerous by all physicians. On the basis of observations by competent physicians all over the world, particularly those in areas where marijuana has been used for a long time, though, there is empirical evidence of its harmful physical effects.

Dr. Winkler's and my remarks received loud applause from the older generation. But most of the questions were directed at Reverend Dennis.

"At what age should smoking marijuana be legal?" asked a boy.

"At whatever the legal drinking age in the particular state," came the reply from Reverend Dennis.

"What about the risk of escalation to other drugs?"

"The risk has never really been proven. Of course, some marijuana smokers might use more dangerous substances, especially if they are dealing with an underground trafficker who tries to push other drugs. But Goode, Grinspoon, Kaplan and others have shown that most smokers are satisfied with pot. . . . We must remember that law and government can never replace the responsibility each of us ultimately bears for our own lives."

This answer won for him a burst of applause. Then a student said to Dr. Winkler, "I've smoked pot for over a year and my school grades are still okay. How can you explain that?" Dr. Winkler's response was based on his long medical practice:

"I have tried for thirty-eight years to make friends with young children and to keep their confidence and friendship through their adolescent and adult years. They do not come as patients but merely to discuss their views on life with an older man. Thus, I have known many people for a long time, not just as a physician but as a friend. Among them there are those who have taken marijuana at one time or another, giving me a chance to observe its effects on the deeper strata of the personality, strata well hidden from a casual observer. In this long experience, I have come to the conclusion that the abuse of marijuana is one of the major tragedies of our time. While hard drugs cause far more obvious physical and mental harm, they are mostly used by people already defeated by life, who seek in them a way to oblivion. What makes the use of marijuana tragic is that it appeals not only to the neurotic and already defeated, but to healthy young people who seek in it nothing worse than diversion or an expansion of consciousness. Unknown to themselves and unnoticed by a generation of parents, teachers and physicians often too busy or uncaring to pay real attention, some of the finest young people are thus condemned by sheer ignorance to a gradual disintegration of their personality."

Our side did not win many points that evening. Most of the youngsters in the audience heard only what they came to hear; namely, a responsible public figure, a clergyman no less, espousing the cause of legalization of marijuana based on "medical" evidence. But if that generation was not impressed by Dr. Winkler's remarks, I was. On the return trip I told him that now, more than ever, I was determined to look into the possibility of physical, even cellular, damage that might accompany the psychological effects he had observed.

Getting started in the laboratory proved to be as difficult a task as convincing the students of Darien that marijuana might have harmful effects. Although marijuana was a controversial subject, it lacked the prestige and respectability of pharmacological research into drugs for diseases of the heart, the lungs, arthritis, cancer, and other catastrophic illnesses. Instead of a staff of eager researchers, the marijuana project was initiated only with the help of one of my staunchest and most capable collaborators in the laboratory, Mrs. Iris Schwartz.

Our first undertaking was strictly bureaucratic: In order to use "dangerous drugs" for experimental purposes, it was necessary to apply for a special license from state and federal authorities. This involved filling out what seemed like an endless stream of forms and answering many questions posed by the special agents of the State and Federal Bureaus of Narcotic and Dangerous Drugs. It's ironic that a physician can prescribe to patients an endless variety of possibly addictive drugs. But the researcher who wants to use relatively small amounts of such drugs in laboratory and animal experiments has to go through the tedious process of getting a license. Any student might have wondered why I bothered with all that paperwork when he could get me all the pot I needed right in his dorm!

The next step in the process was submitting a memorandum to the Center for Studies of Narcotic and Drug Abuse of the National Institute of Mental Health explaining the type of work I planned to carry out with delta-9-THC. At that time this chemical was being manufactured synthetically under contract for the National Institutes which, in turn, distributed it to qualified, licensed investigators. Clearly, as far as the United States government was concerned, marijuana was still considered a dangerous drug to be used only in carefully regulated circumstances.

After several months of inspection by state and federal agents in charge of the control of narcotics and dangerous drugs, and after much correspondence and many phone calls, the license that allowed me to investigate cannabis products

in the laboratory was finally granted. I immediately ordered
THC ampules, and a week later we received our first ship-
ment. We were ready to begin our research!

The first method we used to study the effects of THC was
one widely used by pharmacologists to study many kinds of
drugs in the laboratory. A strip of smooth muscle is removed
from the womb of a rat and placed in a special solution that
allows it to remain "alive" for several hours. The muscle is
then attached to a very sensitive wire that registers any
change in its length. When the drug under investigation is
added, the muscle reacts by contracting or relaxing. This is
recorded automatically on a moving chart. The solution in
the tube can be flushed several times so as to wash one drug
away before experimenting with the next, and the muscle is
allowed to return to its original base line. The advantage of
using this model was that it was relatively cheap: We did not
have to purchase any additional equipment, and one well-
trained person could do most of the work.

Each drug to be tested is prepared in different concentrations in order to establish a "dose-response curve." The
dose-response curve is the standard test of the pharmacologist who must demonstrate that the effect produced by
a drug is related to the amount administered. Furthermore,
the amount of a drug used is related to its biological effect in a
logarithmatic fashion, rather than in a linear one: That is, in
order to double the effect, one has to increase the dosage by
ten until the maximum effect is obtained.

Our first experimental trials with THC were very arduous.
Active THC is contained in an alcohol solution in a small
brown glass ampule about two inches in length. The glass is
tinted brown to screen out the inactivating effects of light. As
soon as we diluted the solution with water (to obtain the
different concentrations for a dose-response curve), it became
cloudy and a blob of brown resin containing the THC appeared in the tube. The reason was that THC is not water
soluble, in contrast to the drugs I had studied previously.
Thus it was not easy to make different solutions containing
precisely known amounts of THC, and we were never able to

predict with complete accuracy how much we were using in each experiment. Our solution to this problem was to dissolve THC in special solvents.

After many attempts we were finally able to obtain dose-response curves relating the concentration of THC to its relaxing effect on the strip of smooth muscle. To our surprise we found this effect of THC to be different from that of other drugs we had used before. Instead of the muscle returning to its original length after removing THC, the relaxing effect was permanent: Once the drug was introduced into the system and the change in muscle relaxation produced, neither could this change be reversed nor could the drug be washed out—even if the muscle was flushed for hours.

We had observed one very interesting effect of THC. Investigators in other laboratories were discovering others: THC decreases body temperature; it stimulates enzymes in the liver to become active; it prevents convulsions in animals; it decreases the heart rate of animals (but increases that of man); it causes changes in blood pressure. Any drug, especially active ones, can be used as a tool in the laboratory to explore the basic mechanisms of body function, and this is the way THC was used.

Obviously the first wave of systematic laboratory work was turning up reactions that nobody had ever suspected or predicted before. But none of these revelations alone explained why they happened or what long-term effects they might have on the human organism. Having gone about as far as we could go with the smooth muscle of the rat, we were anxious to investigate new territory. As a result, we began a search for another experimental model that would allow us to study the effects of THC on a whole animal.

One possible answer came from the work of Dr. Louis Harris, then at the University of North Carolina. At the spring meeting of the American Pharmacological Society, he reported observing the phenomenon of increasing tolerance to THC among rats, pigeons, and dogs who were given the drug over a period of only one month. In some cases, he said, the dosage had to be increased by as much as 100 times in order to obtain the initial effect.

As an example, Dr. Harris described an experiment with a dog who was given a large amount of THC until he was so "stoned" he was unable to stand for several hours. After five days of such a dosage, however, the drug no longer had this effect on the dog. In order to reach the same degree of intoxication, Dr. Harris had to increase the dosage tenfold. This is by pharmacological standards an extraordinary degree of tolerance, and I was anxious to explore it further.

It would be nice to say that we simply went from experiment to experiment, making discoveries and unlocking the biological mysteries of cannabis. Unfortunately, the scientist must at some time or another face the universal problem—where does the money come from? The tolerance experiments I envisioned would require not only a colony of expensive rhesus monkeys, but also the hiring of specialized personnel and the purchase of new equipment. My present funds were not only limited but completely allotted to other projects. Moreover, co-workers did not evince the slightest interest in giving up their present research work in favor of experiments with marijuana.

In the past, luck had been on my side in getting the funding needed for my research projects. My letter of appointment to the Department of Anesthesia at Columbia University in 1959 from the chairman promised me, "You will have complete autonomy in respect to the investigation you wish to pursue and the time you wish to spend on it." Thanks to this liberal mandate, I was able to obtain the monies necessary for organizing a well-equipped laboratory and staffing it with bright young scientists.

Now, however, this halcyon age of unlimited funding was over: Monies were restricted and research programs curtailed. No longer was I free to pursue the research of *my* choice; we were all urged to orient our goals toward solving problems that would produce practical remedies in the near future. The public was demanding more immediate benefits from the millions of dollars poured annually into research since World War II.

Up to that point most of my funds had come from the National Institutes of Health, the federal agency that has supported the bulk of medical research carried out in universities throughout the country. As a rule, NIH awards funds for from three to five years following a peer review of the project of the applying investigator. Our department had received a five-year grant that provided enough money to support most of the activities in my laboratory.

Now, in the spring of 1971, this grant came up for renewal. In order to be ready for inspection by the officials from NIH and peer reviewers from other universities, our future plans had to be detailed precisely and our whole laboratory organization had to be shipshape. Such an inspection is called a "site visit" and is a routine occurrence with all grant applications and renewals.

In the past, when funds were plentiful, these visits were welcome—we were showing off; this time, however, the site visit was fraught with tension and anxiety. Now only a limited number of the hundreds of worthy applications could be accepted by NIH. Would ours be one of them? Obviously, it could hardly have been a worse time to suggest a new research project—on marijuana of all subjects. Even my colleagues in the laboratory and at the university had reservations about my plans. Thus, at the site visit I described only briefly my proposed investigation into the possible effects of THC on body function, and expanded in greater detail reports about the other projects in my laboratory.

Despite these precautions, though, my fears were justified when a few months later I learned that after the expiration of the current grant (we then had two years to go), our federal funds would be discontinued. In spite of these difficulties, I was convinced that I would obtain the financial support needed for this work from some agency or some person who shared my concern about the effects of marijuana.

Despite my own difficulties at that time in finding funds, it was apparent that the government was playing an encouraging and active role in marijuana research. Other studies were going on. In all cases the marijuana being used was standardized, government "issue." As Dr. Edward F. Domino, professor of pharmacology at the University of Michigan

Medical School, told *Medical World News* in July 1971, "I don't think any investigator can say anything but good for the approach the government is finally taking. Our society seems to be at a stage where you're no longer strange if you want to do marijuana research, but a perfectly legitimate investigator."

Dr. Domino, as the medical journal pointed out, should know, because he began working with marijuana derivatives as early as 1954, under a Department of Defense contract. Stressing the need to know more about the rapidly proliferating marijuana smoking habit, he said in the article, "I think that in the next few years we'll see a tremendous burst of energy in this field, particularly directed to determining the place of these substances in medicine."

Almost as he was saying this, some first reports were coming in concerning marijuana's physiological effects. One interesting bit of evidence came from Dr. Domino's own laboratory at the University of Michigan. For decades marijuana users and those interested in the drug had believed that smoking caused dilation of the pupils of the eyes. Narcotics enforcement officers, in fact, often used this sign as evidence that an individual was taking the drug. But photographs showed clearly that when marijuana smokers are high, their pupils actually contract. Moreover, there is a definite, though mild, drooping of the eyelids that gives the user a sleepy appearance.

A more important finding to emerge from this early research concerned tolerance. Marijuana smokers have always been vehement on the subject of how much it takes an experienced user to get high. "The more you smoke," they contend, "the smaller the amount of marijuana needed to reach an intoxicated state."

Controlled medical experiments by reputable researchers, however, could establish no such reverse tolerance. In fact, there was clear evidence that tolerance can be produced in animals—and growing evidence that it happens in man. A team of experimenters at the University of North Carolina found that after a week of regular marijuana administration pigeons developed a marked tolerance to it. Eventually, the researchers reported, a dose even two hundred times as high as the initial amount could no longer produce the responses observed when the birds were first started on the drug. The experiment was repeated in rats and dogs with the same observable effects. And while it is more difficult to duplicate the same conditions in man, studies made by Dr. Reese Jones from the University of California in San Francisco show a similar build-up of resistance in humans to the drug's psychoactive effects.

Perhaps the most important result to come out of the early research done in 1970 was the findings of Drs. Louis Lemberger, Julius Axelrod, and Irwin J. Kopin of the National Institute of Mental Health. Up to that point most scientists had believed that marijuana was "washed" out of the body in much the same manner as the metabolic by-products of alcohol are quickly excreted. Using radioactively tagged delta-9-THC, the NIMH scientists discovered that marijuana's metabolites remain in the body for up to eight days. This represented the first concrete evidence that THC and its metabolites actually accumulate in certain tissues for a week or more.

What does this mean in lay terms? Emphasizing first that these findings are still under intensive investigation by many researchers, it means that even casual smokers who consume no more than two or three marijuana cigarettes a week are never completely free of the drug's active effects. In a sense, this is a form of internal pollution that may have both short- and long-term harmful effects.

Looking back, the years 1970 and 1971 were watershed years for the investigation of cannabis. Although man had been using, talking about, and to some extent studying the drug for almost 2,000 years, only now was cannabis finally coming under systematic scientific investigation. I was certain that the next few years would produce some important results.

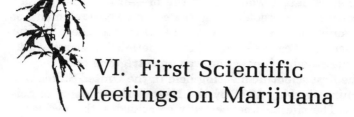

VI. First Scientific
Meetings on Marijuana

In the late spring of 1971, a burst of national concern about the effects of marijuana prompted the release of some federal money for research. Although my own funds were still limited, many other scientists benefited. The new wave of research produced a spate of symposiums. It is important to realize the significance of such meetings to the scientist. He attends them with the fervor of a devoted churchgoer. For this is the forum where he explains his work, discusses his results, and compares them with those of his colleagues and friendly rivals.

One such meeting was organized in London by the Ciba Foundation. Chaired by Dr. William Paton, the distinguished professor of pharmacology at Oxford University, it produced some surprising new findings. A Swedish scientist had injected tagged THC in rats and rabbits. On analyzing the droppings of these creatures, he found that their urine and feces remained radioactive for at least three days. More important, he discovered a similarly lasting concentration of radioactivity in dissected portions of their liver, spleen, kidneys, and adrenal glands. While there had been other reports of the lasting effects of marijuana's metabolites, this was the first time the tagged molecules had been traced to the spleen. The importance of the spleen is that it is closely involved in the body's immunity system. Remembering the phagocytes

and lymphocytes I had observed on the television screen in
Dr. Bessis' lab, I wondered if the presence of marijuana's
by-products in the spleen might affect these basic elements of
our immunity system. At the time, of course, there was no
way for me to carry out this kind of detailed research work.
But the possible connection was an intriguing one.

The first scientific meeting held in the United States was
organized in May 1971 by the New York Academy of Sciences. The timing unexpectedly coincided with newspaper
and television stories of the single largest seizure of
marijuana in America. With public awareness of the existence of grand-scale marijuana smuggling operations,
there was renewed interest in the possible physical effects of
the drug: Besides its action on the mind, did it alter any body
function? Once again, much of the conference material was
familiar, but there was also enough new information to hold
my interest.

The first lecture was given by Professor Norman Doorenbos of the University of Mississippi, the school selected by the
National Institute of Mental Health to grow marijuana ex-
perimentally. The marijuana grown there comes from seeds
collected in different parts of the world. On my visit to this pot
plantation a few months later, I found something that looked
more like a prison than a farm: acres of cannabis plants
surrounded by eight-foot-high barbed-wire fences with
watchtowers spaced every 500 feet. The cost of policing this
area twenty-four hours a day is in excess of $30,000 a year!

The purpose of the Mississippi pot plantation is to provide
scientists with marijuana of known potency and origin.
Using the products grown here, Doorenbos and his colleagues
were able to define in chemical terms the "fiber" and "drug"
types of marijuana by measuring the amount of delta-9-
tetrahydrocannabinol (THC) and cannabidiol (CBD) they
contained. They have learned that while the chemical formulas of THC and CBD are very similar, CBD has one more
hydrogen atom in its molecule. This extra atom changes the
shape of the molecule just enough to effect some important
differences in function.

In recent years pharmacologists have come to know that the general shape of a molecule determines its biological effect on the human body. Drugs that are biologically active molecules can be compared to keys that fit into locks located on the surface of all our cells. These "locks" are called receptors. THC is the only chemical key in the cannabis plant that "unlocks" a receptor in the brain that controls our state of consciousness.

The chemical difference between the drug and hemp type marijuana plants is in the proportion of the amounts of THC and CBD each contains. In the drug type, the amount of the intoxicating molecule THC is greater than the amount of the nonintoxicating CBD. This difference in proportion, however, also varies with the origin of the plant. Marijuana grown from Mexican or Thailand seeds contains enough THC to give a "high" with only one-third of a cigarette. Plants grown from Iowa seed, on the other hand, contain so little THC that they give practically no effect after smoking as many as three cigarettes.

Climatic conditions cause another variation in the potency of marijuana. While drug-type plants have been grown as far north as Iceland, if the climate is too inhospitable they will eventually revert to the fiber-type plant that has little or no THC content. Professor Michel Paris of the University of Paris, in his experimentation with cannabis plants grown in a huge hothouse, called a Phytotron, demonstrated the extraordinary genetic plasticity of the plant. Different degrees of humidity, light, and heat can change the cannabinoid content within a few months.

Dr. Raphael Mechoulam of Israel, who had originally described the chemical cannabinoids, spoke at this meeting, this time about experiments with monkeys. The animals, when injected with THC, showed symptoms similar to those of humans stoned on pot—impairment of motor skills, redness of eye, drooping eyelid, loss of muscle strength, increased heart beat, indifference to environment, decline of aggression. He told the audience that after being injected with THC, the monkeys would assume the posture typical of a habitual

hashish user: a hunched over, brooding position reminiscent
of Rodin's *The Thinker*.

Professor Mechoulam had also continued his research in
cannabis chemistry: He discovered a cause for the variation
in the intoxicating effect of marijuana related to the chemical
composition of THC—any change in the shape of the molecule
can alter the effect of the drug on the mind. But Dr.
Mechoulam could not tell me what kind of biological activity
such a changed molecule might have. This was a question to
be answered by further research.

Thus while the external manifestations of cannabis did not
seem especially serious, the inner effects as reported at the
meeting could be cause for concern. Three scientists, Drs.
Monroe Wall of the Research Triangle Institute in North
Carolina, Erminio Costa of the National Institute of Mental
Health, and Sumner Burstein of the Worcester Foundation,
working independently, told of finding how THC is changed by
enzymes in the body. Enzymes are special substances, produced by cells that have the property of changing the
molecular composition of chemicals so that they become inactive substances, or metabolites. In other words, after a drug,
such as penicillin, for example, performs its designed function, these enzymes come along to render it inactive.

But the three scientists found the body's handling of THC
to be different. Instead of being converted by enzymes into
inactive substances, the THC is actually transformed into
active metabolites that have even greater biological activity.
The next chemical step is for the enzymes to transform the
"active" THC metabolites into nonpsychoactive metabolites.
Because these no longer affect the system, they have been
considered by scientists to be "inactive." But it is these so-
called inactive metabolites that have been shown to linger on
in the body.

What happens to these metabolites was described next by
Drs. Louis Lemberger, Julius Axelrod, and Irwin J. Kopin of
the NIMH. They injected tagged THC into the veins of human
volunteers. Some of these subjects had never smoked
marijuana before, while others had used the substance daily

for at least a year. In both users and nonusers alike, radioactivity in the urine and feces was detected for more than a week. Why did the radioactivity in this experiment persist for so long? Because THC is stored in fatty tissues such as the liver, brain, bone marrow, and adrenal glands and only slowly excreted in feces and urine.

Digressing for a moment, Dr. Lemberger explained why this fact made THC so different from alcohol. "Were it soluble in water, as is alcohol," he said, "it would be eliminated from our body many times more rapidly. Because it is soluble in fat, though, it lingers, and possibly produces effects for days, or weeks, or even months on end."

Interestingly enough, the persistence of cannabis products in the body is not a new idea. It was suspected as long ago as the thirteenth century. Franz Rosenthal, who wrote the book *The Herb: Hashish versus Medieval Muslim Society,* translating from original manuscripts of the medieval Muslim recorder Az Aarkashi, quotes the following observations of a religious leader named Shaykl Ali Al-Hariri:

"This Hariri was very hard on habitual users of hashish. One of his followers sent a messenger to him to upbraid him for his attitude. The Shaykl said to the messenger, 'If the man mentioned is one of my followers, so that I have to oblige him, let him give up hashish for forty days until his body is free from it, and forty more days until he is rested from it after having become free. Then let him come to me so that I shall inform him about it.' "

No one has yet calculated exactly how long it takes to "wash out" THC from the body of a long-term user. When they do, it would be interesting to compare the modern scientist's estimate with that of Al-Hariri's.

Another subject taken up by the conference was the dose of THC necessary to kill an animal. Marijuana smokers have long argued that no one ever dies of using marijuana, in contrast to the many victims of cigarette smoking and alcohol. Experiments by Dr. Robert Forney, professor of pharmacology, Indiana University School of Medicine, tend to confirm this observation. He gave rats and mice a dose so potent that it almost immediately killed fifty percent of them. But when the amount of THC used in this experiment is translated into human terms, it means the smoking of about 100 very strong marijuana joints at one sitting, a dose impossible to reach in man. Except for one instance, there are no thoroughly documented cases of users who have died after smoking marijuana. One case was reported by Dr. Aubin Heyndrix, professor of toxicology at the University of Ghent, of a young Belgian athlete found dead in his room with large amounts of cannabis resins, but no other drugs. When tests were run to detect poisons, the only foreign substances found were cannabis by-products in the urine.

Dr. Forney's work with animals, however, did produce further evidence of tolerance. Among the fifty percent of the rats and mice who did not die from the original amount, larger and larger doses had to be administered before the researchers could achieve a lethal reaction. Thus, even where massive amounts of THC were used, tolerance to the drug developed quickly.

The problem of tolerance raised by the experiments of Dr. Forney and others is an important one for the pharmacologist who seeks new drugs for the treatment of disease. Tolerance of a drug is an unwanted feature of its usage because dosage must continually be increased as the body becomes habituated to it. Early investigators in the United States and abroad stated that long-term users of marijuana did tend to smoke more and more cigarettes. But these observations were discounted after the experiments of Drs. Andrew Weil and Norman Zinberg at Harvard indicated that the habitual user of cannabis experienced a "reverse tolerance"—they required less marijuana to become "high." This concept was accepted uncritically by many sociologists and psychiatrists, who used it as one more argument to demonstrate why marijuana should be accepted as a "recreational drug." Even after reports showed unequivocally that marijuana and THC induce a rapid tolerance in both animals and humans, many of these people refused to give up their reverse tolerance belief.

There were others who presented their clinical observations of increased heart rate, reddening of the eye, uncoordination, muscle weakness, increased passivity. One physician described transient brain wave changes while subjects were under the influence of pot as well as a loss of short-term memory, a faculty that keeps us from rambling in conversation. Still others talked of impairment of motor skills and the slowing of subjective time. This latter effect was illustrated by the story of two "stoned" students watching a jet plane streaking through the sky. "Man," one smoker says to the other, "I thought he'd never leave."

In retrospect, the New York Academy symposium was a scientific milestone, not as a result of any major or conclusive discoveries, but because it offered the first clinically demonstrated, pharmacological evidence that marijuana was neither as simple nor as innocuous a substance as its proponents had proclaimed.

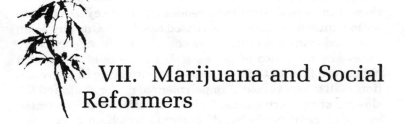

VII. Marijuana and Social Reformers

The next session at the New York Academy meeting would belong to the psychiatrists and sociologists. I went off to dinner with several of my colleagues convinced there could no longer be any effective arguments in favor of the drug. But to my surprise, several people at the table expressed their reservations.

"Interesting reports," said one, "but I've yet to hear really unequivocal medical evidence."

"The only thing we've succeeded in doing," said another, "is to create a climate of uncertainty. In such a climate, the behavioral and social scientists will have a field day."

And so they did. The second session began with a paper entitled "Marijuana Use and Social Control" by the Drs. Richard Brotman and Frederic Suffet of the Department of Psychiatry of New York Medical College. In view of the lack of medical evidence as to the dangers of marijuana, they argued that the current campaign against its use was, first, a reflection of the traditional American distrust of sensual pleasure and, secondly, a peculiarly American fear of inner subjective experience. Since the old-fashioned moral codes were no longer working, the psychiatrists said, society had turned to other means of preventing marijuana use. Among them: treatment of users; economic blockade to keep marijuana from entering the country; and a variety of punitive federal, state, and local laws.

As far as many people in the audience were concerned, Brotman and Suffet were at the very heart of the issue. While the pharmacologists could talk all day about unusual chemical reactions, strange molecular behavior, and the need for more laboratory experimentation, the behavioral scientists addressed themselves strictly to points that could be grasped and understood easily by a generation of actual and would-be marijuana users. Certainly the psychiatrists' arguments were persuasive: How do you "treat" someone for marijuana use when that person does not consider what he or she is doing to be in any way harmful?

Brotman and Suffet criticized the law for its failure to be effective and for its underlying assumption that if marijuana is harmful, then it should be illegal. "An individual should not be punished by criminal law for risking his own health," they stated. While the collection of medical knowledge is right and proper, it should not be used "to sustain the belief that the question of applying criminal sanctions can be answered merely by the accumulation of scientific knowledge. . . . Thus we allow them to defer facing the moral issue involved." The criminal law system should not be used as a means to enforce the moral standards of certain groups.

The last speaker at the New York Academy was Eric Goode, a sociologist and member of the advisory board of the National Organization for the Reform of Marijuana Laws (NORML), who illustrated the behaviorist's basic disregard for biology. He spoke as if man's thought processes could be independent of drug-induced biological changes. Addressing himself to "ideological factors in the marijuana controversy," he said that "the goodness or badness of [the marijuana effect] is not inherent in the drug or its effects, but in the observer's mind." He ended his talk by suggesting that many of the so-called objective truths espoused by the scientists were really based on prejudice.

While no one would deny that scientists, like others, have their prejudices, their research is limited by a rigid set of rules and regulations. On the other hand, the sociologists are not bound by a similar set of constraints, and often do not use any objective yardstick in their observations.

The New York Academy symposium ended, for me at least, on a disquieting note. After the first impression that we were at last making some headway into discovering the biological effects of marijuana, I feared that it might already be too late—that an increasing number of social, behavioral, and legal authorities were already speaking out in a demand for legalization of marijuana. Surely, only in the modern laboratory with all the instrumental innovations and fundamental cellular discoveries of the twentieth century could this question of damage to man from marijuana finally be answered. Thus, in July 1971, I decided to write a technical book for the medical profession that would assemble in one volume all the known facts and myths about the drug. I hoped this effort would help to accelerate the scientific work that was now so desperately needed.

VIII. First Investigations

At this point, it may appear that I spent all my time on the subject of marijuana, making the rounds from symposium to debate to the laboratory. In fact, marijuana research was still only one facet of my work. The bulk of my time was taken up with research and laboratory work in pharmacology as well as in keeping up with developments in my primary field of physiology, but even here, there was a connection with marijuana.

Physiology is the study of the function of the healthy organism as it has developed over billions of years, culminating in that extraordinary marvel, the human body. The physiologist is concerned with the intermeshing of the body's various systems, systems that are regulated as exquisitely as the finest wristwatch.

From my studies with two of the greatest physiologists of our time, Dr. Wallace Fenn and Dr. Maurice Visscher, I know, beyond doubt, that the mind guides the body, and the body influences the working of the mind. For this reason I tend to distrust any unnecessary substance—like marijuana—that disrupts the normal harmony of the body.

In August 1971, though, I put aside my other current projects to attend the fall meeting of the American Pharmacological Society at the University of Vermont. Once again the subject was marijuana. My own experiments were still too fragmentary to report, so I was content to listen to twenty other papers. All these reports indicated that THC was a chemical that had great biological activity. Most of the experiments concerned the effects of a single dose of THC injected into the veins or into the peritoneum (the layer of cells lining the intestine) of animals. THC, it seemed, had an effect on almost all the body functions of the animals studied. It changed heart rate, blood pressure, and respiration; it disturbed sleep and brain wave patterns, and lowered body temperature. It also disrupted the behavior and performance of animals trained to carry out certain tasks, such as pushing a lever in order to obtain food.

When other commonly used mind-altering drugs such as caffeine, alcohol, amphetamine, and barbiturates were added to THC, their effect was increased. One explanation of this "potentiating effect" was that the cells of the liver contain a sort of "garbage disposal system" in the form of enzymes that recognize foreign chemicals such as drugs, and "detoxifies" them into less dangerous substances. When THC is given with another drug, however, this detoxifying capacity is overwhelmed. Therefore a combination of drugs has a much stronger effect than each drug alone.

One report indicated that THC rapidly left the blood plasma, where it is attached to protein and entered the cells of the brain, liver, and lung. This observation, extremely technical in nature, went almost unnoticed during the conference. Two years later, though, it would become the basis for intensive investigation at several laboratories throughout the world.

There were several papers presented on tolerance and development of physical dependence. In rats, dogs, and monkeys, there were indications that THC, given either by intravenous injection or by mouth, produced rapid tolerance. One investigator even reported withdrawal symptoms in monkeys.

After hearing these papers it was hard to believe that any pharmacologist could now doubt that marijuana was a dangerous substance. Furthermore, there was not a single report presented at the Vermont conference that indicated cannabis might have some therapeutic benefit.

On my return from Vermont, I began writing my technical book on marijuana in earnest. Knowing that other scientists would want to know in even more detail the history of cannabis, I turned to the International Bulletin of Narcotics, published by the United Nations Commission on Narcotics, for additional background information to supplement the material I had accumulated for my lecture at the University of Paris and from the United Nations library. That bulletin revealed that the first major field study of marijuana usage was conducted in India in 1893, by Her Majesty Queen Victoria's Indian Hemp Drug Commission. The question the British wished to explore was whether the implied sanction of cannabis use by the British government in the eighteenth century was defensible when weighed against health hazards.

The British method of investigation was to conduct a sort of Gallup poll among Indian cannabis users. This Indian Hemp Commission, as it was called, was comprised of seven members, four British and three Indian. They collected their data by asking some 1,193 witnesses, including 335 physicians, a series of questions. The answers to the questions then became the evidence on which the commission based its medical conclusions.

The observations in this study are interesting, but varied enough to offer something for everybody. Some medical witnesses, for example, ascribed such diseases as dysentery, bronchitis, and asthma to "the moderate use of the drug," while others gave a diametrically opposed opinion. Some of the cannabis consumers maintained that evil effects were produced by the plant; others could find no harm in it. In general, the Commission could find no moral weakness or depravity resulting from cannabis use.

Although many contemporary American writers still quote the Indian Hemp Drug Commission's findings—those statements that conclude there is no mental or physical harm resulting from moderate cannabis use—the commissioners themselves pointed out that their work was based on only flimsy evidence. Since many of those interviewed were illiterate peasants, it was impossible to obtain accurate statistics or reliable impressions. One commissioner wrote that there was no way of dissociating the effects of cannabis from all the other "vices in which a dissipated man indulges." Nevertheless, the commission felt impelled to come up with some sort of conclusion that would give critics something to hang their hat on. Their opinion: Moderate use was harmless while excessive use could cause injury. Just what constituted "moderate" and how much was "excessive" was never established.

The commission initially had attempted to maintain maximum scientific objectivity, demanding absolute visible proof of a cause-and-effect relationship between cannabis and alleged ill effects. When this was not forthcoming, the commission rejected clinical opinions about cannabis. For example, even though the superintendents of twenty-four mental hospitals in India said that cannabis was associated with insanity, this observation was dismissed outright.

It is interesting to note that proponents of legalized marijuana—the so-called pot lobby, which is well supported and highly active in Washington, D.C., as well as in various state capitals—still refer to the "impartial" findings of the Indian Hemp Commission when trying to make a case for their position. The simple fact is that the now-ancient Indian study bears no relevancy whatever to the use of marijuana in the United States today. From a scientific standpoint, moreover, the Indian Commission's conclusions are totally unacceptable because they were made without benefit of either laboratory experiments or clinical studies. Therefore, quoting from or referring to them is no more evidence of marijuana's harmful or harmless effects than relying on the schoolyard information of a teen-ager.

Perhaps the first real attempt at scientific investigation of marijuana's effects in the United States was generated in 1938 by New York's Mayor Fiorello La Guardia. Concerned about the growing use of marijuana in the city, particularly among the black population in Harlem, he asked the prestigious New York Academy of Medicine to find out just how harmful the drug was. Although the study was not nearly as detailed or as thorough as would be required for a drug evaluation today, it did represent the first medically sponsored systematic examination of marijuana's effects.

The La Guardia Report involved 120 prisoner-volunteers, split up into both user and nonuser groups, who were given measured amounts of cannabis in both a smoking and a liquid form. The marijuana used came from material that had been seized by the Federal Bureau of Narcotics in the New York area. After the user-volunteers had either smoked or ingested the drug, both groups were given a series of mental, motor, and physical examinations. Among the findings noted by the scientists who conducted the experiment were the following: Almost all the users experienced some sort of symptom of mental illness, ranging from euphoria to hallucinations to floating sensations to full-blown psychotic episodes. Aptitude and manual dexterity tests showed that despite the widespread belief of increased agility and ability while under the influence of marijuana, users consistently performed their motor tasks with less efficiency than nonusers. Also, regular users experienced a certain amount of tolerance to the drug—a tolerance that required ever greater amounts of the drug in order to get them high. In some cases users had to smoke up to eleven marijuana cigarettes before they were able to reach a fully intoxicated state.

Among the new and then somewhat startling findings of the report were some previously unobserved physical effects. Although the potency of the marijuana used in the study was well below the strength of the cannabis smoked by most people today, virtually all the volunteers exhibited some signs of tachycardia (increased heartbeat) and congestion of the conjunctivae (mucous membranes of the eye) after smoking a few reefers. Moreover, the regular marijuana smokers developed both the heart and eye symptoms to a much lesser extent than those who were new to the substance, another indication of tolerance to the drug.

Although the La Guardia Report was an important first step in the systematic evaluation of marijuana, it should be stressed that the results were far from definitive. There was disagreement among the scientists as to the meaning of some of the observations and data, and there was confusion in the final interpretation of the results. As an example, one physician wrote that "tolerance develops during the period when the drug is being taken and accounts for the necessity of increasing the dosage to bring about the desired results," while another came to the conclusion there were "no evidence ... of an acquired tolerance for the drug." What the report lacked more than anything else was provision for laboratory examination of the tissues and body fluids of the cannabis users, as well as for a follow-up of the subjects for a period of more than one year.

In retrospect, the 1940–41 La Guardia Report is noteworthy more for what it did not reveal than for what it did show us. Like an iceberg, the most important and the most dangerous results of marijuana smoking are hidden beneath the surface. The visible tip of the iceberg shows us clearly that cannabis usage produces temporary mental disturbances, impaired motor functions, some physiological changes and, at least in some persons, a slowly developing tolerance that necessitates more and more of the drug in order to attain a high. The hidden portion of the iceberg, however, is represented by the reasons *why* these symptoms occur and the suspicion that the substance may cause permanent damage.

We know, for example, that pot smoking produces euphoria in some people and hallucinations in others, depending on the strength and amount of cannabis brought into the body. But why do these symptoms occur? Is it the direct effect of chemicals in cannabis that have a sudden and temporary impact on the nervous system? Is it the result of hormones and other body chemicals that are released into the bloodstream because of the inhalation of marijuana smoke? Is it some disruption of the body's metabolism, or is it an action on the brain's cells? More important, are these psychotic-like symptoms only temporary manifestations that last just for the few hours the smoker seems to be under the influence of the drug?

Or is some residue of cannabis, some permanent damage left behind, that, like water dripping onto a sandstone, will eventually erode the body's delicate systems?

Then again, what is there in cannabis that sets the heart to pounding and causes congestion of the eyes almost each time it is used by many pot smokers? Is this, too, just a temporary aberration or is the drug slowly causing some subtle change in the body chemistry? Also, if the substance is causing a side effect, does this deleterious action extend into the very nucleus of our cells where there are critical chemical packages of coded information that not only control our current and future health, but also dictate the form and stability of our unconceived children?

At the very least, the many questions raised by the La Guardia Report and subsequent studies demand more scientific investigation before the drug is even considered for use by the public.

In continued preparation for my book, additional early material that I received indicated that marijuana's use as a "harmless substance," no more potent than legally used alcoholic products, gained almost legendary status in the 1960s. The basis for this reputation, however, was flimsy, to say the least. The 1968 study by Dr. Andrew Weil and Dr. Norman Zinberg, published in *Science Journal,* had observed many of the same mental, motor, and physiological effects of earlier investigations, but had concluded that "marijuana is a relatively mild intoxicant" that produces effects on the order of those created by alcoholic drinks. And a 1969 article in *Scientific American* by Harvard psychiatrist Dr. Lester Grinspoon called attention to a State of Washington motor vehicle department study that showed that marijuana smokers did as well on a driving simulator test as nonsmokers, and better than alcohol drinkers. (More recent studies of marijuana's effects on driving ability, however, have established a definitive loss in both ability and judgment.)

Also, in 1969, anthropologist Dr. Margaret Mead of Columbia University told a United States Senate Committee that "marijuana, being nonaddictive and without any known harmful qualities, is less dangerous than alcohol or cigarettes, and that it should be legalized and sold to anyone over the age of sixteen." Almost as soon as the eminent Dr. Mead had spoken these words, her message went out over the wire services and was featured both on the television evening news shows and on the front pages of morning newspapers. Nowhere did I see or hear mentioned that Dr. Mead's area of expertise was in the study of the origins and development of man. How could she be qualified to make a medical evaluation concerning the lack of harm in marijuana use if she had not attempted to conduct any laboratory or clinical tests before reaching such a definitive conclusion?

I was surprised by Dr. Mead's statement and wrote to her asking for clarification, and sent to her reprints of papers indicating that marijuana use could be dangerous. Her short memo, which was sent to me two months later, referred me to a "Clarification of Press and TV Reports" of her testimony. Essentially it said that she "placed the possible legal limit two years younger than eighteen [the legal drinking age in some states] to stress the fact that marijuana . . . without any known harmful qualities . . . should be accessible earlier." Finally she stated, "I did not advocate the use of marijuana. I did advocate making it legal."

The damage was done: Such a statement, issued by a prestigious scientific personality, may have encouraged thousands of youngsters to try marijuana for the first time.

While researching and writing my book, I continued my experimental laboratory work. With no new influx of funds, we pursued our study of THC on the smooth muscle of the rat, now using a piece of the aorta instead of the womb. But the results failed to show us anything new.

The first major breakthrough in my own research came as a result of my continued association with Dr. William Manger. After my appointment at the College of Physicians and Surgeons, where he was already in the Department of Medicine, we worked together again. Since our time together in the 1940s at the Mayo Clinic in Rochester, Minnesota, he had specialized in research on the disease of hypertension. He brought me up to date about his current studies using a new breed of rat recently developed in Japan. This rat is "genetically engineered" to be born with high blood pressure. They are called "spontaneously hypertensive rats" (SHR), and are used to test the efficacy of hypertensive drugs.

Since several earlier studies of cannabis had indicated that THC lowers the blood pressure of users, it occurred to me that Dr. Manger had just the model I needed to demonstrate why and how THC induces tolerance. We wanted to find the answer to this question: Would THC given over a period of days or weeks keep the pressure low as was true with other hypertensive drugs currently in use, or would it gradually lose its ability to lower blood pressure unless larger doses were given?

Here at last was not only a new and potentially worthwhile project, but also one I could afford! Dr. Manger said he would give me the rats, which meant that I would have to buy only the ingenious new instrument that measures rat blood pressure. It works in this way: The rat is placed in a plastic tubelike cage with a cuff placed around his tail and connected to a recording device. The tail must be heated so that the vessels dilate and blood flows through freely. The recording device can tell us whether pressure goes up, goes down, or remains stable when different drugs are given.

My associate Iris Schwartz and a young Czech worker named Jan Adamec helped me in these SHR studies. Daily feedings of known amounts of THC were given to the rats through rubber tubes inserted into their stomachs. Other investigators had already found that by dissolving the THC in sesame oil, rather than the alcohol that is used for other drugs, it would be better absorbed into the intestine. When this was done we observed that THC did, indeed, lower blood pressure in relation to the amount of the dose administered and that this effect lasted about twenty-four hours.

It took only three or four days before the rat adjusted to the initial amount of THC. After that, the dose had no effect whatever on blood pressure. In order to make the pressure fall, we had to increase the dosage fivefold. Even then, the dose escalation worked for only another three or four days before the pressure went up again.

With this new animal model we were able to demonstrate

that the SHR rat develops a rapid tolerance to THC's effect on blood pressure. This tolerance, as far as I, Dr. Manger, and Dr. Leo Hollister, a veteran clinical pharmacologist, were concerned, made cannabis unsuitable for use against hypertension. We also made another important observation. The SHR rats we used had not yet achieved their full growth. Rats that were treated with THC lost a great deal of weight over the three-week period of the experiment, while those rats in the control group gained weight. Even when THC treatment was stopped and the rats began to gain, they never caught up with the growth of the controls. It was as if their growth had been stunted by THC. My experiments confirmed those published in *Science* by Dr. F. J. Manning of the Walter Reed Army Institute of Research. He attributed the weight loss of their animals to a decrease in appetite caused by THC. Our THC-treated SHR rats, however, seemed to eat as much as the control animals. It seemed more likely that THC was causing some bio-chemical change that prevented their food from being transformed into body-building tissue.

We concluded that in the SHR rat tolerance develops rapidly to THC's ability to lower blood pressure, but loss of weight persists throughout the period of treatment. In other words, if there had been tolerance to weight loss, the rats would have begun to gain weight just as their blood pressure again returned to the hypertensive level. Was this some irreversible change induced by THC? Only more research could answer this question. Our experiments could be expanded further in this area, but I was not sure exactly how.

As my scientific work found new purpose and direction, it occurred to me that I ought to try to visit a country where marijuana has been in use for several centuries. By observing the population at close hand it might be possible to detect some physiological changes that have taken place because of long-term use. Morocco seemed to be a logical choice because most of the reports on long-term cannabis intoxication had come from there. The Moroccan name for locally grown and used marijuana is kif. In the last fourteen years I had read at least four scientific reports that had linked kif to both mental illness and diseases of the leg arteries.

By coincidence, we had a French visiting anatomy professor, Moroccan-born Daniel Zagury, working in my laboratory at the time. When I described my project to him he immediately sent off letters of introduction for me to several doctors who had practiced in Morocco. I again wrote to foundations asking for funds. However, none were interested so I had no choice but to confine my efforts to the rat study.

Late in 1971, the French Ministry of Health invited me to address a meeting in Paris on drug abuse. My audience was made up primarily of school administrators. After describing what was then known about the drug I emphasized that many scientists were continually working to learn more. On the other side of the fence, however, was a psychoanalyst, Dr. M. Bensoussan, who disagreed with my views. Instead, he supported the position of Dr. Grinspoon, stating that marijuana was less dangerous than tobacco or alcohol, and that the more you smoked, the less you needed to reach a high. To make his point more dramatic, Dr. Bensoussan asked any members of the audience who smoked to raise their hand. After a few seconds of suspense, one young man timidly put up a finger—and rapidly pulled it down. Apparently the psychiatrist misjudged the extent of marijuana smoking among French school administrators and teachers! For the first time that I could remember, it was the "other side" that sat down to scanty applause.

Operating on a tight time schedule, I left almost immediately for the return flight to New York. Ordinarily, I might have been fatigued by the trip but new-found support from fellow scientists and the favorable reaction of the audience of school administrators and teachers gave me a big lift. And the flight produced a most fortunate encounter.

My seatmate on the trip turned out to be Pierre Philippe, an investment banker who had created a foundation to support medical exchange programs between the United States and France. During the nine-hour flight I told him about my recent experience in Paris as well as about my current activities in New York. The word "marijuana" struck a receptive chord because both as the father of four teen-agers and as a businessman with many young employees, Philippe was concerned about the spread of drug use. He spoke to me about "the spirit of Munich" among many people who were willing to accept any argument that justified the use of pot.

Before landing in New York, my traveling companion suggested I write to the Philippe Foundation for a grant. Needless to say, this was done within twenty-four hours. My request was approved in time for me to plan my Christmas holiday around a trip to Morocco.

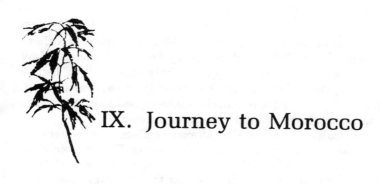

IX. Journey to Morocco

The purpose of my trip to Morocco was to answer two preliminary investigative questions: First, would it be possible to observe physical damage among heavy users of cannabis, and second, would it be possible to carry out a long-term study of a group of chronic marijuana smokers using modern methods of investigation? In planning for the trip I arranged for a stopover in Paris in order to contact friends and colleagues who had once lived or worked in Morocco. They might be able to set up appointments for me with physicians and government officials in the two principal cities of Casablanca and Rabat.

Friends in Paris warned me that the subject of kif is a very sensitive one in Morocco. One doctor who had lived and worked there for twenty years said, "If you do not proceed with great tact, you won't get any information." This was because marijuana is an illegal substance in Morocco and, therefore, is unmentionable. Moreover, because Morocco is a young nation that wishes to be viewed in the best light by the rest of the world, any information that could be even remotely construed as unfavorable to the country is taboo.

My trip began the day before Christmas, 1971. The seaport of Casablanca, Morocco's largest city, with a teeming population of a million and a half, was my first stop. Morocco is a stunning country with a topography that is as varied as anyplace in the world. Along the Mediterranean Sea there are broad stretches of white, sandy beaches punctuated by dramatic rock outcroppings; slightly inland is a fertile coastal plain where fruits and cereals grow readily; and, as a backdrop, there are high, snow-topped mountains, beyond which lies the immense Sahara desert.

Politically and culturally, Morocco reflects the influence of both the native Arab inhabitants and the French colonials. Between 1910 and 1953, Morocco was administered by a corps of French civil servants and the military. The local rulers who remained during this occupation were merely figureheads. As a result, French is the second language of Morocco, spoken by all who have gone to school. The majority of the population speaks only Arabic and is largely uneducated.

My first prearranged contact in Casablanca was with a high administration official, a good friend of one of my relatives. He greeted me with warmth, and soon we were in deep conversation about the many problems facing Morocco. The population explosion (a jump from 5,000,000 to 11,000,000 just since World War II), and the country's limited resources, overshadowed official concern about cannabis. Unofficially, he was quite candid. "Yes, cannabis intoxication represents a major health hazard in this country. But because it is forbidden, no one admits using the drug and few people talk about it openly."

In confidential reports, though, the story is quite different. Figures have been accumulated that show that tons of kif are produced in Morocco. Much of this drug traffic is encouraged by American and British "entrepreneurs" who smuggle large amounts out of the country for international trade. In the mountains of the Rif, where marijuana cultivation is a major occupation, the greatest amount of cannabis use is found. But my contact discouraged my idea of a visit to the Rif area because, as he put it, "Without speaking Berber and without living with the natives you will obtain very little information." Instead of traveling into the mountains, he suggested I interview some of the doctors who work in the country's mental hospitals where a significant portion of the inmates had smoked kif regularly. Then the government official laughed and said, "You scientists are always trying to unlock an open door. You come all the way to Morocco to find out if marijuana is harmful when we could have told you, 'Yes of course it is,' a long time ago."

It was first arranged for me to visit the Psychiatric Hospital of Berrechid, where over 1,000 patients were hospitalized. The director of the hospital was uncooperative, however, and did not care to talk about cannabis. Perhaps he suspected my motives or my credentials. Although I was aware that two studies associating admission to this hospital with cannabis intoxication had been published since 1957, the director would admit only to having *one* patient who smoked kif, but he could not be seen because, "He has left for the day."

The next stage of my journey was along the coastal highway that stretches from Casablanca to Rabat. The modern buildings in Rabat, the administrative capital of Morocco, are designed to harmonize with the elegant palaces and mosques of the old walled city. My introduction to a professor at the medical school came from a native Moroccan, and as a result, he was quite candid with me. "Yes, cannabis is a serious health problem in Morocco, especially from a public health point of view."

He discussed the difficulties in making a study of chronic kif smokers. "Kif smoking is not the only drug used in the cities," he said, "because many of the people also drink wine, a habit they acquired from the French. The ideal situation from a research point of view would be to go to the Rif mountains where nothing else but kif is used."

With his intervention I was able to interview a staff member at a nearby mental hospital. Here I was told that there is a high incidence of cannabis usage recorded in the histories of the patients hospitalized for mental illness. Unwilling or unable to quote percentages, the staff member said that a substantial number of kif smokers were between the ages of eighteen and thirty years. He also said that he had noticed extreme mental and physical deterioration among chronic "old" smokers, whom he identified as men between the ages of thirty and forty.

My next destination, Marrakesh, was reached after a long drive along the high plateaus of the middle Atlas Mountains. Here I interviewed the director of the psychiatric hospital, Dr. M. Teste. He had been studying the subject of cannabis for the past twenty years and he had published the first paper to come from Morocco describing the relationship between kif smoking and mental illness. I took detailed notes as he talked of the problem: Cannabis usage, mostly smoking, produces acute toxic psychosis mainly among young people between fifteen and twenty years old who are in apparent good health, without any symptoms of physical disease. Diet is not a factor, he stressed, because these Moroccans, although poor, are not undernourished. The psychotic episodes last for two to three days and are characterized by agitation, confusion, and paranoia.

How much smoking is needed to produce such toxic psychosis?

"It may occur after even one exposure to the drug," he replied. "Moreover, most are left with a common residual symptom of anxiety. And the intensity of this anxiety often determines whether or not the user will resume taking the drug."

In Morocco, about forty percent of hospital admissions for acute psychosis—mental illness—are related to kif smoking. In some of these cases the acute episode is followed by prolonged classical schizophrenia. Even where the patient does not develop clearcut signs of mental illness, there is a "chronic deterioration of their mental processes." He also mentioned the clearly observed phenomenon of tolerance among kif smokers.

In all his comments he was referring to male smokers. He told me that women, with the exception of prostitutes, are not allowed to smoke.

"You know," he said at one point, "we have a strange situation here today. For the first time within memory, we have a significant number of Europeans and Americans among our patients in the mental hospitals of Morocco. They are young hippies who come to Marrakesh where the drug is easily available." My colleague stressed that the hippies who take multiple drugs were initiating young Moroccans to the use of opium and LSD, creating concern among Moroccan health officials. In addition, the consumption of wine, which is plentiful, continued to increase. In spite of this new phenomenon of multiple drug use, he thought that it might be possible to find chronic smokers in his hospital who used only kif.

My Moroccan journey ended the day after the New Year. At customs all passengers were thoroughly searched. In the attache case of one young man I noted two long kif pipes. He claimed they were souvenirs. Not finding any sign of kif, the customs official shrugged, "Oh well, I guess you can find marijuana anywhere you go these days."

On the flight to Paris, I thought about what I had seen and learned in Morocco. Certainly nothing in my visit produced any definite clinical or physical evidence of the damaging effects of marijuana. Therefore my report to the National Institute of Mental Health concluded only that Morocco offered a unique opportunity to study the effects of long-term marijuana usage and suggested making a feasibility study in the area to see how such an investigation might be carried out. A specific plan would have to include budget, personnel, and a timetable. My proposal produced a steady series of communications with the NIMH. But the national bureaucracy never moves last, and it was not until the following October that I received a go-ahead to make "a feasibility study of chronic kif usage in the Rif mountains of Morocco" with the help of NIMH. At last someone was willing to investigate the other side of the marijuana question!

X. Journey to Egypt

Another land historically associated with widespread cannabis use is my birthplace, Egypt. Thus, when the opportunity to go there presented itself after a meeting in Paris of the French Society of Anesthesia in the spring of 1972 I seized it. Egypt is only three hours by jet from Paris to Cairo, with a fast connection to Alexandria where I still had family to visit. At the same time, I could pursue my interest in cannabis.

Recent publications of Dr. M. Soueif, professor of psychology at the University of Cairo, had described a psycho-social study he had made of 850 hashish users and 839 controls. This was the largest and most thorough investigation of cannabis use ever mounted, and yet, none of these papers were published in an American journal, nor were the results mentioned in the several books on marijuana that appeared during the early 1970s. I have no explanation for such an oversight, unless it is that there is an innate distrust of a study performed in Egypt. In any case, I wanted to check for myself their authenticity.

How things had changed in Alexandria! The world of the wealthy Levantine no longer existed, and all the familiar landmarks of my childhood were gone. I had a pleasant visit with my Uncle Albert in his small city flat. When our conversation turned to my work, I told him that my principal interest was doing research on cannabis. He was amazed that many young Americans were smoking marijuana and that there was a strong movement in the United States to legalize it. "The 500,000 people in the United States who smoke marijuana daily that you say was reported by the President's National Commission on Marijuana and Drug Abuse is more than can be found in all of Egypt! If what you say is true, then America is in great trouble," he exclaimed.

I continued on to Cairo for the primary purpose of my trip. Even though Dr. Soueif had to be out of the country at the time of my visit, he had thoughtfully arranged for me to see his assistants and had prepared a summary of his work in English. Reading it over, I learned many interesting facts about cannabis use in Egypt over the centuries.

For example, according to modern Arab historians, hashish was first cultivated in Egypt about the middle of the twelfth century, during the reign of the Ayyubid dynasty. It was introduced by mystics who came from Syria, and from the very beginning the weed was a source of controversy. The defense of hashish was based on the merits of its behavioral effects—euphoria, independence from the outside world, meditativeness, amiability, and activation of intelligence—as well as on the fact that it was cheap and "did not cause bad breath and thus was not easily detectable." The opponents of cannabis pointed to the ill effects—submissiveness and lethargy, sensory debilitation, organic brain damage, insanity, prostitution and temporary sexual potency followed by impotence.

The Egyptian government first embarked on a definite policy of prohibition of hashish at the end of the nineteenth century, after seven centuries of extensive cannabis cultivation and usage. Laws were passed prohibiting cultivation, sale, transportation, possession, and use of hashish, but they were largely ignored. Each successive legislation since 1874 has carried increasingly severe penalties, but to no avail: If cultivation was eradicated, people resorted to smuggling cannabis into the country, especially from Lebanon. Soon after assuming power in Egypt in 1954, Nasser ordered strict enforcement of the laws banning hashish.

Although most of the laws are still on the books and the government is still strongly opposed to cannabis use, the habit continues unabated among the poorer and less educated classes. To find out what effect hashish smoking has on the population, Nasser ordered a committee formed to conduct an in-depth study. Dr. Soueif and his investigators interviewed hundreds of users and nonusers of similar age and social status, asking each of them 200 specific questions. Then using modern statistical techniques, the answers were correlated and analyzed. The results are enlightening.

The majority of hashish users in Egypt are young men between the ages of twenty and forty years. The peak age for beginning the habit was found to be between sixteen and eighteen, usually as a result of the urging of a male relative or of peer pressure. Hashish users, the study revealed, were more apt to have been neglected by their father and family, or more exposed to interparental conflicts, or more anxious than those in the control group. Under the influence of the drug, they presented the usual symptoms: Their work capacity was significantly impaired in both a quantitative and qualitative sense, and this impairment could be correlated with a deterioration of psychomotor performance. If deprived of the drug for any length of time, the performance of the habitual user was even worse.

I studied the work of Soueif among prison inmates: 850 who had used the drug and 839 who had not. Two standard interview sessions were accompanied by tests that included measurement of speed and accuracy in psychomotor performance, initial reaction time, immediate memory, motor coordination, and time estimation. Subjects were assured law enforcement officials had no involvement whatever in the study.

While the prisoner study turned up most of the same patterns that had been observed in other investigations, there were a few new findings. For one thing, it turned out that the hashish users had lower criminal records than the nonsmokers. Most of them were in prison, in fact, simply because they had broken the drug laws. Moreover, sixty-five percent of the users said they wanted to discontinue their hashish habit but just could not stop.

Soueif explains this craving: "Among hashish users there is a definite pattern of oscillation of temperamental traits, swinging between two opposite poles: that of social ease, acquiescence and elation when under the immediate effects of the drug; and that of ascendancy, seclusiveness, negativism, depression and pugnacity when the subject is deprived of it."

Focusing on the heavy users, Soueif found that the frequency of smoking and the number of attempts to stop were directly related to the age of onset. The earlier an individual had begun smoking hashish, the higher his frequency of use and the lower his desire to stop smoking. They also tended to drink more alcohol, coffee and tea, and smoke more cigarettes.

Another finding to emerge from the prisoner study was an association of hashish use with opium taking. I was shown a graph, called Soueif's Curve, that indicated that thirty-two percent of 850 habitual hashish users admitted taking opium—with the greater number of opium users concentrated in the heavier smoking range. In addition, the heavier the hashish habit, the more likely the user was to take other kinds of drugs.

The observation that I found most interesting in this study had to do with the results of various objective tests given the volunteers. While I had expected that psychomotor tests would show hashish smokers to have lower performance scores than controls, the finding that this differential is related to the level of education was a surprise. According to Soueif's data, the more educated the user, the greater the percentage of impairment caused by the drug. While an illiterate peasant might perform five percent less efficiently than a nonsmoking control of the same educational background, a man with the equivalent of grade school education might do thirty percent less well than his nonsmoking counterpart. It would seem the drug is more taxing on those who have the most to lose.

Thus, the Egyptian data showed that chronic cannabis use among a large segment of the population produced noticeable and measurable changes in psycho-motor skills and personality. I could not help but wonder what significance these studies might have for modern, technological countries like the United States. On my return to New York, I made it my first task to write a letter to the prestigious *New England Journal of Medicine*'s section devoted to current medical topics in which I summarized the Egyptian studies and decried the fact that they had been ignored by all the American social researchers who had performed surveys at great public expense.

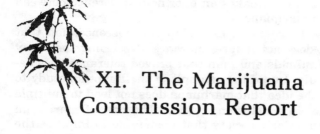

XI. The Marijuana Commission Report

In mid-April the New York Chapter of the National Association of Social Workers invited me to participate in a workshop on "Controversial Issues on Marijuana." The program was part of an all-day workshop on "The Influence of Government and Politics on Drug Treatment." Other members of the workshop were Michael Sonnenreich, the executive director of the National Commission on Marijuana, and Professor Robert Salmon from the Hunter College School of Social Work. The meeting was limited to an audience of thirty people, primarily social workers plus a few journalists.

My talk stressed the three major areas of misinformation then in existence about marijuana. My corrections of this misinformation were based on the results of recent research, both my own and that published by other scientists. First, tackling the misconception that marijuana is a simple substance similar to alcohol, I described the complex chemical composition of the cannabis plant and explained the difference between the two types grown. "If you are talking about the hemp-type marijuana that is grown widely in the United States," I said, "then that is truly harmless. If, however, you are referring to the drug type, which is being used with increasing frequency by pot smokers today, then there is a significant and harmful difference involved." I went on to explain how the drug-type plant varies widely in potency and

83

why this variation makes an enormous difference between alcohol and marijuana.

Secondly, I addressed myself to the misconception that marijuana does not induce tolerance, describing the many studies in animals and man that proved tolerance does develop. Finally, I used the example of the Egyptian study to contradict the idea that marijuana does not lead to multiple drug abuse. In conclusion, I said, "The cost of marijuana usage to an orderly society that is striving to improve the quality of life of all its citizens would be enormous. The social erosion that we already see around us can only be increased by extensive marijuana usage. Legalization would certainly be accompanied by increased consumption."

Professor Salmon spoke next. His thesis followed the lines previously set down by Alfred Lindesmith, Lester Grinspoon, and John Kaplan. Among the themes he stressed: The overriding issue is a legal and social one; the present laws are disregarded by the young because they are unjust; and making marijuana smoking a criminal act causes considerably more damage than the smoking itself.

"The young people of today," said Professor Salmon, "will be the jurors of tomorrow. If they are drug users, there is every reason to believe they will be sympathetic to those charged with possession or use. We would be better able to control marijuana use if it were legalized and licensed. The social benefits of legalization would greatly outweigh the social costs. Another positive change would be control of marijuana potency through licensing. The punishment of the marijuana user is in no way justified by the harm he may cause. Although there is some danger in excessive use of marijuana, it does not seem to be in the same category as the dangers of nicotine or alcohol."

It was a familiar theme; namely, that alcohol and tobacco are just as bad as marijuana, if not worse. My studies in the past few months had taught me that the theme was based only on inaccurate information, in itself a kind of wishful thinking.

Michael Sonnenreich, a young lawyer, spoke with the authority conferred on him as the executive director of a national presidential commission:

"Dr. Nahas is blowing up out of all proportion the potential harm of marijuana use to man and society. Millions of people have smoked it and we cannot see any signs of severe damage. Our Commission has shown that marijuana use is not related to crime, no more than pot smoking is related to escalation to harder drugs. Yes there is tolerance, but only among heavy users." Sonnenreich also cautioned those who believed the study published in *Science* by Professor A. Crancer from the University of Washington that smoking did not impair driving performance. The commission had concluded, said Sonnenreich, that there was a danger in driving an automobile under the influence of pot and that such behavior should be penalized just as drunken driving is penalized.

He next pointed out a misinterpretation of the Commission Report that, while it did recommend removing criminal penalties for possession and private use, it did not recommend legalization as proposed by Professor Salmon. "We would like people not to use marijuana and we are opposed to legalizing it. We want to discourage its use. But we do not want all the people who smoke [marijuana] to go to jail."

During the question and answer period that followed, Professor Salmon admitted that he was personally against marijuana use, and had told this to his three daughters and hoped they would not use it. In answering a final question about the possibility of legalization, he predicted a basic change in the law within the next ten years. Drug control through punishment would move eventually to control through licensing. "Meanwhile," he said, "we need to concentrate on the factors of our society that cause people to turn to drugs in the first place."

On this point I agreed with Salmon. Certainly if the present trend of popular thinking is not reversed, the sale of marijuana will be legal in the near future. Such a move, however, should not be taken on the fallacious pretext that marijuana is a harmless drug. Historically and clinically marijuana has been shown to be destructive both to man and

to society. Because of this I criticized the extraordinary ambiguity of the Marijuana Commission Report, which contained something both for those who were for marijuana and
for those who were against marijuana, and I stated my belief
that decriminalization could only lead to legalization.

Sonnenreich did not agree with me, and repeated the commission's position of "decriminalization without legalization." He believed that the commission's position was not as
far removed from my own as I thought, and promised to send
me the Summary Report. A week later, when I received it and
began studying it in earnest, my initial impression of its
ambiguity was confirmed. In my opinion, the report could
only compound the prevailing general confusion about
marijuana.

The reason for the report, commissioned by President Nix-
on, is obvious. By 1971, it was apparent that marijuana
smoking among teen-agers and young adults in this country
had taken on huge proportions, with the number of one-or-
more-times users estimated at anywhere from 8,000,000 to
20,000,000 people. Studies taken on some college campuses
showed that over eighty percent of the students had tried the
drug at least once. There were rumors that the figure was
almost as high on many high school campuses. Equally disturbing, the pattern of marijuana arrests for use, possession,
or sales varied tremendously, punishing scores of youngsters
in some states with jail sentences of many years' duration
while allowing young offenders in other areas of the country
to go free. Thus, there was a critical and long overdue need for
a national study designed to find out (1) how many people
were smoking marijuana, (2) what age groups they represented, (3) how much marijuana they consumed, (4) what
effects were caused by the drug, and (5) what changes, if any,
should be made in the federal marijuana laws.

The commission appointed by the President was, as a television newscaster put it, truly "a blue-ribbon panel." Chaired
by former Pennsylvania Governor Raymond Shafer, it also
included: Vice-Chairman Dr. Dana Farnsworth, a psychiatrist and public health expert who had been director of Student Health at Harvard College for several decades; Dr.

Maurice Seevers, professor of pharmacology at the University of Michigan, who had been working with cannabis for years; Dr. Henri Brill, one of the most respected names in American psychiatry; Dr. Thomas Ungerleider, professor of psychiatry at UCLA; Mrs. Joan Ganz Cooney, the creator of the "Sesame Street" television program; Senator Jacob Javits from New York; Senator Harold Hughes from Iowa; Representative Paul Rogers from Florida; Representative Lee Carter from Tennessee.

But the staff of fifty-five, who did most of the research, had little medical or scientific background. Sixteen youth consultants and eighteen student researchers, who were supposed to bridge the generation gap, were included. Among the thirty-eight contributors listed in the report were seven psychiatrists and six sociologists, three of whom were already known for their views favoring the legalization of marijuana. The forty-six consultants listed included representatives of the social and behavioral sciences, but the specialties of pharmacology, pathology, and internal medicine were not in evidence. Of the two physician-pharmacologists asked to testify before the commission, one of them had publicly expressed his views favoring leniency toward marijuana use.

The formulation of a balanced report ought to have been ensured if the earlier views about the harmful effects of marijuana of Dana Farnsworth and Maurice Seevers had been allowed to prevail. In an article written in 1968, Dr. Farnsworth agreed with the statement of the American Medical Association and the National Research Council that "Cannabis is a dangerous drug and is a public health hazard. Practically all societies in which it has been extensively used have found it necessary to impose legal and social sanctions on users and distributors. Legalization of marijuana would probably create a serious abuse problem in the U.S." In 1970, I heard Dr. Seevers give a talk entitled "Drug Dependence and Drug Abuse, a World Problem," in which he clearly spoke out against the philosophy of making drugs readily available, and singled out cannabis as one of the severely destructive ones.

The first job of the commission, as the report revealed, was to estimate and to categorize the number of marijuana users. The raw data came from surveys conducted on junior high, senior high, and college campuses throughout the country. To the surprise of many, though not all, the commission members, the totals showed that the drug already had reached a huge segment of the population. Fully 24,000,000 Americans, fourteen percent of them between the ages of twelve and seventeen, had tried marijuana at least once. More disturbing, over 12,000,000 of these people were now using the drug more or less regularly. According to the commission's report, approximately 7,750,000 teen-agers and adults were smoking marijuana "intermittently" from two to ten times a month; 4,500,000 were using it "moderately" from eleven times a month to once a day; 500,000 were "heavy users" who smoked several times daily; and a "very small fraction" of the "heavy users" were "very heavy" users, described as being "rarely drug-free."

While I have no argument with the figures, the use of categories that give the illusion that the divisions are clear, and that each group is a distinct entity, is misleading. To even suggest that "moderate," for example, is a better or safer category than "very heavy" is highly misleading. In fact, there is irrefutable medical evidence that smokers in both categories are under the influence of the drug for as long as they continue the marijuana habit.

In 1971, radioactively tagged delta-9-THC showed clearly that the active metabolites of marijuana are stored in the tissues, including the brain, for as long as eight days after initial entry of the drug into the body. This means that a so-called moderate smoker who has only three or four marijuana cigarettes a week would never really be totally free of its effects. And although an individual who smokes one or more marijuana cigarettes a day might experience a greater high at any given time because of the larger concentration of active chemicals in his body than in that of the intermittent smoker, both would have to be considered to be under the influence of the drug.

Another shortcoming of the commission's report is the sloughing off of the 500,000 people listed in the heavy or very heavy categories. The commission takes the attitude that this is an insignificant percentage of the overall total. Harvard psychiatrist Dr. Grinspoon, in an editorial analyzing the report, which appeared in *Saturday Review,* says "only a small number use it excessively, and they are people who, because they are already emotionally disturbed or suffer from personality disorders, would compulsively use some other psychoactive agent, quite possible a more dangerous and truly addicting one, such as alcohol."

As a physician, it seems to me that a half million people, most of them teen-agers in a drugged state because of the several marijuana cigarettes they smoke each day, is neither an insignificant problem nor one that can be written off because these youngsters would probably turn to some other psychoactive substance. It is, instead, a national tragedy. If as many cases of measles, influenza, or any other disease were diagnosed, it would be called a runaway epidemic. And that, in fact, is what these 500,000 daily smokers represent—a runaway epidemic!

Rather than simply accept the sanguine conclusions of the commission, I wanted to look at the record. Dr. Henry Brill, a member of the commission, had told me that he did not agree with a number of interpretations of the data as they were reported in the published recommendations. He gave me the two volumes, 1,252 pages in all, containing the detailed reports of the studies on marijuana. Through careful analysis of the data contained in these reports, it was possible to find support for a conclusion different from that of the commission. And so a colleague, Dr. Albert Greenwood, and I wrote a detailed rebuttal of the conclusions of the Marijuana Commission based on their own studies. The rebuttal was published in the *Bulletin* of the New York Academy of Medicine in January 1974.

In our reading of the unexpurgated commission report, Dr. Greenwood and I sought the answers to several specific medical questions:

What is the relationship, if any, between the use of marijuana and the use of other psychoactive drugs?

The report itself is ambivalent and unclear in this area. It presents a series of sociological and psychological arguments to justify why only certain individuals who smoke marijuana are liable to turn to other, harder drugs (heroin, cocaine, amphetamines etc.) rather than state definitely that a clear relationship does, in fact, exist. But if one reads the report carefully, evidence needed to support this association can be found. For example: The survey shows that "marijuana users are about twice as likely to have used any illicit drugs than those who have ceased using marijuana." Later it states that "four percent of current marijuana users have tried heroin" and, still later, warns that "to assume that marijuana use is unrelated to the use of other drugs would be inaccurate. As mentioned earlier, the heavy or very heavy users are frequently users of other drugs.... The other drugs ... vary according to the social characteristics of the population in question. Within some groups, heroin may be the choice; in other groups it may be LSD." Nevertheless, the investigators seem to go out of their way to minimize these important findings by then adding, "The fact should be emphasized that the overwhelming majority of marijuana users do not progress to other drugs."

My own research on this question has turned up ample support for the linkage between marijuana and other hard drugs. In a 1971 study of the use of cannabis in Egypt, for instance, Dr. Soueif found that twenty percent of hashish users turned to opium within ten years after starting their smoking habit; and forty percent were using opium after twenty-five years of smoking. In the United States, Drs. E. Crompton and N. O. Brill, publishing their findings in the *Annals of Internal Medicine,* surveyed college students and reported that 100 percent of the daily smokers and twenty-two percent of the monthly smokers also ingested other psychoactive drugs. Thus, despite the report's rather offhanded treatment of this important question, there can be little doubt that there is an association between marijuana and other mind-altering drugs.

What effect does chronic marijuana use have on brain function?

In trying to judge the chronic effects of marijuana, the commission sponsored an experiment, called the Boston free-access study, in which the drug was made freely available to twenty young volunteers. They were divided into two groups, casual and heavy users. The objective was to find out what effect, if any, chronic use had on the life style and intellectual abilities of the subjects. And while the evidence presented could leave no doubt that habitual smoking had a profound effect on these people, the subjective evaluations of some committee members virtually obscured these critical findings.

Consider how the National Commission on Marijuana describes the subjects in the study, and what we discovered from close reading of the data: The commission says that the subjects were "a group of individuals whose life styles, activities, values, and attitudes are representative of a segment of the unconventional youthful subculture." Because it was difficult to enlist people who smoked marijuana once a week or less, "the intermittent users studied appeared to be similar to, rather than different from, the moderate and heavy users studied. Both groups had used marijuana for an average of five years."

The data, however, showed that if these subjects were truly "representative of a segment of the unconventional youthful subculture" then, indeed, the problem was even more serious than we thought. Of the ten users in the "casual" group, five admitted to experience with other drugs—two of them having tried cocaine two or three times, one having used barbiturates two or three times, another admitting to cocaine once and barbiturates two or three times, and the fifth having snorted heroin. Among the heavy users, six told of using cocaine and barbiturates, and one person said he had smoked opium twice. The heaviest user in the group said he had taken three bags of heroin intravenously for a period of eight months, although he claimed to have taken no heroin at all for the past thirteen months. All in all, a sordid picture of drug use among at least one group of marijuana users—and a puzzling omission of facts in a report that was supposed to be "the last word" on the subject.

Moving on, the commission describes the education and employment record of the subjects this way: "The mean age ... was twenty-three. Based on I.Q. testing, they were superior intellectually, although they had completed on the average, only two-and-a-half years of college. Their job histories were rather erratic, characteristic of a pattern of 'itinerant living.' Despite a relatively high level of scholastic attainment and superior intelligence, many of the subjects were performing well below their intellectual capabilities, usually working at menial, mechanical, or artisan tasks."

Our examination of detailed data presented in the appendix volumes showed that the commission had glossed over some rather meaningful facts. Although the subjects may have "averaged" only two and a half years of college, four of the ten "casual" users had had four years of college and one had earned his degree. What were these college-educated people doing today? One worked as a carpenter's assistant, the most recent of the three jobs he had held during the past three years; the twenty-three-year-old graduate, with an I.Q. of 128, had had four jobs during the past four years and was now doing office work; another subject, with an I.Q. of 139, did "odd jobs"; and a college graduate among the heavy users was an attendant in a parking lot. Thus, when the commission said that "the social adjustment of the daily users ... was impaired," they were putting a very mild interpretation on what some people think is a serious judgmental and intellectual impairment secondary to chronic marijuana use.

Although the report mentions the serious personality changes observed in heavy users, the commission qualifies the finding by restating the proposition that "heavy users represent only a small proportion of the total number of users." Once again, it is important to remember that this "small proportion" is a half million young Americans.

Finally, in summing up their observations of the long-term effects of heavy use, the commission says, "In the past few years, observers have noted various social, psychological, and behavioral changes among high school- and college-age Americans including many who have used marijuana heavily for a number of years. . . . These individuals drop out and relinquish traditional adult roles and values . . . appear alienated from broadly accepted social and occupational activity and experience . . . [and] show reduced concern for personal hygiene and nutrition."

While I agree with these findings, my inclination would be to state them in terms unvarnished by sociological and psychological jargon. Namely: The long-term users who were studied by the commission drop out of college, go on public welfare, dress in a slovenly manner, renounce responsibilities, and occasionally take menial jobs despite their high-level educational background.

Should alcohol be brought into the discussion as a standard of comparison?

One of the favorite arguments of marijuana proponents is to say that alcohol presents a far greater problem. The report also recognizes that "many young people perceive that marijuana is less dangerous than alcohol in terms of its addiction potential and long-term physical and psychological consequences," and seems to sanction this belief in its conclusion that "the use of marijuana by the nation's youth must be seen as a relatively minor change in social patterns of conduct and as more of a consequence of than a contributor to these major changes."

As a physician who is fully aware of the human wreckage caused by alcoholism in Western nations, I still can see no rationale for making it a standard of comparison with marijuana. If marijuana is legalized, our country would be the only Western nation to have accepted the large-scale use of an additional stupefying drug that has been proven harmful to health and destructive to society. Clearly, trying to compare alcohol with marijuana only clouds the issue.

Are we punishing the educated, occasional user by forbidding the sale of marijuana?

In its conclusion, the commission has taken into account the insistent demands for legalization made by educated and articulate occasional users. These people point to their own well-controlled use as proof that the dangers are overrated. But their self-confident viewpoint overlooks the half million heavy users in the United States who had at one time or another graduated from the intermittent, occasional group of smokers. While there certainly must be some persons capable of using low-potency marijuana for a long time in a controlled way, who is to know in advance which people can resist the drug and which will fall victim to an escalating habit? Is it only those from the lower socioeconomic groups who find themselves trapped by the drug? Not when you remember that a sizable number of the 500,000 heavy users and the millions of moderate users were once college students from middle-class backgrounds. And to underscore the fact that serious drug problems can develop among the so-called better classes, a study of the effects of chronic marijuana use on thirteen adults published in the *Journal of the American Medical Association* included several upper-middle-class housewives and a thirty-eight-year-old English professor, all of whom experienced severe drug-related reactions after smoking only moderate amounts of marijuana for a few years.

Rather than punishing the educated users, it seems to me that preventing the distribution of marijuana would be doing them a service.

Does tolerance, in fact, develop?

Once again the commission seems to lean over backward to make a case for intermittent use. On page fifty-two of the report: "With regard to marijuana, present indications are that tolerance does develop to the behaviorally and physically disruptive effects, in both animals and man, especially at high frequent doses for prolonged time periods. Studies in foreign countries indicate that very heavy prolonged use of large quantities of hashish leads to the development of tolerance to the mental effects, requiring an increase in intake to reach the original level of satisfaction. However, for the intermittent use pattern and even the moderate use pattern, little evidence exists to indicate the development of tolerance to the desired 'high,' although the high may persist for a shorter period of time. During the Boston free-access study, no change was apparent in the level of the high produced by a relatively large dose of the drug over a twenty-one-day period of moderate to heavy smoking."

Now look at the details of the record. The psychiatrist who interviewed the Boston subjects reported that fourteen of the twenty subjects found that the marijuana they smoked was losing its potency as the study progressed. To make up for this loss, they tended to smoke more. The commission's report explains this increase in need by the "study's confined conditions." Exactly what is meant by "confined conditions" and how or why it should affect usage is not explained. What is clear, though, is that intermittent, moderate, and heavy users all had to increase their use of the drug during the study in order to achieve an acceptable high. Thus the fiction that tolerance does not develop for intermittent users is shattered by the fact that when marijuana is freely available, tolerance to the drug shows a definite pattern of growth.

Why make such a big point about tolerance? The explanation needs very little elaboration: If the dosage must be increased in order to repeat the initial effect, then sooner or later the heavy user may be tempted to move on to the next higher class of mind-altering drug in order to gain the effect he is seeking.

After my thorough study of the commission report, I put some of my questions in writing to Governor Shafer, Dr. Dana Farnsworth, Dr. Maurice Seevers, and Mr. Michael Sonnenreich. Neither Governor Shafer nor Dr. Seevers answered my letters. Michael Sonnenreich replied in only general terms. However, Dr. Farnsworth agreed to publish my criticisms in *Annals of Psychiatry,* of which he is the editor. My concern with the report as it stands today is the many errors, incorrect conclusions, and ambiguities that paint marijuana in a far more positive and harmless light than it deserves. What I urged in my article was further analysis of the hidden facts of the record—to be carried out by a nonpolitical and completely objective body of medical experts. If this were done I am certain the results would call for strict regulation and prohibition. In any case, in 1975, three years after the publication of the recommendations of the Marijuana Commission, which purported to discourage marijuana use, the work has had little effect: The use of marijuana has increased fivefold.

The Canadian equivalent of the Marijuana Commission Report, the Le Dain Commission Report, appeared shortly after and it is subject to the same criticisms. The methods of investigation and sources of information were very similar. However, it would appear that the Canadian commissioners were somewhat more sensitive to the issue of possible potential physical harm resulting from chronic marijuana use, especially by the young, and consequently, the Le Dain report is more cautious in its recommendations than its American counterpart.

XII. A Working Summer

My response to the bland conclusions of the Marijuana Commission Report was a determination to study the immune system. I felt that there might be found the key to marijuana's damaging effect on man.

Scores of scientists had shown that there are two kinds of lymphocytes involved in the immune system: the T lymphocytes, which are manufactured by the thymus gland located at the base of our neck, and the B lymphocytes manufactured in the bone marrow. The T lymphocytes function like a surveillance system, protecting the identity of our cells. These T lymphocytes act against both the cancer cells that every one of us manufactures at one time or another, and against viruses. The B lymphocytes produce the antibodies that neutralize toxins secreted by bacteria that invade our body.

My first attempt to find out if marijuana affects the lymphocytes was to work again with the SHR rats. In this new work we gave them measured amounts of THC combined with a drug called azathioprine, which is known to interfere with the immune system. We observed that when the two drugs were combined, THC not only lowered blood pressure, but the blood pressure remained lowered even after ten days. Remember, THC given by itself had been shown to lose its effect the longer it was given. In our new experiment, however, this tolerance did not occur when THC was given with azathioprine.

It was obvious that what was needed now was a new experimental model that would measure directly the effect of THC on the immune system. And this is where my problems began because I was confined both by limited funds and by the general indifference of my laboratory colleagues.

In the late spring I conferred with Professor Daniel Zagury of France, who was visiting the United States. Zagury, a professor of anatomy in Reims, had once spent a sabbatical leave in my laboratory. Since then he had specialized in the study of lymphocytes and returned regularly to this country to confer with his colleagues in this field at Rockefeller University. "If marijuana interferes with T lymphocytes," Zagury said, "it should be easy to find out by using mice. I could do this in my laboratory without much difficulty." His offer was the answer to my dilemma.

We briefly discussed the protocol. Zagury would give the mice some THC. After a few weeks, he would study their lymphocytes. "If marijuana does interfere with the immune system," said Zagury, "it must react with the T lymphocytes." Arrangements were made for him to obtain the necessary THC in France from Dr. Michel Paris, who was licensed to handle this substance.

A useful professional conference took place in July. This one was given by the International Congress of Pharmacology in San Francisco. Three special sessions of the congress were devoted to further studies of marijuana. The more than thirty papers given at these sessions were highly technical. Some of the subjects covered were: the effect of a large dose of THC on heart function; the effect of THC and hormone levels in dogs and rats; the disruptive effect of THC on the behavior of pigeons, rodents, and chimpanzees. Although many papers described tolerance development in animals, none hypothesized about the possible mechanism of this tolerance.

One report of tolerance in pigeons was especially interesting. The authors had shown that the behavior of a pigeon trained to peck a key in order to obtain food was disrupted at first by a very small dose of THC. Over a period of a few days, though, a dosage of THC ten times greater than that originally given no longer affected the bird. But this development did not mean that the birds had less THC in the brain. On the contrary, by means of radioactive tagging, it was shown that the drug continued to accumulate in the brain even though it no longer had any disruptive effect on behavior.

Another report described the transformation of THC in the body as it was rapidly distributed to the tissues where it then formed metabolites that, upon entering the cells, attached to fatty particles. I guessed that the body must have a mechanism to neutralize the effects of an accumulation of THC. Was it the immune system? Was there damage to the cells? None of the papers presented, not even the most sophisticated, gave any indication.

One paper advocating the view that marijuana could be useful received a lot of publicity in the lay press. Marijuana was shown to have the effect in man of lowering the intraocular pressure of the eye, the pressure exerted by the fluid contained in the eyeball. The author reported that a practical application of this observation was the use of marijuana to help one of his patients with glaucoma, a disease that is, in effect, an increased pressure of the fluid in the eyeball. After smoking just one marijuana cigarette, the symptoms were relieved.

I asked the author of this report if he had noticed any tolerance development, and also what advantage marijuana had over the more conventional drugs already in use. He did not have a satisfactory answer to either question. The media, however, seized upon this therapeutic application of marijuana. The next day one newspaper headlined, "Pot, A New Cure For Glaucoma!"

Trying to keep an open mind, I asked one of my colleagues at Columbia's Eye Institute, Dr. Harold Spalter, what he thought of these findings. He was skeptical. Then, two years after the announcement, this particular "cure" had not gained any acceptance among the specialists, and side effects such as "red eye" were reported following this treatment.

In the midst of such meetings and my own laboratory work, I kept up a continuing correspondence with the NIMH regarding my proposal for a Moroccan study on long-term marijuana use. We had already agreed that, in addition to pharmacologists and biologists, the survey team should include specialists in the fields of anthropology and ethnology. Anthropology involves the study of the customs, development and beliefs of man, while ethnology is concerned with man's origins, institutions, relations, and speech development. The ethnologist is to man what the ecologist is to nature. In addition, we would need a psychiatrist to administer and evaluate various kinds of psychological and physiological tests. I enlisted the aid of Dr. Philip Zeidenberg, associate professor of psychiatry at Columbia's College of Physicians and Surgeons and attending psychiatrist at New York Psychiatric Institute, for this part of the study. In addition to his training in medicine and psychiatry, he held a Ph.D. in biochemistry. The Moroccan study would give him the opportunity to pursue his interests in the biochemical aspects of normal and abnormal behavior.

For the ethnological side of the study, I enlisted as our consultant, one of the world's leading authorities in this field, Professor Claude Levi-Strauss, chairman of the department of social anthropology at the College de France in Paris. His chosen field gave him an overall grasp of problems related to the study of man; thus, he would be the ideal one to guide us in the best way to proceed with the ethnological part of this study.

In late July, Dr. Zeidenberg and I met with officials of the NIMH for a long briefing session. Essentially, the aim of our study would be to investigate the effects of chronic marijuana smoking on the major physiological functions of a selected sample of Moroccan villagers. The sample would include 100 long-term kif smokers and 100 nonsmokers. Levi-Strauss would help us to find among his associates field workers familiar with the Berber language and culture.

When I left the NIMH building with Dr. Zeidenberg that afternoon, we had assurance that our study would be funded, and that we could make the preliminary arrangements. Soon, however, we received a surprising report from the NIMH entitled "Ganja in Jamaica" by two social scientists, Dr. Vera Rubin and Dr. Lambros Comitas. The authors of the study had concluded: "Chronic use of potent cannabis is not toxic to the human mind and body."

Such a conclusion did not jibe with my own experience at a symposium held in 1971 where I met Dr. John Hall, chairman of the Department of Medicine and physician in chief of the Kingston Hospital in Jamaica. In his presentation at that symposium, Dr. Hall described the damaging effects of ganja that he had observed in the farmers of Jamaica: emphysema, gastrointestinal problems, impotence, personality changes, and mental illness. Thus the Rubin and Comitas report contradicted Dr. Hall's findings. I wondered why. As I read the report, however, I became aware of many shortcomings in its preparation, methods, and conclusions. "Ganja in Jamaica" was not a longterm in-depth study, the number of subjects studied was small, and sophisticated tests in cellular biology were not used. The willingness of the NIMH to commission Dr. Zeidenberg and me to do a feasibility study of chronic kif consumption in Morocco indicated that the government also recognized the need for a more comprehensive study than the one of Rubin and Comitas.

"Ganja in Jamaica" can be divided into two parts: an anthropological section and a medical one. The medical part of the report, something I was competent to judge, appeared to me to be fragmentary. In comparison to my plans to study 100 smokers in Morocco, a thirty-person sample was small indeed. The subjects were mostly unskilled farmers, and the medical examinations given them were little more than routine checkups. In order to find a particular pathology, such as the effects of ganja smoking, testing methods have to be more sophisticated. One finding of possible harm, an impairment of gas exchanges through the lungs leading to a lowered oxygen level in the blood, should have led to more extensive tests to determine the cause of such an abnormality, but these were not included. Chromosomal studies, which claim to indicate absence of genetic abnormalities, were completely inadequate. For example, twenty-eight out of sixty

cultures did not grow, indicating unsolved technical problems; and only between six and twenty-five cells per culture
were analyzed, an inadequate number to express such definite results. Other methods and the statistics used in this
study are not suitable for the detection of early symptoms of
the underlying pathology that is associated with heavy smoking of ganja. The authors had not analyzed cells of the body
taken from the lungs, the blood, and the testis. Perhaps the
medical team did its best with the material available, but
now that newer, more revelatory methods are available, their
study is out of date.

One conclusion of the report, "The general decline in the
skills of these men, masks the subtle differential effects related to the use or nonuse of ganja," fascinated me because it
was a confirmation of Soueif's Egyptian study. But Soueif
had added an important observation: "The higher the initial
level of proficiency, the larger the amount of impairment."

Still, when looked at as a whole, the "Ganja in Jamaica"
report is an interesting document. In its own way, in fact, it
confirmed some of my own conclusions. I had written earlier:
"The use of cannabis in poor, agrarian societies, is not so
much for pleasure as it is for an aid to perform menial tasks.
The symbiotic relationship of man and cannabis allows him
to tolerate both the drug and the dreariness of his daily
existence. From a sociological point of view, the daily use of
cannabis in a warm climate can be compatible with the performance of unskilled tasks, although a certain inefficiency
and lower productivity does result. In those countries the
existence of a man daily dependent on cannabis use is
stabilized at a marginal subsistence level."

Naturally I corresponded with Dr. Hall to find out what he
felt were the shortcomings of the "Ganja in Jamaica" report.
"Such a study, which is not a longitudinal one, carried out
over a longer period of time, is bound to omit from its sample
all of the marijuana smokers who have shown pathological
symptoms such as we see in our clinic." I was incredulous
because his answer meant that the sample was not representative of the ganja-smoking Jamaican population, since those

who had been sick due to ganja were not included—further evidence of the faulty quality of the study. Because of the wide area of disagreement between John Hall and Rubin and Comitas, I decided to go to Jamaica and see for myself the real situation.

Dr. Hall and members of his staff met with me, and during our long conversation, I learned much about the history of ganja in Jamaica. Briefly, I found out that ganja was introduced to Jamaica by indentured workers from India. Historically, ganja has been used mostly in a few areas by mountain farmers. As long as it was limited to this class, there was no problem. During the postwar period, however, this situation changed with the industrialization of the island. As farmers drifted to Kingston to find employment, the resulting new urban proletariat also began to use cannabis and it was necessary to stem this tide. Certainly, in a burgeoning technological society the end result of ganja smoking would be very different than in a poor agrarian one. Sugar-cane workers use marijuana to endure the drudgery of their occupation. But imagine going a few steps up the economic ladder to a skilled occupation such as printing. Imagine the following commentary: "The Linotype operators expended more energy at their work while smoking marijuana but were less efficient and made useless motions; as a result, printing took longer and the paper was filled with errors." In countries over-burdened by teeming masses, I can understand why the problems of daily existence are so overwhelming for some, especially the unskilled, that they have to escape into the pleasant stupor of cannabis intoxication. But a progressive society cannot justify the use of marijuana. Thus "Ganja in Jamaica" only convinced me further that longitudinal studies such as the one we planned on marijuana smokers in Morocco would show results far different from the ones reflected in the Jamaica report, that, in fact, smoking marijuana will cause physical and mental deterioration.

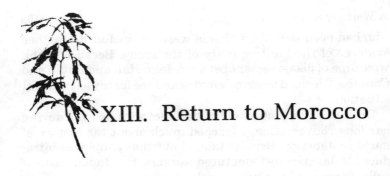

XIII. Return to Morocco

My second trip to Morocco, in October 1972, to make the preliminary arrangements for our study of the effects of long-term marijuana usage, began with a stop over in Paris where I contacted Dr. Levi-Strauss at the College de France. Dr. Zeidenberg and I were ushered into a spacious study where the walls were literally covered by mementos of his various expeditions to remote parts of the world. Dr. Levi-Strauss, an impressive man with piercing eyes that looked out from under a crown of white hair, spoke to us in accentless English.

"As I informed you, Dr. Nahas, the Berber tribes of North Africa are not the area of my primary expertise. In order to help you, I have selected two of my associates, Pierre Bonte and Claude Lefebure [both ethnologists], who are thoroughly familiar with the Berber language and culture. I'll be pleased to give you any support or advice you may need in your study."

Pierre Bonte, a pupil of Professor Levi-Strauss who had earned a doctorate in anthropology, had just returned from southern Morocco where he had studied the economic organization and customs of slavery among the Touareg Il Ken, a nomadic Berber tribe. He was, indeed, the right person to brief us and also accompany us to Morocco. His colleague, Claude Lefebure, an ethnologist who was working in the field, would then take us to the areas of kif cultivation and consumption. We flew the next day to Casablanca and from there traveled by car to Marrakesh. Bonte expressed a keen interest in our study. "You will see," he said, "the villagers in the mountains are very secluded from the rest of the world. They represent an ideal social laboratory."

In Marrakesh we rented a Land Rover for the next leg of our trip. At daybreak we were on a road that winds tortuously through the Atlas Mountains. The only vegetation to be seen was the irrigated terraces where the Berbers grow wheat and barley, fruits and vegetables; and the only dwellings were one-story stone houses clustered along the streams that cut through the valleys. We passed many women and children carrying large bundles of twigs and branches for their winter fires. Bonte explained that the bare spots we could see on the mountains were caused by deforestation that had been going on for years.

Ouarzazate is a striking city located on the eastern slope of the Atlas Mountains at the edge of the Sahara desert. The surrounding landscape is reminiscent of parts of Arizona— flat and covered with brown mushroomlike mounds that jut out against the blue sky. There are few streams to water the dry land.

At one local hotel we joined up with Claude Lefebure. Bonte greeted him with enthusiasm and then made the introductions. Lefebure had already received a letter from Levi-Strauss describing my study. He readily agreed to delay his current work for a week or ten days in order to accompany us to the two areas where kif smoking was prevalent: the lower slopes of the middle Atlas Mountains, near Beni Melal, and the central Rif, near Ketama.

As we sat in the lounge of the hotel, Lefebure filled us in on the tribes we would be visiting. It was evident that he had great affection for the rugged mountain people, referring to them as "my Berbers." "The tribes of these mountains are made up of proud, ascetic people who live in a structured, medieval setting. They scrupulously follow the religious traditions of their ancestors and claim to be descendants of the prophet Muhammad or of saints." He assured us we would not find kif smoking among the tough mountaineers of "my Berber tribes," but that we would probably uncover quite a bit of usage among Moroccan soldiers who are stationed in the area.

After listening to our plans, Lefebure and Bonte both agreed to delay their next projects in order to participate fully in our program, starting in July or August of the following year. We planned on a one-year study with an anthropological phase followed by a medical one. Phase I of the study would involve Bonte and Lefebure, who would live with the Berber tribes for a period long enough to enable them to describe the daily life of the people and determine how kif smoking affected their interaction with society. Toward the end of this period (an estimated eight months), they would then be able to select 100 smokers and 100 controls, and brief the subjects on what would come next.

With appropriate and well-documented subjects selected, Phase II could then concentrate on the medical aspects of the study. This would mean a series of mental and physical examinations as well as immunological tests, over a period of perhaps three months, to determine what, it any, physiological effects could be observed in long-term kif users.

As we drove back to Marrakesh with Lefebure, Bonte pointed out the multistoried castles of pounded earth that had been built by the Berbers for defense and for the winter storage of food. In the summertime, because the nomadic Berbers take their livestock up into the mountains to graze, their dwellings are black goat-hair tents. We arrived at our destination at sundown, somewhat shaken up by the 200-mile drive over the rough mountain roads.

We discussed and debated our plans far into the night. How could we best structure our study? What would be the timetables of Phase I and Phase II? What personal equipment would be needed? What type of studies and tests should be performed? At the end of our discussion, the only major point that remained to be solved was which of two locations we would use for the study. The consensus was that we should visit both before deciding. We would have to do this preliminary work without Bonte, who had to return to Paris to finish work already begun on another study.

When we drove to the provincial capital of Beni Melal a day later, Lefebure, wearing his jellaba (the typical native costume), left us in a little motel. We had already agreed that he would do some investigation on his own while we waited for him. With his command of the language, he could learn the extent of kif usage, where it is cultivated, and its patterns of use, according to age and sex, far easier without us in tow. It was his intention to obtain samples of the kif as well as some cannabis seeds. Off he went, quickly blending into the stream of people who moved through the town.

But Dr. Zeidenberg and I were not idle while he was gone. We went to the administrative center in Beni Melal to meet with the chief public health officer of the province. In very general terms we explained the aims of our prospective study. We were told that although health statistics were available for the province, they did not include the mountain region we were interested in. Indeed, there was as yet no medical service available in the mountain villages.

Casually, we inquired about the problem of kif intoxication in the province. The officer was emphatic that the problem did not exist because the laws forbidding cultivation of the plant were strictly enforced. The major health problems that concerned him, he said, were similar to those of any underdeveloped country: infant and maternal morbidity, and contagious diseases such as tuberculosis, gonorrhea, and malaria. Nevertheless, he was interested in our study because of what information we might be able to gather about the health needs and problems of the Berber mountaineers. He was pleased to note that we would have ethnologists involved who spoke Berber. Certainly, he said, he would cooperate in the medical phase of our study. He told us that it was a rare occurrence when a Berber, even those very sick, could be brought in for treatment.

During the afternoon we rented a car and drove to a neighboring village. Attracted by a plant growing by the roadside that I took to be kif, we stopped for a close look. It turned out to be something else, but the halt gave us an opportunity to talk to some of the villagers. I asked other questions before getting around to my main interest in kif. I said that we were botanists interested in the local flora. The man I was questioning, a former construction worker who spoke excellent French, told me that to find kif one had to go north to the Rif. Another villager, joining our conversation, said he knew where to find kif if we wanted some. He said it was grown in a village about ten miles up the mountain. The driver of our car, however, refused to go there because the road was very bad. So we returned to the hotel and waited for Lefebure.

Lefebure came back with a report on the three villages he had investigated. They were located at the foot of the slope of the middle Atlas, populated mostly by Berbers who were in the process of migrating down from the upper regions toward the more fertile plains. The social structure of these newer settlements, Lefebure explained, is no longer as rigid as those farther up the mountain, because the newer villages are influenced by the cities in the valley. He confirmed that the Berber tribes who lived in the high vallys of the Atlas mountains did not use kif. But in the villages he had just visited, he learned that twenty-five to forty percent of the male population smoked the drug. Although he had met some of the smokers, they were abstaining at the time because of the Moslem annual fast of Ramadan, which prohibits smoking, eating, and drinking during the daytime. Nevertheless, he did get some information about the general habit.

Kif smokers begin as early as age ten, but most start at age fifteen. They give the usual reasons for acquiring a drug habit—unemployment, boredom, peer pressure. The only women who smoke are prostitutes. Some men, after prolonged usage, actually give up the habit. Lefebure spoke with a schoolteacher who claimed he had finally stopped smoking because it "disgusted him." But such claims are difficult to verify. In this respect, all the Moroccans we spoke to described the smoking of kif as deviant behavior, one that went against the Islamic moral code and against civil law, and few of them admitted using it.

"Pure kif" is a powder that generally is mixed with tobacco (in a ratio of three parts kif to one of tobacco) and smoked in the stone cups of pipes with stems from ten to twenty inches long. The cup of these pipes are quite small and contain the equivalent of one American joint. An average smoker will smoke twenty to thirty pipes a day, but some boast of as many as sixty or seventy!

A twenty-four-hour dose was prepared for Lefebure by some young people he met in one of the villages. The group included a twenty-four-year-old professional soccer player, a drop-out student of fourteen, and two teen-age European girls who joined in for the fun of it. They showed him how to separate the dried flowers from the leaves of the plant, how to sift out the stems and seeds, and how to mince the residue into a fine powder. It took about an hour to make ten grams of powder or one day's dosage. Most smokers need two pipefuls an hour in order to stay high. Lefebure brought us samples of the different stages in the making of kif, which I planned to send to the analytical laboratories of Dr. Coy Waller in Mississippi, Dr. Paris in Paris, and Dr. Braenden in Geneva, in order to determine the composition of Moroccan kif.

We discussed the possibility of using the area around Beni Melal for our study. There were some obvious advantages: The villages were easy to get to and the weather was good most of the year. We also saw many disadvantages that had nothing to do with the logistics of our study, but with the social and cultural aspects. We really wanted a "pure and unspoiled" population for our sample and this was not the case here. The easy access meant that there was a lot of contact between the villagers and the more sophisticated city dwellers of Beni Melal. The main roads were heavily traveled by people going between Fez and Marrakesh. Because of this interaction there could not be a clear delineation of influence or of patterns of drug use. Obviously, we needed to press on to the north and investigate the Rif mountain villages where cannabis not only was cultivated, but also was a major source of revenue for the Berber tribes living there.

Early the next morning we began the journey. In order to save time, Zeidenberg went to Rabat to meet the public officials we had to interview, while Lefebure and I went to the Rif mountains to explore the villages around Ketama.

For nearly fifty years, until 1953, Spain occupied the Rif area of Morocco. But, unlike France, Spain invested little in her colony that was of benefit to the people. As a result, the countryside is destitute. Roads, washed out and rutted, wind through mountains laid bare by erosion and deforestation. Sparsely populated, there is little traffic except for overladen donkeys led by ragged farmers. At a crossroads a group of soldiers stopped us, but after speaking with Lefebure in Arabic they let us proceed. As we drove closer to the center of the Rif mountains, the landscape became greener and the trees more numerous.

We stopped at Ketama, a mountain station where there is a pleasant hotel. We had our supper and retired to the bar where we invited two of the villagers to take mint tea with us. One was a handyman and the other, Ahmed, was a native of Ketama who worked in the area with the agricultural service. It turned out that the latter fellow was familiar with every kif field cultivated around the district!

The agricultural worker Ahmed offered to take us wherever we wanted to go and we accepted his offer, making an appointment for the next morning. Accidentally, we had found a dependable and useful guide. As we talked, our conversation limping along in snatches of French, Spanish, Berber, and Arabic, we explained our mission. Our new friends spoke freely, giving us useful information. They told us that kif was the only cash crop cultivated in the area. At least half of the growers of kif also smoked it. Ahmed claimed he was one of the few who did not use kif, but he had plots that he harvested every year. He gave his reason for not smoking: "It is not good. If you smoke kif, you have to eat a great deal and wear warm clothing. Otherwise you become very thin and waste away. You can't work very well." The handyman agreed that he could not function very well if he smoked kif. Toward the end of the evening, four young men walked into the bar. They had long hair and were dressed in jeans and sweaters. "These men are millionaires, thanks to the profits they make from trafficking in kif," Ahmed told us.

At nine the next morning we met our guide, Ahmed, who was dressed in pants with a heavy jacket and an embroidered hat. Lefebure and I had donned jellabas so we would look less obvious in the villages. We drove first to a mountaintop where a few piles of stones were all that remained of Spanish fortress. We could see all around us the rounded tips of the Rif mountains, dotted with clusters of villages and a few isolated farms. Ahmed pointed out greenish terraces on the slopes where kif is grown. He told us that the king of Morocco once had come here and, after looking around at the barren hills, had asked, "But what do these people eat?" To Ahmed the answer was clear: To alleviate their extreme poverty the people of these mountains must grow kif.

We next stopped at Ahmed's village, a dozen dilapidated one-story stone houses with corrugated tin roofs held in place with heavy rocks. A barbed wire fence surrounded the perimeter of the village. As we approached, the stench of human excrement assailed us. Ahmed went to get his brother, a tall, lanky Arab in his thirties, who came out to escort us into the low-ceilinged house. There we were amazed to find two young European men, one a Dutchman and the other French. They were sitting on the floor surrounded by "bricks" of kif and smoking with typical long-stemmed pipes as well as with a device called a *chillum,* a six-inch cone made of terra cotta. They both nodded at us, and we watched as one of them took the tazli and stuffed the opening with powdered kif that he had loosened from one of the bricks. After placing a piece of cloth on the smaller end, he lit the kif, took a deep drag and passed it on to his companion.

We were curious to know why the two young men were there. The Frenchman, the more garrulous of the two, told us they had arrived two days before and planned to stay a few weeks. He turned out to be nineteen, a high school dropout whose family lived in Dakar. Having begun smoking at the age of fifteen, he said his greatest thrill was to ride his motorcycle at night when he was high. His Dutch friend was about twenty-five, and had arrived from India where he had gone to sample their hashish. The two of them had already been smoking for two hours and were planning to continue for the rest of the day. I asked them what else they did. "Oh, we play a little music and relax," said the Frenchman, pointing to a guitar resting on the floor. I inquired if they used other drugs. They told me yes, LSD and mescaline. Breaking his silence, the Dutchman added, "LSD is really good, very, very good." Whereupon the Frenchman whispered in my ear that his friend was a little stoned.

Since we had declined to smoke his kif, Ahmed's brother hospitably offered us some mint tea. Because it was Ramadan, our host did not join us. He could not eat, drink, or smoke from sunrise to sunset. "Otherwise I would be smoking kif with the boys," he said. "In one night, I can smoke as many as eighty pipes." He showed us an autographed picture of his girl friend in London who was also smoking kif. It appeared that he traveled widely, thanks to his profits from the sale of kif.

Lefebure was disappointed. "This is not the village for us. It's invaded by foreigners. One of the natives even travels to London!" He turned to Ahmed and asked him to show us another village. He agreed to take us, but it was heavy going once we left the main route. The road was plagued by potholes and crisscrossed with water-filled trenches. At times, two of us had to push the car out of a rut while the third held the wheel. It took us an hour to cover six miles. Finally we decided to walk the rest of the way. It was not long before we caught site of the village of Azilah, nestled at the foot of Mount Tidirine. We hoped that this would be our model of a well-settled, stable village, isolated from outside influences.

As we approached the village, many people joined us, including two young men who were riding a brand-new motorcycle. At one point we noticed some women bent and practically hidden under huge bundles of weeds. "Kif, kif," whispered Ahmed. In the middle of the village, parked alongside of the road, was a new Renault, half-hidden under a plastic cover. How on earth did they manage to get it there?

We were led to the house of a major kif producer. He greeted us on the terrace of his house and offered mint tea. Drinking the tasty brew, I spoke to Ahmed in Spanish while Lefebure carried on an animated conversation with our host in Berber. In a little while we were joined by a Canadian, a Senegalese, and a Swede who sat down on the porch where small bags of kif were piled. The Senegalese picked up one of the bags and kissed it. The Candian told us that in his country all criminal penalties for possession and use of marijuana had been removed. If caught, the penalty was now no worse than receiving a parking ticket. But even that, he felt, was a nuisance. "Why should there by any penalty when marijuana is completely harmless? Look at me and my friends, we've been smoking your kif here for ten days and we're fine. And this is really strong stuff—no comparison with the grass at home!"

Meanwhile, in his discussion with our host, Lefebure tried to find out what proportion of the villagers smoked kif. Since Ahmed had told us previously that half of the male villagers smoked, Lefebure was surprised when our host said practically no one in the village used the stuff. But when we asked a young villager sitting near us if he smoked, we got a different answer: "Sure I do, everyone around here does." Our host was furious and began yelling at the young man, and Ahmed had to serve as a peacemaker.

We were taken on a tour of our host's factory, located on the top of his house. There we saw three men with shaven heads sitting in the middle of piles of flowering tops of kif. They were rubbing the flowering tops over sieves. The powdered residue was funneled to the floor below and transferred into plastic bags by means of a huge hand press. Then the finished product was formed into flat bricks weighing about a pound, the most convenient form for export.

There was no doubt that kif was the major, if not the only, produce here. We thanked our host for his hospitality and started out of the village. On the way back two European women appeared in the doorway of one of the crude houses and watched us silently. When we went by the Renault, there was a wheelbarrow full of kif bricks next to it, ready for loading. Lefebure laughed and said, "I wonder how those guys expect to get their car back over that road loaded with 600 pounds of kif?"

We then drove back to Rabat, discussing our survey of
Azilah. Lefebure described the features of Azilah that made it
perfect for an ethnological study. "Its isolation, ethnic and
linguistic character, and ancient settlement are all qualities
associated with confirmed social structures. In other words,
an ideal setting to observe the interaction of kif consumption
with the individual and his society." Even though as in
Ahmed's village there were some influx of foreign visitors
(mainly at kif harvest time), this was not enough to disturb
the ethnological characteristics necessary for our study.

The relative inaccessibility of the village posed a problem,
however. In a few weeks rain or snow would effectively seal
off the community from the outside world for months. And
this meant that the medical phase of the program would have
to be held off until the following summer.

We arrived in Rabat in the middle of the night. There we
found Zeidenberg, who told us he had been in touch with one of
the highest public health officials in Morocco, the secretary
general, who had published several articles on the subject of
kif. That official believed the problem to be second in important only to tuberculosis, and he quoted a well-known expression, "Le kif fait le lit de la tuberculose" (Kif makes a bed for
tuberculosis). As a physician I could easily understand how
the apathy and malnutrition resulting from extended cannabis use could make these people more susceptible to diseases such as tuberculosis.

One other important bit of information picked up by Dr.
Zeidenberg was the estimate that sixty percent of hospitalized, mentally ill patients in Morocco used kif. This is a
huge number that certainly would bear consideration in our
studies.

We met for our last planning session in the morning. We
were agreed—the proposed study of chronic kif usage and its
effect on man was definitely feasible. All factors considered,
the Rif mountain location was the best. Depending on the
availability of the ethnologists, the study could begin in the
spring or summer; Lefebure, at least, said he would be available.

In Paris we met again with Bonte, and gave him copies of our Moroccan findings. He then would detail our proposals and budget the projected study. One further loose end had to be tied before I could leave for the States. I had to find out about Daniel Zagury's progress with his studies on the immune system of rats treated with THC. As I suspected, he was able to show that THC definitely interfered with the immune system. It was logical that the next step in carrying these results further ought to be the study of THC's effects on human lymphocytes.

My efforts, both scientific and ethnological, came full circle when Zagury agreed to participate in the Moroccan study if it was approved and funded.

Bonte's detailed proposal arrived within two weeks after our return to New York. He had estimated that the cost of the study would be about $400,000, equally divided between the ethnological and medical phases. Although this would be a tight budget, it would be sufficient to set up a field hospital near the villages and transport medical specialists to it.

You can imagine the tremendous letdown, the frustration, the despair I felt when, in August 1973, the NIMH turned down our proposal after funding our exploratory trip and after indicating their real interest in our study. Moreover, our disappointment was compounded by the news that the government had just allocated $3,000,000 for purely sociological study of marijuana use in the United States and Israel. It was a mystery. How could the government think it more important to fund a Gallup Poll–like study that would merely sample the drug-using habits of different sections of the population, instead of our Moroccan Study, which would have given them real scientific data?

XIV. Marijuana and the Immunity System

One of the advantages of being involved in research is that there is always something new to be learned. Although NIMH's cancellation of the funding of our Morocco expedition rankled, concentrating on my laboratory work became a way to overcome my disappointment. My concern at this point was still the effects of long-term marijuana smoking on the immunity system of man. In order to make up for a lack of detailed knowledge in this field, I spent a great deal of time studying the latest publications and talking with some of the experts at Columbia's College of Physicians and Surgeons.

One such expert, Dr. Elliot Osserman, a specialist in the study of lymphocytes and the associate director of Columbia's Cancer Institute, told me, "You might be correct in supposing that fat-soluble substances, such as marijuana products, could interact with the cells of the immune system after prolonged absorption and storage in the plasma membrane."

The experiments completed recently by Daniel Zagury in Paris gave some indication that this idea was a possibility. Mice who were given small amounts of THC had been sensitized to the point where more and more of the drug was needed to produce an effect on the mice. When treated lymphocytes of these mice were then collected and incubated, the researchers were able to stimulate them to grow and multiply by new additions of THC. This is akin to an army bringing in reserves to repulse an attack. Meanwhile, the mice lymphocytes that had not been already treated with THC—those from the controls—did not grow and divide when THC was added. Our conclusion was that THC acted as a stimulant to lymphocyte activity.

Osserman thought the experiments sounded interesting but was unable to help me in his own laboratory. Instead, he introduced me to Dr. Nicole Suciu-Foca, who was in charge of the laboratory of clinical immunology just down the hall from his own labs. Dr. Suciu-Foca's special area of expertise is the study of the immunity system of cancer and kidney transplant patients. In both cases, the patients have a lowered immune response, the former because their lymphocytes are overwhelmed by cancer cells and the latter because of the drugs given to suppress the body's natural reaction to the foreign kidney. When the lymphocytes from these patients are stimulated in test tubes with special substances called mitogens, they do not grow and divide at the same rate as do those from normal control subjects.

Dr. Suciu-Foca showed me the new micro method she used to analyze blood samples. It involved a machine called the Multiple Automatic Sample Harvester, MASH for short, which is a method faster and more accurate than previous techniques. Watching a demonstration, I realized that it could be easily adapted to the study of how THC affects the lymphocytes.

Would Dr. Suciu-Foca be interested in applying her techniques to my projects? Yes, but she would need additional help in the lab to handle both her present workload and the new tasks. Probably one highly skilled postdoctoral fellow would do it. I asked two fellows from my alma mater, the University of Toulouse in France, who were working in my lab if they knew an immunologist from their university who might want to come to the United States. "We know one," they replied. "His name is Jean Pierre Armand. He would be perfect because he not only speaks English but he likes to travel."

When I contacted Armand he was excited by the idea of

coming to this country for eight months or so, and in turn, I was impressed by his qualifications. He had just completed a chief residency at a university hospital. Next, I approached the Philippe Foundation to see if they would grant a fellowship. They approved my request and Armand soon arrived in New York. During his first few weeks he learned the new techniques available in Suciu-Foca's laboratory.

After a prolonged planning session with Dr. Suciu-Foca, we decided to compare the immune response of marijuana smokers with that of age- and sex-matched nonsmokers, as well as with cancer patients and patients treated with immunosuppressant drugs. In this way we would be able to take full advantage of Dr. Suciu-Foca's previous laboratory experiments and further our own interests at the same time.

Through his personal popularity, Armand was able to enlist the cooperation of members of the staff at Columbia who smoked marijuana at least several times a week. We knew that this could not be an ideal sample because there was no way to be absolutely certain that our subjects did not use other drugs, nor could we know exactly the amount and potency of the pot they smoked. But, we had to begin somewhere! Eventually we hoped to be able to correct these deficiencies with a study of marijuana smokers in a controlled environment. Certainly there was some empirical evidence that our subjects were not using stronger substances than pot because of the nature of their work as medical students or laboratory technicians.

Armand sampled blood from the subjects and studied their lymphocytes. When we looked at the results, Dr. Suciu-Foca pointed out that the lymphocytes from the marijuana smokers had a cell-division activity significantly *lower* than the lymphocytes from the controls.

This was a surprise! Judging from Zagury's limited experiments, using very brief exposure to THC (three times in as many weeks), we had hypothesized that there would be a greater activity from the lymphocytes of marijuana smokers. But in these new experiments, this hypothesis turned out to be incorrect. The effect was just the opposite. In contrast to Zagury's experiments, ours were based on prolonged exposure to marijuana (an average exposure of four years in man) and used more accurate methods. In scientific research, as this test situation shows, a wrong hypothesis can still lead to a right answer, in any case: Chronic marijuana smoking does have an effect on the immunity system.

Thus encouraged by our findings, we decided to expand our experiment by using a larger number of smokers and nonsmokers. We wanted subjects who had been smoking marijuana once a week for at least six months, and who did not take other drugs. Our one problem in selection would be the difficulty of determining the amount and potency of the marijuana that our subjects used and whether they used any other drugs. We were sure only that they were not shooting heroin as there were no needle marks on their arms. Since none of the subjects were drifters (all were students or had jobs), we felt we had fairly reliable credibility.

We advertised for male volunteers in *The Village Voice*. The study was limited to males only, but not because of male chauvinism or a lack of awareness that many women smoke pot. Our reasons related to the fact that estrogen levels in the plasma of women change the rate at which lymphocytes divide: the higher the estrogen level, the lower the rate of division. For the time being, this variation would not be helpful in our experiments.

When the issue of the *Voice* with our ad reached the newsstand, the phone kept us hopping. We eliminated two out of three applicants through questions. A further reduction occurred when we set up appointments to see the volunteers; only two or three out of four actually showed up at the office. We, of course, promised them complete anonymity and immunity from officials.

A short interview preceded the sampling of blood from the arm vein. The questions were: How long had they been smoking pot: How often? Did they use other drugs? Did they smoke tobacco or drink alcohol? How was their health? Did they suffer from a recent virus infection, mononucleosis, or had they recently been exposed to X-rays? If they passed the interview, samples of blood were taken and collected in a sterile syringe that contained heparin, an anticlotting chemical. The samples were then placed in a centrifuge that rapidly spun off the lymphocytes from the red blood cells.

Before describing the "recipe" used to test lymphocyte activity, it would be helpful to understand the different phases of cell division. First, there is the *prophase* when the cell is quiet, resting. Secondly, the *S-phase* when the cell draws in chemicals from the outside to double its amount of DNA, the chemical in the nucleus that carries the genetic code. Among the chemicals drawn in to effect this doubling is thymidine. We used thymidine in our experiments and call the process "thymidine uptake." Thirdly, the *metaphase* when the cells start dividing and the strands of DNA split apart. This is the only time when you can actually see, under a microscope, all forty-six pairs of chromosomes that are found in a normal dividing human cell. Fourthly, the *anaphase* when the chromosomes migrate toward the two poles of the cell and fifthly, the *telephase* when the cell pulls apart to make two identical daughter cells.

In our experiment we placed equal amounts of lymphocytes that had been drawn from marijuana smokers, and non-marijuana smoking controls, into 100 wells of a transparent plate, which looks something like a mini-egg carton. Substances needed to nourish the cell, and a stimulant to make the lymphocytes grow and divide, were added. The "egg carton" was then placed in an oven and incubated for three days.

The stimulant added to the wells performs an important function because unlike other cells in our body, lymphocytes divide very slowly in culture. We added to the wells very small amounts of one of three different chemicals or mitogens to stimulate lymphocyte growth and division. The first, called Phytohemagglutinin (PHA), is a molecule extracted from the navy bean; the second is Mixed Lymphocyte Culture (MLC), which is made from lymphocytes sampled from several normal subjects and treated with an antibiotic that kills the cells but leaves their ability to stimulate other lymphocytes (antigenic property); the third is Pockweed (PWM) which, as its name implies, comes from a weed.

During the last few hours of incubation, radioactive thymidine was added. Then the cultures were "harvested" and washed until only the cells, free of the culture media, remained. This is where Dr. Suciu-Foca's MASH machine was used to suck the lymphocytes into test tubes and get them ready for the scintillation counter that would measure the amount of radioactive thymidine taken up by the different kinds of cells. In this manner, the scientist can follow one of nature's most deeply buried secret mechanisms: The rate of formation of DNA in dividing cells. The scintillation counter gives a printed readout of the counts per minute (abbreviation CPM) obtained from the different vials: the higher the count, the greater the incorporation of thymidine and the greater the formation of DNA.

When we read the printout from the various lymphocytes, a pattern seemed to emerge: The marijuana smokers had a lower count per minute and therefore a decreased lymphocyte response than the nonsmokers. Later, the results were compared by Dr. Suciu-Focca to the lymphocyte response of cancer and kidney transplant patients which did indicate a somewhat similar effect.

Since our initial experiment included only twenty marijuana smokers, and since the results of this small sampling were so encouraging, we decided to increase the size of the group in order to heighten the statistical significance of the results. Our goal now was to enlist 100 marijuana smokers who met our stringent requirements. To this end we placed another advertisement in *The Village Voice*.

In the midst of all this my technical book, *Marihuana, Deceptive Weed,* was published. My hope as the author was that the contents would make a useful contribution to science and stimulate other scientists to investigate the mechanism of the slow debilitating effect of prolonged marijuana use.

But both my optimism and a campaign to reach influential people met with failure. Only one newscaster, Lowell Thomas, who had observed at first hand the effects of marijuana in other countries, recognized the message I was trying to convey. Otherwise the book was met either with silence or negative criticism. Dr. Grinspoon, who reviewed it for *The New England Journal of Medicine,* said, "What Nahas produces is a kind of psychopharmacological McCarthyism that compels him to use half-truths, innuendo and unverifiable assertions." With this kind of ammunition the National Organization for the Reform of Marihuana Laws (NORML), a pro-pot lobbying group based in Washington, D.C., had a field day.

XV. From Texas to Alaska to Washington, D.C.

As a result of the Marijuana Commission Report and an aggressive campaign by NORML, many states began to reconsider their marijuana laws. Actually, such an action was long overdue. Ever since the federal Marijuana Tax Act had been enacted in 1937, most states dealt with marijuana offenders as felons. Texas, for example, had laws on its books that carried sentences up to life in prison for conviction of simple possession. Indeed, in 1973, there were over a dozen young men languishing in Texas' prisons with ten- and twenty-year sentences because they were caught with a few marijuana cigarettes. Such examples were seized upon by NORML and other groups as demonstration of the need to reform or abolish the marijuana laws.

Certainly these prisoners were an unfortunate illustration of the legal "overkill" that existed in many areas. What distrubed me, however, was how their plight was now being used by some people as a wedge to promote legalization of marijuana cultivation, sales, and smoking. In addition to NORML, the American Bar Association, the American Public Health Association, and the Civil Liberties Union were all calling for repeal of marijuana laws. The basis for their arguments was the old and familiar position that "marijuana is an innocuous substance, less dangerous than alcohol or tobacco."

In late March 1973, Texas' Governor Dolph Briscoe and state congressman Bill Meier asked me to testify before a committee that was considering changes in the state's marijuana laws. The governor was supporting a bill that would reduce the penalties for a first possession from a felony to a simple misdemeanor. Other voices, though, were calling for repeal of all laws, thus producing de facto legalization of marijuana. Governor Briscoe and Congressman Meier needed medical authorities to aid them in the counterattack of the "total repeal" side.

And so I arrived in Texas. In the hearing chamber, the galleries were packed, mostly with long-haired youths. The joint committee of the Texas legislature—no pun intended—sat around a long table in the center, surrounded by staff members, press representatives, and other members of the legislature.

The first two witnesses argued that the punitive approach had not worked, and would not work. One of them was a young man, the son of a state politician, who had received a long prison sentence for growing marijuana on his farm. His gaunt appearance and obvious nervousness underlined his argument that jail was far worse than the effects of occasional pot smoking.

As one of two expert witnesses called to present the medical case against marijuana, my testimony concentrated primarily on the damaging effects of cannabis that I had observed in both my own and other research.

I was followed by Dr. Forest S. Tennant, director of the University of California Drug Treatment Center in Los Angeles, who had been a medical officer in the army from 1968 to 1972. Dr. Tennant told him he had examined the lung tissues to soldiers stationed in France, aged nineteen to twenty-four, who had been smoking hashish for a period ranging from six months to one year. "The lining of the lungs of these young men," Dr. Tennant told the committee, "resembled what you might expect to see in people who have been heavy cigarette smokers for twenty years." Moreover, he added, some of the lung tissue he had observed in the soldiers gave evidence of precancerous lesions.

On the pro-pot side, a spokesman of the American Public Health Association disagreed with Dr. Tennant's and my own testimony. He was particularly critical of my findings that linked marijuana with the immunity system, saying, "I've never heard that one before!"

As Dr. Tennant and I were leaving the Senate chambers, a tall, powerfully built young man wearing a ten-gallon hat and cowboy boots approached us and said in a pleasant drawl, "Man, you really are full of shit! I've been smoking marijuana and hash for a long time and, man, I really feel fine." In spite of his words, his Texas charm was as heavy as his drawl, and it was impossible to take offense; instead we all laughed.

The officials thanked us for our testimony and told us that it would be several weeks before the committee made its recommendations. After my return to New York, Governor Briscoe wrote, saying, "Your statements were very effective in rebutting the widespread notion that marijuana is harmless." More important, he informed me that while his bill lowering the penalties for simple possession had been passed, marijuana still retained its status as an illegal drug.

Meanwhile, my second series of experiments to test marijuana's effects on the human immune system started. From the response to our ad in *The Village Voice,* we selected fifty-one marijuana users, aged sixteen to thirty-five who had smoked an average of three cigarettes a week for four years. This was not the 100 we had originally intended, but lack of funds and the loss of the help of Dr. Suciu-Foca due to illness caused us to decrease the number. Some of the subjects had long hair, beards, and wore unkempt clothing; others were neat, close-shaven, and short-haired. All, however, were well-mannered and even-tempered. In both groups we found individuals who were extremely anxious about their health and eager to know the results of our tests.

The same trend that we had noticed in the first series of experiments continued among the new volunteers: Three out of every four of the marijuana smokers had a clearly discernible decrease in their "cellular mediated immunity" when their lymphocytes were compared to those of nonsmokers. In short, seventy-five percent of the pot-smoking volunteers in our study showed some cellular impairment as a result of their drug habit.

While these laboratory results were being recorded, I received a letter from the district court of Anchorage, Alaska, in connection with a law suit that challenged the state's marijuana laws. Briefly, the story was this: The attorney of a man who had been arrested for possession of marijuana was arguing that the state did not have the authority to regulate a "harmless" substance. In attempting to prove his case, the attorney had enlisted the aid of several nationally known authorities, including Drs. Joel Fort and Lester Grinspoon. Representing the State of Alaska was District Attorney William H. Bittner. It was Mr. Bittner who contacted me, saying, "It is my responsibility . . . to rebut this testimony. After reading the literature in the field, I decided that you clearly appeared to be one of the most well-versed authorities on marijuana, as well as a physician-researcher who would be most familiar with those studies past and present involving marijuana."

He concluded his appeal for my help with the statement: "If any state were to legalize marijuana through the courts, Alaska in my opinion is the most likely to do it first."

This seemed like the most serious challenge to date concerning the legalization of marijuana and I agreed to fly to Alaska. Fortunately we had the results of our second series of immune-response experiments. With the help of Dr. Suciu-Foca, I was armed with microphotographs of the cellular damage we had observed, as well as the draft of a statement that would explain in lay language the implications of our studies.

Flying to Alaska can be an adventure in itself. Even though it was June, my journey was delayed almost one day by weather cancellations and missed connections. I made it into the courthouse just as the district attorney was rising to ask the judge for a trial delay because of a "missing" witness. We were given a thirty-minute recess while Mr. Bittner briefed me and the other witnesses for the state, Drs. Hardin Jones and Harvey Powelson of the University of California at

Berkeley, about what we might expect when called to the stand.

In the first part of my testimony, I went into some detail to explain our current findings, using our recently prepared illustrations. As I talked I glanced at the defendant, a waxy-faced young man with shoulder-length dark hair. I could not help feeling sympathy for him. He was, after all, nothing more than a pawn in a controversy that transcended the charge against him.

District Attorney Bittner asked me many questions about my work and scientific background, skillfully establishing my expertise and eliciting information at the same time. When we broke for lunch, though, he warned that the lawyer for the defense would try to irritate me by asking questions not related to the point under consideration.

The defense attorney, an alert-looking man who wore his hair in a ponytail, started slowly. He asked if I had written the technical book, *Marihuana, Deceptive Weed,* and presented the book to the court as Exhibit I for the defense. Then he pulled out several reviews that had criticized the book, including an *unpublished* one written for the *New York Times*. After that, extrapolating odd lines and paragraphs from the book, he tried to convince the court that I was nothing more than a rigid Victorian and dyed-in-the-wool Puritan.

There was really only one point of agreement that I can remember from that long afternoon: Both the defense attorney and I were in accord on the fact that alcohol, barbiturates, and amphetamines were also dangerous drugs. Otherwise, my only thought when court adjourned was to return to the hotel and get some sleep.

From Alaska I flew directly, via the polar route, to a meeting in Paris. The court case and its decision, I knew, would drag on for several more months. Eventually the judge sustained the statute that considers marijuana to be a dangerous drug, saying that in accordance with the Single Convention of the United Nations, it should be kept under strict control. (However, in May 1975 the Alaska Supreme Court reversed its earlier decision and Alaska became the first state to

legalize marijuana possession for personal use on the erroneous premise that its use "does not constitute a public health
problem of any significant dimension. . . . It appears that
effects of marijuana on the individual are not serious enough
to justify widespread concern, at least as compared with the
far more dangerous effects of alcohol, barbiturates, and amphetamines.")

My technical book had now made me a sought-after witness
and panelist. From legislative hearings and a courtroom witness stand, my next assignment was to present the case
against marijuana to a church group and a national woman's
organization in Washington, D.C.

An old wartime comrade, Herbert Stein-Schneider, pastor
of the French Protestant Church in Washington, invited me
there to address a group of his parishioners. The congregation
which uses the facilities of the famous St. John's Episcopal
Church in Lafayette Square across from the White House, is
made up of French-speaking people who live and work in the
capital. Once my family had been his parishioners during my
tenure at the Walter Reed Army Institute some years ago.

My slide-illustrated talk went over well to the small but
receptive audience, and two months later I received another
invitation from a far more ambitious Washington gathering.
This one came from radio personality Martha Roundtree on
behalf of a national convention called "Crusade Against
Moral Pollution," sponsored by the Leadership Foundation.
According to Mrs. Roundtree, my primary audience would be
representatives of social and civic women's clubs throughout
the United States who would be convening in Washington to
discuss a number of topics, among them: the equal rights
amendment, crime, abortion, and marijuana.

To counter my hesitation because of a busy schedule, Mrs.
Roundtree used some flattery. "The future of America could
well be at stake," she said, "if the youth of this nation is told it
is all right to smoke marijuana. We need expert opinions. We
will be covered by the press, and you will have the opportunity of reaching an ultimate audience of 30,000,000. With the
machinery of this organization, we could make a big difference in the final outcome of proposed legislation."

How could I refuse? Looking back, though, the most fortuitous result of my accepting Martha Roundtree's invitation was a meeting with David Martin, an investigator for the Senate Subcommittee of Internal Security. Known around Washington as a "champion of lost causes" because of his frequent but unsuccessful fights for the subjugated people of eastern Europe, Martin was to be my partner in a debate against Michael Sonnenreich, the former executive director of the National Marijuana Commission.

During this panel discussion Sonnenreich belittled those who used "scare tactics" in relation to marijuana, claiming that there was not enough medical evidence against the drug to justify any hysteria. Looking directly at me, Sonnenreich said, "I'm glad that you have given up the idea of locking up all those who smoke a joint."

David Martin was on his feet defending my position—apparently the idea that marijuana was harmful was his new "lost cause." Having read my book and other of my material, he knew that Sonnenreich was misinterpreting my position. He spelled out the necessity of humane legislation that would make marijuana smoking a misdemeanor. But he also emphasized that legal pressure should be backed up with social pressure against its use.

At lunch, David Martin, Herbert Stein Schneider, and I agreed that the tide of marijuana usage and acceptance was still on the rise. "Why not get as many of the world's marijuana researchers together," suggested Stein Schneider to Martin, "and let them present their viewpoint before your Senate committee as you already did a year ago?" Martin's enthusiasm for the idea could not prevent the Watergate scandal from taking precedence over our concerns, and the hearings were delayed for almost a year—until May of 1974.

XVI. Marijuana and DNA

As the summer of 1973 approached, we encountered irritating problems with our volunteer experimental work on marijuana. Many of our participants had left the sultry city for cooler and greener climes. We also had problems in the laboratory. First, a worker inadvertently threw away the plates containing lymphocytes that had been taken from five smokers. After that, Dr. Suciu-Foca told me she soon would be on leave for medical reasons and that she expected us to complete our work in her laboratory before she entered the hospital.

Faced with these roadblocks, there was nothing to do but write up the observations we had made on the first fifty-one volunteers. These were consistent with the results we had found in the initial series of experiments. That is, three of every four smokers studied had some lymphocytes with a lowered rate of cell division.

Some months before, Dr. Morton Stenchever, professor of obstetrics at the University of Utah, had suggested that if lymphocytes showed a loss of function, they might also exhibit some abnormalities in structure. He found, for example, that when lymphocytes of marijuana smokers were cultured for three days, they showed an abnormally high number of chromosome breaks. Chromosomes are the strands of DNA that carry the hereditary characteristics of our cells. When such a strand is broken, one of three things can happen: The cell can repair itself; the cell can die; or the cell can live with its abnormality, which it transmits to other cells.

It occurred to me that breaks in the DNA strand might account for the lowered rate of cell division we had observed among our fifty-one marijuana smokers. What was needed at this point, though, was some expert assistance. My own knowledge of cytogenetics—that branch of genetics concerned with cellular heredity—was marginal. For this reason I sought out Dr. Akira Morishima, an authority in this field at Columbia.

I explained to Dr. Morishima why I thought the lymphocytes of marijuana smokers might exhibit some chromosome abnormalities. He agreed that the impairment we had seen among our fifty-one smokers might be associated with DNA strand breakage. "At any rate," he said, "I've been studying the lymphocytes of heroin addicts for several years and have some techniques that might be useful in your kind of research."

After some persuasion—it was a matter more of his time than his interest—he agreed to help me. Because of the exacting nature of his techniques, though, he would be able to study the lymphocytes taken from only four smokers and four controls of similar age and sex. The reason for the small number of subjects was that Dr. Morishima did not depend on automatic machines for his research. "I prefer macro samples so that I can see what I am doing and can get a good statistical evaluation," he said.

We provided Dr. Morishima with millions of lymphocytes isolated from the blood of the four smokers and four controls. He took the cells and both stimulated and incubated them in a special nutrient "broth." Then using the drug colchicine, he "fixed" the cells in the midst of their dividing or metaphase condition by spreading them on slides. He examined the cells individually under a microscope to find out how many had less than the normal complement of forty-six pairs of chromosomes; such incomplete cells are called micronuclei.

Normally, seven to fifteen percent of the cells in a sampling would contain less than the requisite forty-six pairs of chromosomes. In the lymphocytes of the marijuana smokers, however, Dr. Morishima observed that as many as thirty percent contained less than the normal amount. "In fifteen years of experience as a cytogeneticist," he told me, "I've never encountered a comparable phenomenon."

This was the start of a very productive association with Dr. Morishima. With his skills and cooperation, we were able to accelerate our research. Moreover, he agreed to let me share his laboratory facilities, an arrangement that solved the problem of where to go when we left Suciu-Foca's lab.

But we were not the only ones to notice the effects of marijuana on cellular function and structure. While doing research on a paper on the subject for the journal *Science,* I came across several recently published reports that linked cannabis with impaired cell division. One report from Dr. Arthur Zimmerman at the University of Toronto showed that THC in very small amounts prevented the division of a micro-organism called Tetrahymena, a single cell endowed with a rudimentary digestive tract. And another paper, published by Cécile and Rudolph Leuchtenberger, a distinguished husband-and-wife team of biologist and pathologist working at the Swiss Institute for Experimental Cancer Research, found that marijuana smoke produced a marked increase in the number of abnormal micronuclei in cell cultures.

While awaiting the return of our test subjects from their summer haunts, setting up our experiments in Dr. Morishima's lab and attending a round of medical meetings kept me busy. Among the gatherings was an International Workshop on the current status of marijuana research organized by the United Nations and chaired by Dr. Olav Braenden in Geneva. Among the twelve participants who had specialized in the marijuana research were Dr. Paton from Oxford, Michel Paris from Paris, and Bob Willette from Washington. We spent two days discussing the chemistry, pharmacology, and biological effects of cannabis and noting that the following areas of research demanded priority concern: Determination of the chemical characteristics of the cannabis plant and its preparations in different parts of the world; the development of appropriate methods for such studies and the standardization of research methods; the continuation of efforts to establish the biological activity of components other than delta-9-THC; the development of methodology for the detection of cannabinoids and their metabolites in body fluids; analysis of the effects of the smoking process on biologically active compounds in cannabis preparations with basic biological systems and physiological regulation; and the effects of long-term cannabis use in man.

The meeting in Geneva also served as a first step in preventing unnecessary duplication of effort by holding such gatherings from time to time in order to discuss and compare individual efforts. In short, for the first time in cannabis research some mechanism was set up to allow the left hand to know what the right was doing.

While in Switzerland I took advantage of some spare time to visit the Leuchtenbergers at their laboratory in Lausanne. Utilizing very sophisticated equipment, they are currently engaged in studying the effects of both tobacco and marijuana smoke on rodents and on human tissue cultures. As they showed me around their laboratory, I saw machines that "smoked" mice and rats for days, and other instruments that measured the amount and frequency of smoke delivered to cells in culture. What intrigued me most, however, were slides of dividing cells taken from human lungs that had been exposed in culture to marijuana smoke. Many of these dividing cells, called micronuclei, had fewer numbers of chromosomes than the normal forty-six. Morishima had observed similar abnormal cells in lymphocytes of marijuana smokers placed in culture.

On the basis of their observations, the Leuchtenbergers were convinced that marijuana could induce cellular damage when used on a long-term basis. "And," added Rudolph, "marijuana is certainly worse than tobacco, which, after all, does not alter perception or affect mind or work."

After my return to the Columbia Medical Center a few

weeks later, I scrimped to buy my own MASH machine so that our work could proceed at the fastest pace possible. With this device Armand and a new research worker, Joy Hsu, were able to perform a "counter proof" of our initial experiment in order to answer the following question: Is the decrease of lymphocyte division in marijuana smokers really due to marijuana products and especially to THC? If so, would normal lymphocytes sampled from subjects who do not smoke marijuana show abnormal cell division when exposed to tiny amounts of THC?

The answer was yes. Within a week, Armand had made this observation and had established what is called a "dose-response curve relating the decrease in incorporation of thymidine in normal lymphocytes of non-marijuana smokers to an increase in dosage of THC." In simple terms, when normal lymphocytes sampled from healthy volunteers who did not smoke marijuana were exposed to very small amounts of THC (a few millionths of a gram), they did not divide normally and their growth was markedly decreased. This was a result similar to the findings of Zimmerman in his experiments to decrease the growth of tetrahymena.

It was now possible to think of many different experiments that would show how marijuana products interfere with cell division and function. While this may seem like unnecessary repetition, a scientist is seldom content with one or two observations. And now, more than ever before, we were making important progress. I was able to carry out most of this work up to now thanks to the Philippe Foundation, which paid Dr. Armand's salary, and the generosity of a dedicated friend, Mr. Henri Doll, who believed in the importance of such an investigation.

But still more funds were needed. With Morishima, I applied to the National Institute of Mental Health for more research money. In January, the NIMH sent a group for another site visit. Marijuana research, we then were told, just did not have a high enough priority. We would have to get funds from another source.

XVII. From Vancouver to Baalbek

In the midst of these developments I had to travel to Vancouver, invited by Dr. Conrad Schwartz to participate in a symposium on "Nonalcholic Drug Abuse in British Columbia." Dr. Schwartz, a professor of psychiatry at the University of British Columbia, had for some time been keeping tabs on the growing use and effects of marijuana among students at the university. In many ways, his concerns paralleled my own, and we had been keeping each other informed of our observations and research.

Vancouver is a visually impressive city, spread out between forested slopes and snow-covered mountains on the one side, and the Pacific Ocean on the other. Thanks to a mild year-round climate and a bountiful surrounding area that provides farm goods, coal, steel, oil, hydroelectric power, and huge forests, Vancouver is the busiest Canadian port on the Pacific coast and a major commercial and industrial center. It is difficult to think of this rich and lovely setting as the source of a major drug problem. Yet it has one of the worse in the world.

Ever since the Chinese laborers were imported to Canada to build the railroads that connect Vancouver with the Canadian islands, opium and heroin smuggling and use has been a persistent problem. In recent years, though, a new element has entered the picture: hashish and marijuana

135

smoking. The symposium set up by Dr. Schwartz was designed to assess the extent of the current drug problem in British Columbia. Earlier local police authorities had reported that marijuana and hashish use had more than tripled during the past two years, with the biggest jump among high school students. In 1972, for example, a diligent police force sized almost three tons of illegal marijuana in the city and surrounding areas; in 1973, they had confiscated over nine tons of illegal cannabis. And there was no end in sight to this escalation.

How to cope with the drug problem? One by one, the participants got up to suggest various enforcement measures. One speaker suggested that instead of jailing drug addicts they should be quarantined and treated in special centers. Another suggestion came from Dr. Tsutomu Shimomura, deputy director of the National Institute of Hygienic Sciences in Tokyo. The basic premise of the Japanese approach to illicit drug use is a program of forced hospitalization and cold turkey withdrawal. This method, reported Dr. Shimomura, stopped an epidemic of amphetamine use that was far greater than anything experienced in either Canada or the United States.

My talk was on the cellular damage produced in man by marijuana. The next speaker was Dr. Tennant, who reported on the lung damage he had observed among heavy users. Two biochemists from the University of British Columbia, Dr. Patrick McGreer and Dr. Alexander Jacubovic, discussed their experiments with animals that showed cellular damage as a result of marijuana usage.

A few weeks later I landed at still another beautiful seaport in a similar setting of sea and mountains. This time the sea was the Mediterranean and the city was Beirut, capital of Lebanon. For years a distant cousin, Dr. Hector Nahas, a chest surgeon in Beirut, had invited me to visit him. Christmas, 1973, was a good time for me and my family to accept his invitation for the holidays. As usual, my visit had a twofold purpose—I wanted to learn how much of a problem hashish represented in Lebanon. My courteous reception by the director of the school of pharmacy and the head of the department of pharmacognosy (branch of pharmacology that treats or considers the natural and chemical history of unprepared medicines), did not mask the fact that the purpose of my visit was embarrassing to them. Hashish is an unmentionable subject in Lebanon. "No, I was told, "we have no information about hashish because it is strictly regulated and there is little, if any, use."

Later, however, I did see a report that indicated that the drug was being smoked at the American University in Beirut. In an anonymous survey of 429 students at the school, it turned out that twenty-six percent of the young men and women enrolled there who were from the United States or European countries had tried hashish at least once, while only seventeen percent of the students from the Middle East said they had tried the drug. Such figures were quite low when compared to those from American universities, where as many as eighty percent of the student body had experimented at least once with marijuana.

When I asked why more students did not smoke, particularly since the drug-type cannabis plant is grown in the area, I was told, "Traffic in the drug is very strictly controlled. Penalties are severe. Several American students, in fact, are presently in jail for trying to smuggle large amounts out of the country. As for the native population, repression is aided by social disapproval."

In a sense what was happening in Lebanon was a reversal of the pattern found in other areas of the Middle East. In Morocco, for example, many young Europeans were being introduced by natives to the centuries-old habit of hashish smoking. Here, however, it was the Americans and Europeans who were initiating their Arab classmates into the world of "hash."

In my quest for information about the areas in Lebanon where hashish is grown and serves as a cash crop, I approached my cousin, the chest surgeon. He looked at me as if I had gone mad." "The subject is strictly taboo. Either you deal in the trade according to certain rules or you keep your nose

out of the business unless, of course, you want to get it cut off.
That is it, cousin," he said with a chuckle.

Dissuaded from a trip into the growing region, I settled for
a visit to my colleagues at the Université de Beyrouth, the
French-speaking university. But no one there was currently
studying marijuana. The last report on the subject, in fact,
was a Ph.D. thesis written in 1935 that covered the local
history of cannabis. This document revealed that the plant
had been introduced into Lebanon around 1860 and was
grown in the high valley of Bequa. The drug content of the
plant, according to the author, was equal or superior to the
quality of cannabis that came from India or Turkey.

The Turks, who ruled the country until World War I, tolerated cannabis cultivation until they realized that the drug
represented a threat to their control of the people. At this
point they cracked down by the simple expedient of burning
all crops. When the French took over after the war, though,
this threat was ignored and the poor farmers of the Bequa
valley had a field day growing and exporting large amounts
of the potent resin. The cannabis crop was an important
source of revenue for Lebanon until 1924 when, as a result of
the Second Opium Conference in Geneva, cultivation was
banned again. Nevertheless, it was never really eradicated
from the remote valleys where generation after generation
has made a living from the yearly crop.

Warned by several people that researchers would not be
treated hospitably by the growers, I decided to visit the Bequa
valley in the guise of a tourist. After all, there were many
legitimate ruins in the area, including the temple of Baalbek,
constructed in the second century A.D., during the apogee of
the Roman Empire. After viewing the ruins, however, my
chauffeur refused to drive me to the hashish country of Her-
mel. "Ordinary tourists don't go there," he said. Discretion,
they say, is the better part of valor, and I decided to heed that
advice. A journalist in Beirut, however, who had spent some
time living with a grower did give me some information. Here
are excerpts from a story he wrote:

"The largest of the villages in the area has a population of a
few thousand. It is one of the most destitute sections of the

country, with no electricity, no public water distribution, no hospital, not even a pharmacy. Most of the land where hashish is cultivated is owned by tribes made up of groups of families, most of them related to each other and bearing the same name. The cultivation of cannabis enables these people to live at a bare subsistence level."

The methods used for cultivation of cannabis are extremely primitive. According to the journalist, the land is churned with ancient plowshares and fertilized with manure. April or May is the planting season, with seeds sown every two feet in parallel rows. At first the growth is very slow. After the seedlings reach a height of about five inches, the plant grows very rapidly, shooting up to six or eight feet within the next four months. At this point the male plants are taken out and thrown away. The female plants, which produce a greater concentration of the active intoxicating ingredient, on the other hand, are dried in the sun and stored in special bins until they are ready for transformation into hashish. As in Morocco, this is done by rubbing the flowering tops over sieves.

The quality of the drug taken from these plants varies depending on the amount of irrigation. In a heavy rainfall season, the crop will be larger but less potent. In a dry season where the bulk of the moisture comes from light rain or the morning dew, the yield is less but the hashish is stronger. The popular name for the product grown here is "Lebanese red" and it is usually smuggled out at night, in compressed resin form, by small bands of people called *abad hoys* or, freely translated, "tough guys." One rigid rule the smugglers abide by is that hashish is never consumed locally and cannot be sold within the country.

Hashish is sold for export by the "quintal," which measures fifty liters or about 120 pounds. Although prices fluctuate under the same supply and demand conditions of other crops, a quintal usually brings about 1,000 to 1,200 Lebanese pounds, or about $80. Compared to the grower's meager income, the smuggler or trafficker takes the major share of the profits.

Until recently, most of the Lebanese hashish was smuggled

to Egypt. When Nasser assumed power, however, he initiated a campaign to eliminate hashish consumption and asked neighboring Lebanon to stop exporting the substance. Although the Lebanese government agreed to cooperate, it had little effect in halting the traffic. As a result, relations between Egypt and Lebanon became very strained, and only the war with Israel plus the opening of American and European markets for marijuana eased this tension.

From my travels around Lebanon, it is evident that hashish smoking is confined to only a very small segment of the population. In that country, the social taboo against the drug is very strong. Nevertheless, there is not doubt that the Lebanese government does look the other way when it comes to the growth and distribution of the drug abroad. Like so many "pushers," the Lebanese recognize the dangers of the product they are selling, but are more than willing to profit from the weaknesses of others.

There was much time to reflect on this sorry state of affairs, however. On my return to my laboratory at Columbia, I learned that our article on the effects of marijuana on immunity had been accepted for publication.

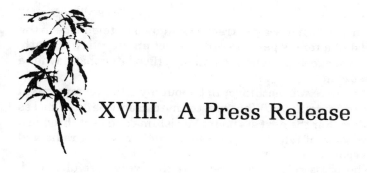

XVIII. A Press Release

When an original medical finding of general interest is reported in a scientific journal, it is customary for the institution that has sponsored the work to release it to the press. Dr. Morishima and I had agreed that it was time the general public knew of our findings concerning marijuana as they were to appear in the February 1 issue of *Science*. The fact that our work was at variance with widely held current views was what made it particularly newsworthy.

On January 25, with the agreement of Columbia University, we released a statement to the press that described our experiments and our findings concerning marijuana. While it is difficult to accurately translate the language of the scientist into a language comprehensible to a layman, we think we succeeded in explaining that "habitual marijuana smoking weakens the body's immunology defenses and inhibits the division of the cells that specialize in the defenses. This is the first evidence that marijuana usage induces cellular damage in man.... Furthermore we have observed that marijuana products accumulate in the testes and ovaries. It is therefore most urgent to find out to what extent chronic marijuana use will impair the genetic equilibrium and the DNA metabolism of the dividing germ cells and possibly affect adversely the offspring of the marijuana user."

The first indication of the impact of the press release was

141

when a radio newscaster tracked me down by telephone in the midst of a tennis game in order to get an interview. Breathless, I suggested he meet me in my office later that day for a quiet chat.

But there was nothing quiet about my office on my arrival forty minutes later. What greeted me can only be described as bedlam. For the next six hours Morishima and I sat through a succession of television interviews and answered radio and newspaper inquiries.

The press release had been written very carefully, with qualifications where we thought they were needed. Newscasters, however, want to inform the public with direct, precise answers. In their thirst for hard news, they are impatient with scientific nuances such as "potential" or "seemingly." As a result, we were faced with a new problem: How to speak to the press without compromising the true meaning of our findings? Should our personal view that long-term use of marijuana would result in serious effects, especially if the habit were started in the formative adolescent years, prevail over the unemotional, rather pedantic words that appeared in *Science*? We tried to take a middle course.

Meanwhile, the partisans of NORML, caught unawares by the original release, were regrouping for an attack. The first "shot" fired by them was a letter to the chairman of my department that questioned my abilities as a researcher as well as my findings.

NORML attacked me in other ways. A letter similar to the one sent to the chairman of my department went to editors of major newspapers, denouncing what the NORML publication *The Leaflet* called "the great Nahas red herring." *Playboy* magazine, the major source of funds for NORML, published letters written by NORML people who were on their own payroll, and who derided our scientific findings.

Since my detractors could not argue with scientific findings that contradicted their own assumptions, they attacked those who had made these new observations. They confused the scientific issue with the legal one, claiming that I was a spokesman for those who wanted to maintain harsh penalties for private possession of marijuana. My true position has always been a steadfast one: I am as strongly against legalization of marijuana as against the free availability of barbiturates, amphetamines, LSD, or heroin. But I have never ventured opinions as to what kinds of laws there should be nor have I indicated a desire to make "criminals out of recreational drug users." My concern has always been that if marijuana is a harmful substance, then people should know it and should be cautioned against its use.

XIX. The Senate Hearings

In the midst of the press furor over our controversial laboratory findings, David Martin called with good news from Washington. "Senator Eastland, chairman of the Committee on Internal Security, has given us the go-ahead to hold hearings on the marijuana epidemic," he said. "Senator Eastland is concerned about the large amount of illegal marijuana seized by the Drug Enforcement Agency (DEA) during 1973 and wants to find out what is behind it all."

Astonishing figures released by the DEA had caught Senator Eastland's attention. These figures showed that confiscation of marijuana by governmental authorities had increased from 85,715 pounds in 1968 to 1,261,259 pounds during the first nine months of 1973. According to projectionists, the resulting figure was enough to make *five billion* marijuana cigarettes—thirty joints for every man, woman, and child in the United States!

"There doesn't seem to by any question that marijuana use is widespread in America today," said David Martin. "But what we don't know for sure is if it is causing the kind of cellular damage that you and some other scientists claim it is. Can you provide me with a list of researchers of impeccable scientific repute who may shed some light on this question? Meanwhile, I am going to contact several psychiatrists and psychologists who might be able to clarify the issue from their point of view."

During the next few days I listed the names of scientists throughout the world who I knew were working on the cannabis question. It was a list that included a Nobel Laureate and professors from many leading universities. The results were sent on to Martin, with the notation that "any or all would make a valuable contribution to the hearings."

The first meeting was scheduled for May 9 and, the night before, I flew down to Washington, D.C., with Dr. Morishima. After checking into a hotel, we taxied over to the new Senate office building where about a dozen scientists were waiting in Martin's office. Over dinner at a nearby restaurant, we compared notes on our individual progress.

The next morning, under the glare of television lights, the first United States government hearing into the medical effects of marijuana use began. What emerged during the six days of hearings and testimony of twenty scientists, representing six countries, was a picture of a widely used psychoactive drug that carried with it seven clear-cut biological hazards.

1. THC, the major psychoactive substance in cannabis, tends to accumulate in the brain, sex glands, and other fatty tissues of the body in much the same manner as DDT is stored.

This observation, which has been reported in recent years by several investigators, was established beyond challenge at the hearings by Nobel Laureate Dr. Julius Axelrod and his colleagues at the National Institute of Mental Health. Here is how Dr. Axelrod described the work: "For many years our laboratory has been involved in biochemical and pharmacological investigations on drugs affecting the mind. We have developed very sensitive methods for measuring LSD and amphetamine in blood, urine, and tissues. These studies made it possible to establish how long these psychoactive drugs remain in the body, how much gets into the brain, and how the body disposes of them."

When the marijuana controversy heated up a few years ago, Dr. Axelrod and his associates decided to apply the investigative techniques they had applied earlier to LSD and amphetamines ingested by volunteers to the active ingredient in cannabis. They recruited volunteers who were injected with measured amounts of THC. Then, over a period of time, blood samples were taken to determine exactly how much of the substance still remained in the body and how much had been either burned up or excreted.

"After an intravenous injection of THC," Dr. Axelrod reported to the subcommittee, "the amount of this compound in plasma rapidly declined during the first hour, with a half-life of thirty minutes. This means half the drug disappeared within thirty minutes. After one hour the THC disappeared from the plasma and presumably from the body much more slowly, with a half-life of sixty hours. THC and its biochemically transformed products continued to be excreted in the urine for more than a week. The initial rapid decrease in the plasma represents a redistribution of marijuana-active products from the blood into tissues including the brain; it also means a chemical transformation."

What this meant to the NIMH scientists was that a significant amount of THC and its transformation products remained in the body for long periods of time after the drug was taken. What happened to these products? Where did they go between the time of ingestion and final excretion? To find out, Dr. Axelrod used radioactively tagged THC which, with the aid of special instruments, can be followed and measured as it moves through the intricate systems of the body. In this case, the tagging showed that the transformation of THC into metabolic products took place in the liver, while during the week or more these products remained in the body, storage was in the brain, gonads, and fatty tissues.

2. Regular use of marijuana may cause damage to the process of cell division.

This finding was observed independently by five of the scientists who testified before the subcommittee: Marijuana products prevent normal cell multiplication of lymphocytes as well as other cells in culture. Moreover, each of the researchers expressed fears that such cellular damage could lead to cancer, increased susceptibility to disease, and an increased possibility of genetically damaged offspring.

An explanation of why such abnormalities might occur among chronic pot smokers was given by Dr. Akira Morishima, a specialist in the study of genetics, who reported the results of our joint studies. "When the specimens of three marijuana smokers were compared with those of nonsmokers of the same age and sex, the mitotic index, or the proportion of these cells in process of cell division, was noted to be only 2.3 percent in marijuana users, compared with 5.9 percent for the controls." This means that the rate at which cells give birth to new cells—a continual process in man and essential to life—was significantly lower among marijuana users. And while this alone is enough to cause concern to anyone familiar with the human body's complex processes, the next finding was even more startling.

"In the marijuana samples," Dr. Morishima said, "we noted that a large proportion of metaphase nuclei contained a significantly decreased number of chromosomes when compared to the normal human complement. Metaphase is a brief stage of cell division during which each chromosome is clearly visible."

That statement had an evident effect on the subcommittee. Here was actual pictorial evidence indicating that the incidence of cells missing a full chromosomal complement was twice as great among marijuana smokers as in nonsmoking controls.

At this point Senator Edward J. Gurney had some questions. But Dr. Morishima anticipated most of them with this closing remark: "Since lymphocytes constitute an essential component of cellular immunity and since chromosomes are basic units of inheritance at the cellular level, it seems logical to anticipate potential danger in the immune defense system, development of cancer, germ cell production, genetic mutation, and birth defects. Unfortunately, little is known of the effects of cannabis in these areas . . . it is prudent to keep in mind possibilities of long-term effect that can be studied only by long-range epidemiological investigations."

My own testimony, which actually came before that of Dr. Morishima, anticipated many of the points he told the subcommittee. Most particularly, I described the effects we had observed on the T-lymphocytes of marijuana smokers. After examining my figures, Senator Gurney asked if this amount of smoking represented heavy marijuana usage. "No," I replied, "not as defined by the President's Marijuana Commission. By their standards, these people would be classified as moderate smokers."

In addition to describing the work we had performed that had been published in *Science,* I described another set of experiments that showed that other cannabinoids besides THC impair dividing cells. This time we took lymphocytes from nonsmokers and incubated them in a test tube with three different chemicals of marijuana: Delta-9-tetrahydrocannabinol (THC), cannabinol (CBN), and cannabidiol (CBD). The THC, as we knew, was a proven psychoactive substance. The CBN and CBD, however, were considered to be nonactive components of marijuana that seemed to have no effect whatever on the body. To our surprise, the CBN and CBD molecules were even more potent than THC when it came to inhibiting DNA production. In other words, in a test tube they were just as active, and just as dangerous, as THC.

When this evidence was presented to the subcommittee, they wanted to know how this reaction would compare to the side effects created by other substances. "It would take about fifty times as much aspirin or caffeine to do the same amount of cellular damage," I replied, "and about 10,000 times as much alcohol. This amount of alcoholic beverage, though, would probably kill the subject."

3. There is evidence that marijuana may cause irreversible damage to the brain, including actual brain atrophy, when used daily for several years.

Several psychiatrists testified that there were many cases on record of brilliant young people who had gone on a cannabis binge and then found they could no longer perform at their previous level of efficiency. Dr. William Paton, professor of pharmacology at Oxford University, described animal experiments that showed that rats exposed to marijuana had smaller brains than those raised in a cannabis-free environ-ment. He also referred to another controversial English study that found brain atrophy in a group of young smokers equiv-alent to the amount usually found in people aged seventy to ninety. Still another experiment, conducted by Dr. Robert G. Heath of Tulane University, found highly abnormal brain-wave patterns that persisted long after marijuana was withdrawn in a group of rhesus monkeys exposed to the drug.

4. Marijuana adversely affects the reproductive process, and it poses potential genetic damage, to the offspring.

Five scientists working at as many different medical schools found: evidence that the male hormone level was reduced by forty-four percent in young males who had used marijuana at least four times a week for a minimum of six months; evidence that the sperm count in this same group dropped in proportion to the amount of marijuana smoked, falling to almost zero—or sterility—in some very heavy smokers; evidence that sperm cells in some animals exposed to marijuana carried reduced amounts of DNA; evidence that regular marijuana use resulted in roughly three times as many broken chromosomes as are found in nonusers; ev-idence that in some animal experiments marijuana caused an increased incidence of fetal deaths and fetal abnormalities.

5. One year of cannabis smoking often—twenty cigarettes a day—can produce as much sinusitis, pharyngitis, bron-chitis, emphysema, and other respiratory conditions, as would be expected from smoking twenty to forty tobacco cigarettes daily for twenty years.

It was also pointed out that emphysema, which is normally a condition of later life, is now being found with increasing frequency among younger people who are regular tobacco smokers. Now the lung damage observed among heavy mari-juana smokers could open up the prospect of "a new crop of respiratory cripples".

6. Marijuana smoke, particularly when it is mixed with tobacco smoke, is far more damaging to lung tissues than tobacco smoke alone.

Professor Cécile Leuchtenberger, head of the department

of cytochemistry of the Swiss Institute for Experimental Cancer Research, and Dr. Forest S. Tennant, former chief of the Special Action Office for Drug Abuse of the United States Army in Europe, both came to this conclusion as a result of independent research. Dr. Tennant based his observation on the examination of over 5,000 army members who are marijuana users. Dr. Leuchtenberger's concern came from a series of laboratory experiments conducted with mice and human lung-tissue cultures: "Marijuana cigarette smoke has a harmful effect on tissues and cells of humans and animals," she said. "The observation that marijuana cigarette smoke stimulates irregular growth in the respiratory system that closely resembles precancerous lesions would indicate that long-term inhalation of marijuana cigarette smoke may either evoke directly, or may at least contribute, to the development of lung cancer. The observation that marijuana smoke interferes with DNA stability in cells and in chromosomes, that is, it disturbs the genetic equilibrium of the cell population, strongly suggests that long-term inhalation may alter the hereditary material DNA and may also have mutagenic potentialities. Consequently, further extensive research is urgently needed to explore chronic effects of marijuana cigarette smoke on cells and on tissues. In particular, studies should be carried out that are concerned with the problem of possible mutagenic properties of marijuana."

7.Chronic cannabis use results in deterioration of mental functioning, pathological forms of thinking resembling paranoia, a progressive and chronic passivity, and lack of motivation.

Of all the observations made at the Senate hearings, this one is in direct contrast to the popular myths about marijuana. The proponents tell us that marijuana is far superior to alcohol as an intoxicant because it does not make you sick, it has no hangover effects, it does not make people mean or obnoxious or dangerous. All it does, they say, is to bring light and love and peace.

But eleven of the scientists who testified before the subcommittee, several of them professors of psychiatry, presented a long line of evidence and observations of dangerous aberrant behavior even among moderate smokers. The population that Dr. Tennant had an opportunity to observe at close range consisted primarily of young army members in West Germany. Confronted by tedium, homesickness, and the language barrier, and strongly influenced by the actions of their peers, a large percentage of the soldiers graduated rapidly from being experimenters with marijuana to regular users. The hashish they found in Europe, however, was far more potent than the usual marijuana sold on the streets in the United States. As a result, the escalation process was pronounced. Dr. Tennant described some of the violent behavior observed in soldiers whose consumption of large amounts of hashish had lead to the commission of serious crimes. Frequently, the combination of alcohol and cannabis in many cases of criminal behavior had a compounding effect. In other words, not two and two equals four, but two and two equals six.

Tennant's testimony indicated that there could be danger of violence if marijuana were made freely available to the armed forces as the result of legalization. He further testified to the real possibility that the alertness and combat efficiency of soldiers would be affected were marijuana to be sold at cut rates in military post exchanges.

Additionally, Dr. Paton told the subcommittee, "Alcohol is taken ... and is eliminated [from the body] in a few hours [while] cannabis ... is cumulative and persistent ... The price for overuse is paid in early life ... it can predispose to the use of other drugs." And Dr. Tennant added, "the major [personality] manifestations [in marijuana users] were apathy, dullness and lethargy, with mild to severe impairment of judgement, concentration and memory ... physical appearance was stereotyped in that all patients appeared dull, exhibited poor hygiene, and had slightly slowed speech...."

The Senate hearings, it must be stressed, were not designed to give the final word on marijuana but to call attention to the fact that most of our knowledge about the effect of cannabis still lies hidden. The scientists who testified before the subcommittee were uniformly agreed that the hazards of the drug were much greater than had been originally thought, and that the evidence to date demanded continued prohibition of the drug, as well as a broad-scale education program to deter nonusers from experimenting with marijuana. It seemed to me especially, that time was running out. We could no longer afford to wait for massive doses of positive scientific evidence against cannabis. There was enough known right now to justify an all-out effort to halt the spread of this dangerous drug.

XX. The Quest Continues

The continued public controversy over marijuana did not distract me from pushing ahead with more experimental work. After studying the effects of THC, we also had found out that the other cannabinoids, which are not psychoactive, produce an impairment of DNA formation in dividing cells as we had testified at the Senate hearings in Washington.

THC also produces in the body by-products that are called metabolites. Some of these metabolites are classified as active because they produce the same psychological or behavioral changes as does THC. A few researchers have even argued that these active metabolites are responsible for the mind-altering properties of marijuana. Other metabolites, such as cannabinol, are called inactive. They do not affect the mind. But they do affect cell division. In our experimental model all the products of marijuana and their metabolites, the so-called active as well as the inactive ones, prevented cells from dividing. Therefore, the slowing down of cell division and the impairment of DNA formation that we had observed was an effect of marijuana that could not be attributed entirely to THC.

Until our observations, THC had been considered by most marijuana researchers to be the major biologically active substance in the plant. But a few scientists had cautioned against this simplistic view. They were right: We had ob-

153

served that a fundamental biological property of marijuana was shared by many of its major constituents. This property could be called "antimitotic" because it prevents mitosis, or cell division.

Our next step was to try to determine the molecular structure common to all of these cannabinoids and how this structure was responsible for their antimitotic effect. The answer came during one of the weekly informal conferences attended by the dozen or so people who were now working on our experiments. I started the meeting by drawing on the blackboard the chemical formulae of all of the cannabinoids we had used. It appeared that all these compounds had in common a certain chemical structure or ring. This ring turned out to be a very simple chemical, olivetol, which is available commercially and used for industrial synthesis of the cannabinoids. THC and the other natural cannabinoids that are used in the laboratory are not extracted from the plant because this would require a tedious and cumbersome process of purification. Instead, they are synthesized or made in the laboratory by a chemist who uses olivetol as his first building block. We tried olivetol in our experimental system and found that this simple chemical also impaired DNA function in lymphocytes.

At this point Akira Morishima contributed some important information. In his examination of thousands of cells, he showed that the functional impairment produced by marijuana is also accompanied by structural changes in the cell—that the incidence of micronuclei (cells in metaphase with less than forty-six pairs of chromosomes) in lymphocytes sampled from marijuana smokers was related to how much and how strong was the dose of marijuana taken by the subject. Those who smoked three cigarettes or more a week had a marked increase in the incidence of micronuclei (thirty-six percent) compared to the incidence in a paired control group (fifteen and one-half percent) who smoked less; and cultured lymphocytes of light smokers (less than three cigarettes a week) had an incidence of micronuclei greater than that of paired nonsmoking controls, but less than that of heavy smokers. In addition, Morishima observed that adding minute amounts of THC or of olivetol to normal lymphocytes in culture produced a very marked increase in the incidence of micronuclei. In each of the experiments the number of cells examined by Morishima varied between 1,000 and 10,000.

The implication for all marijuana products appeared quite far-reaching to me. It meant the so-called active as well as the presumed inactive components of the drug impaired cell division from the time they entered the body until they were eliminated. This period of time would be several days after a single administration, and there would be continued storage in tissues if the substance were taken at less than weekly intervals. Could this explain the slow, progressive, debilitating effects of marijuana on mind and body reported throughout history?

At the time we were making these observations, we were pleased to hear that others were confirming some of our earlier findings. Dr. Paul Cushman, from our own institution, who worked in St. Luke's Hospital, used a different test from ours to evaluate the immunity response of marijuana smokers. This test, which is also performed *in vitro,* is called "rosette formation." When lymphocytes are placed in a test tube with red blood cells taken from an animal, such as a sheep, they have the ability to attract these foreign sheep cells in a form that appears to be a rosette. This property of attracting foreign cells is considered to be an index of cellular immunity. Healthy lymphocytes with good immunity potential will form many rosettes. In Cushman's experiments, lymphocytes sampled from marijuana smokers had lost part of their ability to form rosettes, and this was an indication that these cells had a lowered immunity. The results of his study were published in the *New England Journal of Medicine.*

A group from the Lilly Laboratories in Indiana, headed by Dr. B. N. Petersen from Indiana University Medical School, reported that macrophages taken from the blood of marijuana smokers have an impaired function. Macrophages are the large white blood cells that move around in our tissues like amoebas to swallow up foreign substances, such as dead bacteria. Dr. Petersen showed that the migrating ability of the macrophages were reduced in marijuana smokers.

At the University of Virginia where he had just moved, Dr. Louis Harris, a veteran researcher in the pharmacology of marijuana, approached the study of marijuana's effects on the immunity system from still another angle. White mice were given skin grafts from black mice, and at the same time were injected with THC. The immune system of the treated mice did not reject the skin grafts as soon as that of the untreated mice. In studying the lymphocytes sampled from the spleen of mice treated with THC, he showed a decrease in thymidine incorporation, just as we had found in our experiments with human lymphocytes. Pushing the results of these experiments to their logical conclusion, Dr. Harris thought of using THC and other cannabinoids to control the growth of abnormal cells. And when THC was administered to malignant tumors implanted in rats, the rate of cell growth in these tumors was decreased. This finding raised the possibility that cannabis products could be used with other drugs to control malignant growth in man.

Not all experiments agreed with our findings, however. Dr. Melvin Silverstein of Los Angeles reported that twenty-two marijuana smokers who had used the drug for at least six months did not show any change in their immune response as measured by a skin test called the denitrochlorobenzene test or DNCB. In this test, the chemical DNCB is injected under the skin of a subject. In patients with a good immune response, a red flare and hardening of the area around the injection will occur within fourteen days and persist for a few days. Then a second, smaller injection is given at another site on the body. In normal patients, there will again be redness at the injection site. But if this reaction or delayed hypersensitivity is absent, then it would mean a profound decrease in the patient's immunity defenses. It has been shown, for example, that the absence of a delayed hypersensitivity response to DNCB is associated with a poor prognosis in patients with cancer. Dr. Silverstein showed that marijuana smokers had a normal DNCB test—a reddening of the skin at the site of the injection. My answer to the results of these experiments is that our findings indicated a *depressed,* not a suppressed, immune response. And such a depressed response might not show up with a DNCB skin test.

We were still on the investigative trail to find out *why* DNA formation was impaired. Do the cannabinoids attach to this basic molecule in the same manner as chemicals used in the treatment of cancer attach to malignant cells to stop their division and growth? Or do the cannabinoids impair the energy-producing machinery of the cell? In our exploration of these possibilities, we found a less complicated answer: The cannabinoids and olivetol act in a more general way—they dissolve into the membrane of the cell. All the nutrients and building blocks of the cell must pass through this membrane, which is surrounded by a fatty layer. Remembering that the property of the cannabinoids is their ability to dissolve in fat, we were able to show that the entry of basic building blocks into the cell was slowed markedly by the cannabinoids and by olivetol.

The next question is, since all drugs added in large enough amounts will also produce cell damage, why is the damage caused by THC significant? In answer to the latter consideration, we did test other drugs in our particular system and found that their effects nowhere matched the cellular damage done by THC. First we used aspirin. We found that although aspirin does have an effect on the replication of lymphocytes, it took amounts equivalent to the ingestion of five or six grams a day (ten to twelve tablets) to depress lymphocyte function. Next we tried caffeine. Since caffeine is rapidly inactivated by the body, it never reaches sufficient concentrations in tissues to produce a change in lymphocyte function. When we added alcohol in concentrations rarely reached in the bloodstream of man, the division of lymphocytes was not impaired. We even tried LSD and found that it too never reaches a high enough level in the tissues to cause cell damage *in vitro*. Only cannabis, then, causes this kind of cell damage.

The next question is, since all these studies on the components of cannabis were performed in test tubes, what is the clinical significance? First, it must be recognized that when marijuana products are added in concentrations that would develop in the body of a smoker, they do not destroy even a larger number of cells. Since there are 100,000 trillion cells in our bodies, only some will be permanently impaired by marijuana, and many of those that are impaired would die anyway. But, and here is where the danger is: Over long periods of prolonged usage of marijuana, this slow cellular erosion might well become clinically apparent if a serious disease should develop. The critical result is that permanent damage will have been done to the immune system—without which man cannot survive. Thus, when I observe the effects of marijuana products on dividing cells, I feel more than justified in cautioning, in declaiming, against the use of cannabis.

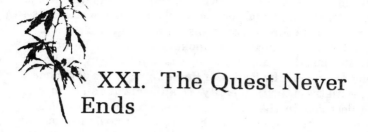

XXI. The Quest Never Ends

Wilkinson Island, off the Georgia coast, was the scene of a three-day international gathering of some 100 scientists in December 1974. The subject—the pharmacology of marijuana—at a symposium organized by the United States government agency, the National Institute on Drug Abuse. All the familiar names were there, plus a few selected nonscientific observers such as David Martin. The participants heard no less than sixty-seven papers. One of the participants summed up the consensus of this meeting when he said: "Marijuana is a drug with multifaceted action on nearly every body function: brain, heart, lung and endocrine. No scientist can refer to it as a 'mild intoxicant.' "

Dr. Morishima and I discussed the effects of cannabis products on DNA and cell division and our conclusion that, unlike other more toxic drugs, marijuana interferes with and depresses cell function, but it does not suppress it; this explains its slow and progressively debilitating effect.

Our results were confirmed by experiments performed by Dr. Cécile Leuchtenberger who showed in cell cultures that marijuana smoke impaired the formation of DNA and damaged cells even after having been filtered through water, indicating that the damaging substance is not soluble in water. A Greek psychiatrist, Dr. Costas Stefanis, found abnormal white blood cells in chronic hashish smokers. The

abnormality was in the form of appendages made of chroma-
tin, a genetic material, on the nucleus of the white cells—
another indication of marijuana's effect on cell division.

That chronic marijuana smokers present a lowering of
testosterone, the male hormone, was confirmed by Dr. Robert
Kolodny and also by Professor Reese Jones of the department
of psychiatry of the University of California at San Francisco.
The decrease in the male hormone, according to Kolodny,
seemed to be traceable to the effect of marijuana on the
pituitary, the master gland in the brain that controls the
endocrine secretions. He also reported in several of the
marijuana smokers he studied a decrease in sperm count,
and in two instances complete impotence. Jones also reported
a marked development of tolerance in individuals given up to
210 mg THC to ingest in a thirty-day period. He commented,
"three out of twenty-one subjects claimed that they did not
reach a dose level that they habitually used in their everyday
consumption of marijuana. In our experiments we may be
nowhere near the dose limits preferred by some users." Jones
also found that his subjects experienced withdrawal symptoms ascribable to a physical dependence similar to that of
other sedative-hypnotic drugs.

Still, the scientists assembled in Savannah were far from
agreed on the "abuse potential of cannabis" or the potential
damaging effect of its prolonged use. Dr. Melvin Silverstein
stated that marijuana smokers did not present a *gross* impairment of their immunity. He had found a decreased lymphocyte response in his marijuana smokers, but not of the
extreme, frequently irreversible, nature found in his cancer
patients. This report, however, did not really contradict our
own observations. The report was an additional indication of
the depressant action of marijuana on cell function and its
slow debilitating effect on the body. Other scientists still
compared cannabis to tobacco and alcohol, unwilling to single
out marijuana as a particularly dangerous drug. This cautious attitude of many scientists was illustrated by a small
incident: One of the organizers of the meeting handed me a
copy of a newspaper article concerning an interview with

David Martin in the *Savannah Morning News*. His reaction to Martin's remarks about the dangers of marijuana as they had been described by many scientists in the May Senate hearings was to warn me against being "used" or "ruined" as a scientist! I discovered that many scientists at the meeting resented this interview because, indirectly, it linked them with a position they were not ready to assume.

When Martin was made aware of this sensitive issue, he obligingly went into a huddle with the organizers of the meeting and the reporter of the paper in order to draft a new article to correct any misinterpretation of the first. At the meeting itself, he was given the chance to apologize for any embarrassment his original interview might have caused anyone attending the meeting. He did not, however, neglect the opportunity to point out to the audience that the government was disturbed by the fact of ever-spiraling seizures of marijuana and hashish of an increasingly potent variety.

I did not feel the same way as the other scientists about Martin's strong views as expressed in the "unfortunate" interview. For me, the scientific evidence presented at this conference as well as at previous ones all pointed to only one conclusion: Marijuana is dangerous to man and to society!

In the plane on the return trip to New York, one of my young colleagues remarked, "Dr. Nahas, we admire you as a scientist, but we don't like your rhetoric. Why don't you stick to science?"

How to answer him? "There must be some of the crusader in me," I told him. "My concern is for all of those teen-agers who are smoking a drug that I believe is just no good for them. How can they find this out if some of us don't speak out publicly?"

When the controversy about tobacco cigarette smoking was raging in the late 1950s, some eminent medical scientists came to the defense of cigarettes, the way others do to marijuana today. For example, Dr. Ian McDonald, chairman of the Cancer Commission of the California Medical Association and one of California's foremost cancer specialists, made this sweeping statement before a congressional committee:

Not only did he believe that cigarette smoking bore no relationship to lung cancer, but he would venture that "a pack of cigarettes a day will keep lung cancer away."

At the same time I was a fellow at the Mayo Clinic, where the controversy was also very much alive. Some of the clinic's chest surgeons believed that there was a link between heavy cigarette smoking and cancer of the lung. They were aware that most of the patients operated on for lung cancer had smoked two packs of cigarettes or more a day for twenty years!

It still took until 1963, as scientific evidence mounted, before the association of cigarette smoking with lung cancer was clearly established by the Surgeon General's Special Committee on Tobacco and Health. It is worth recalling that the Surgeon General's study was carried out in the greatest secrecy by scientists who were able to work shielded from the media and the emotional reactions of the public.

And so it was eighty years before the damaging effect of the "mild-cured, inhalable tobacco cigarette" could finally be established—eighty years of scientific investigation in the most technologically developed country in the world!

And, unfortunately, before it was possible to prove *scientifically* that cigarettes are harmful, the habit had become part of our Western culture. Today, despite the Surgeon General's warning printed on every cigarette package, youngsters continue to begin smoking at an early age, and overall cigarette consumption continues to increase. This entrenched use of cigarettes has created an enormous public health problem that has thus far resisted all attempts at eradication.

The tobacco debacle should be a warning to those who elect today to ignore the danger signals of marijuana. Should marijuana be legalized in this country, it would become part of our culture, thus joining alcohol and tobacco as a third major public health hazard. And marijuana is perhaps the most dangerous substance because it never leaves habitual users free of its effects and may cause damage to brain, germ cells, and lungs. It may possibly affect the learning processes of the young or the development of the unborn. In this respect, the limited number of germ cells in women (400,000 eggs at birth compared to 300 million sperm per one ejaculation in men) makes these germ cells more vulnerable to toxic substances like marijuana which affect DNA. Do we have to wait another eighty years for incontrovertible proof of the irreversible damaging effects of marijuana on the mind and the body?

While I have always believed in the ascendancy of science and its ability to point to the truth of an issue over and above the opinions of a fickle public opinion, the abuse of a socially disruptive drug is not a matter for science to resolve, but a social problem. The scientist should not be asked to cast himself in a role that should be assumed by the legislator. Marijuana use or abuse in a society is determined not by the scientific merits of the case, but rather by society itself. The citizens in a democracy are free to choose the kind of society in which they wish to live. The modern scientist recognizes that knowledge and wisdom are not necessarily synonymous with the power to influence social issues. Citizens will make their critical choices based on the type of society in which they wish to live, but they must also remember that future generations will have to contend with the results of those choices. As the social scientist Robert Heilbroner has said, "The fate of your grandchildren will be sealed by the decisions taken today."

Those momentous decisions required to ensure the very survival of our society can come only from minds unfettered by the distorting effects of marijuana. The place awarded in a society to such a drug, which is used only for chemical self-gratification, is in the last analysis symbolic of the mental and physical health of its citizens, of their short-term motivation and of their long-term goals. Throughout history, the social acceptance of marijuana in a society appears to set citizens on a one-way downward street. In the past there has been no way of turning back once embarked on such a course. For the future, the time for unlimited experimentation with marijuana is rapidly running out: We have enough evidence at hand in the laboratory to indicate that marijuana damages cells and slowly erodes vital functions. The time for action is now—before it is too late for America.

XXII The Helsinki Conference

In late April 1974, I was notified of a grant award from the National Institute on Drug Abuse (NIDA) for the research project, "Effects of marijuana smoking in a controlled environment on T lymphocytes and zygotes." This was a joint collaboration: I was the principal investigator, aided by Dr. Philip Zeidenberg, Dr. Akira Morishima and a new member of the team, Dr. Wylie Hembree, from the departments of medicine and obstetrics and gynecology of Columbia University.

Finally we had the chance to isolate marijuana smokers and overcome the disadvantages that had been present in our earlier studies. We planned to select five men to be housed in a research ward at the New York State Psychiatric Institute for a period of ten weeks. During four of those weeks the volunteers would be given marijuana of known potency ("government issue") to smoke, with two three-week periods of "wash-out" (no smoking before and after). Exhaustive medical and psychological tests would be run, and once weekly blood samples would be taken for analysis.

In addition to the studies of the immunity system, we decided to investigate the reproductive or gonadal function of our subjects. This phase of the study would be the contribution of Dr. Wylie Hembree, an endocrinologist who at Columbia had specialized in the study of male fertility. For Dr. Hembree's gonadal function studies we measured the concentration in the blood of the male hormone, testosterone, and that of the pituitary hormones that regulate the production of testosterone. These hormones had been found to be disturbed in heavy marijuana smokers by some scientists. In addition, Dr. Hembree was anxious to study the production and formation of sperm in these young men. In some reports, impotence has been mentioned as a long-term effect of marijuana use.

At the end of four weeks, when the flow of marijuana cigarettes abruptly stopped because our entire stock had been consumed, none of the subjects showed any withdrawal symptoms. There were no signs of severe physical or psychological discomfort similar to that seen when the use of opiates, such as heroin, is discontinued. But, as in the period of abstinence before smoking, the subjects were restless, bored, and demanding, and had many complaints.

Again we conducted routine tests after the five stopped smoking marijuana, and again the results fell within the normal range. In the blood tests we made for the immunity system, however, as in our previous report, we did find a decrease when the marijuana smokers were compared with normal controls. But this decrease was not associated with any clinical symptom of disease. None of the subjects developed any infections during this time. We do feel that the decrease in immunity found in the lymphocytes can be interpreted as a danger signal for future years, although it is not necessarily an immediate cause of illness.

Another significant result was observed in the tests for sperm count and quality. After the period of marijuana smoking, concentration and number of sperm cells collected from the five was markedly reduced in each man, and the reduction was dramatic: a fifty percent average decrease. What concerned Dr. Hembree, who had not anticipated such a drop, was that, as a general rule, decreased sperm production is associated in men with abnormal sperm—germ cells of poor quality. He carefully checked and re-checked the count of all subsequent samples gathered during the "recovery" period. All of them continued to show a significant decrease.

The day before they were discharged, the five volunteers

met in my office, learned about the results of the tests they had undergone, and were thanked for their cooperation. Now that it was over, they seemed pleased to have been a part of the study. Then I tried to explain what our more sophisticated tests had shown about their immunity system by showing them the chart of the measurements of immunoglobulin levels in the marijuana smokers and in the controls, and pointing out that the line representing the smokers was consistently below that of the controls. Basically, the volunteers were unimpressed by our findings. Still I pleaded with them, "Now we can detect only danger signals present in some of your dividing cells. But in ten or twenty years, you might develop some serious disease." Alas, to a young man, ten or twenty years sounds too far off for immediate concern.

As they filed out of my office, I felt perplexed and saddened. Our experiment was a "scientific success." We had obtained hard data indicating the damaging effects of marijuana smoking on some of the key cells of the body. But we had not been able to alter the unhealthy habit of the five young men of our study. What will happen to them in ten or twenty years if they keep on smoking marijuana? Their future is not, strictly speaking, a problem for the scientist to resolve, unless he feels like the Roman playwright Terence of 2,000 years ago who observed, "I am a man, and nothing which concerns man is alien to me." Again I was brought up short by the limitations of science and the frailty of human nature.

These same frustrating limitations, compounded again by the distortion of the marijuana issue by the press, were obvious when the four-year-old "Ganja in Jamaica" study suddenly received national prominence in *Science* magazine in a review by Eric Goode. Goode, a sociologist and member of the advisory board of the National Organization for the Reform of Marijuana Laws (NORML), wrote a rave review of the report in which he carried every bland conclusion of Rubin and Comitas one step further. For example, because in the Jamaica study no other drugs were used by the subjects except for aspirin, alcohol, and tobacco, Goode uses this fact to rebut the stepping-stone hypothesis that he says "is presented by Gabriel Nahas in *Marijuana, Deceptive Weed*. The more one smokes, tolerance to the effect of the drug sets in, and users search for more drugs." But I had written an important qualification—cannabis consumption is associated with multiple drug use *"when these are available."* There is evidence that other kinds of harder drugs are *not* available to the poor farmers in Jamaica. The report "analyzed" by Goode states: "The use of hard drugs is as yet virtually unknown among working-class Jamaicans . . . most had never been to a doctor or taken medication of any kind. In every instance cannabis use was preceded by cigarette smoking." So cigarettes were available, cannabis was available, and both were used; as hard drugs were not available, it is difficult to claim that users do or do not "search for more drugs."

Another conclusion of Rubin and Comitas, that "chronic use of potent cannabis is not toxic to the human mind and body," is expanded to mean that the smoking of marijuana helps to motivate the workers rather than give them an "amotivational syndrome." But nowhere does Goode qualify his conclusions with the fact that this study concerned only poor, illiterate farmers. No hint of the feasibility of having an equal study of the effects of marijuana on a more intellectually oriented group. The fact that he is a sociologist perhaps contributes to Goode's belief that the effects of marijuana are mainly influenced by the sociocultural context in which it is used. It is the environment, not chemistry or biology, that determines the reactions of an individual to marijuana. This kind of thinking completely ignores the many studies of the cellular effects of marijuana on DNA that have proliferated since the Rubin and Comitas study was made.

With Goode's stamp of approval of the "Ganja in Jamaica" study, other publications have taken up his campaign for the decriminalization and eventual legalization of marijuana. A *New York Times* article appearing shortly after Goode's review states, "Fear in the United States that [the use of marijuana] leads to lethargy is not borne out by life histories of Jamaican working class subjects or by objective measurements." There is no mention of the lack of productivity of those same farmers, which is certainly not compatible with a modern society concerned with economic growth and full employment. In typical journalistic fashion, the claim or suggestion that marijuana is harmless is "proved" by a series of omissions and selective quotations.

Despite the continuing distortions, I am convinced that through scientific studies the truth of the effects of marijuana will prevail. And toward that highly desirable end, I was eager to attend the VIth International Congress of Pharmacology in Helsinki, a meeting important to me because of its "satellite symposium" on marijuana. This is a scientific gathering, held every three years, in which a new discipline has emerged, that of clinical pharmacology—the study of the way drugs act on the human mind and body, how they are absorbed, and how eliminated, how they interact with hormones, as well as with other drugs. With this interest has come a concern for establishing a code of regulations aimed at protecting the patients who are given any new drug.

In Helsinki, in the summer of 1975, 3,000 pharmacologists from all over the world gathered for a week. Each day hundreds of papers in dozens of sessions were presented. Taking a cue from the new interest in the quality of our environment as it is affected by modern technological discoveries, for the first time sessions were devoted to the long-term biological and toxic effects of plastics, plasticizers, and food additives. There is a growing concern now among many scientists over the widespread use of substances that might alter the fine genetic equilibrium of living cells through slow accumulation in the body. It is this same concern that has kept me active in the fight against the use of marijuana and that made the inclusion in the congress of a symposium on marijuana so timely.

Throughout the preceding year, I had spent many hours organizing this meeting on marijuana with the help of Dr. William Paton of Oxford University, and Dr. Juhana Idanpaan-Heikkila of the State Medical Board of Helsinki, Finland. We limited our selection of investigators to those who had focused their attention on the identification of the different chemicals contained in marijuana or on the examination of the subtle changes produced by cannabis products on living cells. We did not include the behavioral or psychological aspects of marijuana because of the ambiguous conclusions reached by so many investigators.

Our conference was not to be held in obscurity: Helsinki journalists had noticed the marijuana symposium in the program of the Pharmacology Conference they had received. As this was a topic that even in Finland was newsworthy, the journalists insisted on meeting some of the organizers and speakers. So we had to call a press conference the first day. The questions that most interested the press were, "How harmful is marijuana smoking? Is it as bad as alcohol or tobacco?" Basic scientific mechanisms that we participants of the symposium planned to discuss were not "newsworthy." The one bit of concrete evidence they wanted that I was able to give them was the result of our Columbia study where we had found that five young men had a marked decrease in their sperm count after one month of heavy smoking of marijuana. This fact was immediately recorded and headlined in the local papers.

The chemistry of marijuana occupied the attention of participants at the opening session of the meeting. What are the main chemicals that can be extracted from the marijuana plant? How can they be identified? Many more chemicals are involved than scientists were aware of at first. As methods become more precise they can be isolated. Further questions about chemical contents were: What happens to these chemicals when they are burned in a cigarette? How many new products are formed and how many actually are destroyed? Then what happens to these chemicals when they enter the body and are transformed into new substances as they pass through our different organs: lung, liver, intestine, and kidney? The scientist is working with new techniques to detect these different substances, and many of the answers to these questions are still forthcoming. The composition of new molecules formed in the body from marijuana products can be described, as well as the pathway followed by marijuana chemicals through the body before elimination—a process that can take more than a week. Mass spectrometry and immunoassays are new techniques that can be used to measure the infinitesimal amounts of marijuana chemicals in blood and urine.

So far, however, these techniques of detection are not sophisticated enough to distinguish between by-products of marijuana that act on the brain and those that do not. And this brought up an argument between those scientists who felt the results of present analyses were inconclusive because of a lack of this distinction, and those who felt that *all* the by-products of marijuana seem to have biological effects that may be debilitating. In any event there is as yet no simple way of determining the amount of marijuana products in the body similar to tests that have been established to show the amounts of alcohol in the blood that impair judgment and behavior.

The second part of the meeting was devoted to the cellular and biochemical effects of marijuana—how it affects living cells. In the first session, investigators reported studies in which they had exposed different cells to minute amounts of different cannabinoids (chemicals derived from marijuana) in test tubes, or, in scientific terms, *in vitro*. In every instance, these cannabinoids prevented normal growth of the cell and disturbed its division. This was of great satisfaction to me because many of my detractors have questioned the validity of my experiments with the action of THC on lymphocytes because they had not been duplicated by others. Here in Helsinki were no less than twelve studies that were similar to mine!

The high point of the session was a striking movie. It showed a white blood cell (our body's first line of defense against infection) that had been removed from the lining of the lung. In a natural medium, the cell and all of its parts were moving continuously. After a small amount of THC was added, the cell became completely paralyzed, as if it had lost all life.

My friend Cécile Leuchtenberger, who was unable to attend the symposium, nonetheless contributed a paper describing her latest observations of what happens when some cells from the testis are placed in tissue culture and are exposed to marijuana smoke while other cells from the testis are exposed to tobacco smoke. The result is that the former had a marked decrease in DNA whereas the latter did not. In further experiments, using male mice inhaling smoke from marijuana cigarettes, a disturbance in sperm formation as well as an increased number of cells with a reduced DNA content were found. An inevitable conclusion is that this effect may have serious consequences for future offspring if a sperm with altered DNA content fertilizes an egg. From these presentations come the now obvious, inescapable fact that a basic effect of marijuana products is to prevent the normal formation of DNA and protein by cells, with a resultant slowing down of cell division and the production of abnormal cells.

Since these findings were all reports of test tube experiments, the next question was to determine to what extent these observations apply to the entire organism. Some of the papers that were given gave a partial answer to this question. Certain experiments using rats showed a decreased immunity, while others using rabbits showed an increase in the incidence of abnormal offspring. Other investigators found that this basic cellular effect could be used to slow down abnormal cancer cell division in rodents. The finding of an increased incidence of abnormal offspring in rabbits was challenged by other scientists who did not see such an effect in rats exposed to higher doses of THC than had been given to the rabbits. However, I was reminded of the experiments of a number of years ago with thalidomide when malformations were produced in rabbits with a seventy-five percent smaller dose than that given to rats to produce a similar effect. From my own observations, it is logical that a substance known to slow down the division of cells could affect the fetus, an organism in which cell division is occurring at a very rapid rate. Other *in vivo* experiments (those outside of the test tube) showed evidence of a permanent learning impairment in young rats exposed to marijuana during their early development. Earlier experiments with monkeys had shown the same effect. Dr. Robert Heath, whose paper had been sent to be read at the symposium, reported that brain alterations can be induced in monkeys by prolonged administration of the active ingredients of marijuana in amounts equivalent to what moderate to heavy human smokers of marijuana might use. Yet the impairment was not severe enough to prevent the animals from eating, sleeping, and performing their daily gymnastics.

The first documented observation directly linking heavy marijuana use by men to the impairment of the amount and content of sperm cells was presented at the last session. This was the paper by Dr. Wylie Hembree, my colleague at Columbia, entitled "Effects of Marijuana Smoking on Gonadal Function in Man," which I had received just the night before, and presented to the symposium in Hembree's absence. His results gave clinical significance to the *in vitro* studies of some of the other investigators.

After my reading of the Columbia study, two of my Greek colleagues, Professor Costas Stefanis, a psychiatrist, and Professor Marietta Issidorides, a cell biologist, reported finding basic chemical changes in the white blood cells and sperm cells of chronic hashish users indicative of an abnormality of the nucleus of the cell. Although hashish smoking is condemned in Greece as a deviant and harmful habit by the majority of the population, there is a small group of unskilled laborers who live in the Piraeus area of Athens who smoke it regularly. They have been studied for the past ten years by a group of Greek and American investigators under the direction of Professor Costas J. Miras and Professor Stefanis from the University of Athens. With impressive slides, Stefanis was able to show the basic cellular changes brought about in white blood cells and sperm cells by marijuana use that could be traced to the interference of marijuana with the formation of the basic chemicals of the cell. This report gave further corroboration of our findings at Columbia. It was most significant that these basic cellular changes were observed in the same hashish users who had been given a near clean bill of health a few months earlier when examined with conventional clinical methods. The previous study was performed by Professor Stefanis in cooperation with Professor Max Fink of the New York Medical College under the sponsorship of the National Institute on Drug Abuse.

Finally, after a century, the Columbia and Athens studies had ushered in a new era of basic scientific investigation of chronic cannabis use: the impairment of cell division by marijuana. I was satisfied that the Helsinki meeting had firmly established the scientific basis for the long-term damaging effects of marijuana use: a damage to germ cells and a slow erosion of life that could be transmitted to future generations. I thought that my quest was drawing to an end.

Some time later, Dr. Hembree, Dr. Morishima and I decided at this time not to continue the practice of exposing paid volunteer marijuana smokers to their drug of choice, in order to study them in a "controlled hospital environment." Hembree had observed under such conditions that marijuana smoking decreases quantity and quality of sperm cells. Morishima had reported an impairment of division of white blood cells. Basic biochemical processes required for orderly division of fast-growing cells had been disrupted. The long-term consequences of these temporary disruptions were not known. None of the subjects studied manifested any desire to give up their habit when they left the hospital. Quite to the contrary, they planned to use a good part of the money they had earned to purchase the best quality of cannabis available. We believed that the cellular changes observed following marijuana smoking were serious enough to justify the termination of our studies. We would have liked however, to follow up our original subjects over the years, and call them back for regular studies of their white blood and reproductive cells. But NIDA was not planning, at that time, long-term follow-up studies.

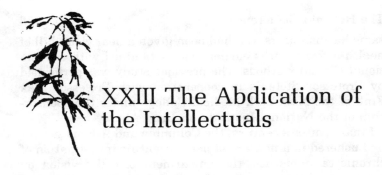

XXIII The Abdication of the Intellectuals

Dateline January 1976: another conference on the chronic use of cannabis, sponsored by the New York Academy of Sciences. Its organizers were Doctors Alfred Freedman, Max Fink, and Rhea Dhornbush, Professors of Psychiatry at the New York Medical School, who in recent years had concentrated their research efforts on the study of acute effects of cannabis intoxication in college students. They had come to the conclusion that cannabis was a benign drug, quite harmless to the user. Upon reading the program received in the mail, I felt that the conference needed more substantive scientific input and wrote to the organizers asking if the Columbia University study of the effect of marijuana on reproductive function could be presented. Our examination of ten more smokers had confirmed the results we had presented previously at the Helsinki World Conference of Pharmacology in 1975. My request was politely turned down, however, under the pretext that this particular conference would be restricted to the study of the effects of the chronic use of cannabis on behavior patterns.

As expected, this meeting, dominated as it was by sociologists, psychiatrists, and psychologists, did little to penetrate the biological mysteries of cellular damage caused by chronic use of cannabis or the possible long term effects of the drug. Thus, the conclusions of the reports presented were predetermined by the sociological orientation of the participants.

There were opposing opinions, however. On the one side, some studies determined that cannabis was harmless to the users in terms of behavior and health, both physical and mental. One such report, that of Rubin and Comitas, even claimed that the use of ganja by Jamaican farmers increased their motivation so they were able to cut more sugar cane! This despite a contradictory opinion by one of their associates who demonstrated that these same farmers were actually less efficient in the fields after having smoked cannabis. Another study from Greece, by Doctors Fink and Stefanis, also concluded that a group of heavy hashish smokers showed minimal physical and mental disturbances when compared to a non-smoking group.

In contrast, Dr. Soueif of Cairo, reporting his observations for the first time in the United States, had found in his study that Egyptian hashish smokers did have measurable psychological loss coupled with considerable dependency on the drug. Lending further credence to his conclusions were those of Professor G. S. Chopra of Calcutta, who described psychological disturbances and psychotic disorders among 275 chronic users of cannabis in India.

Unfortunately the many newspaper, radio and TV reporters present at the conference, disregarded the Soueif and Chopra studies, headlining only the Jamaican and Greek reports. The *New York Times* was the most unequivocal in its appraisal, proclaiming through its science editor that "Marijuana, even in heavy daily doses rarely reached in the US, produces no physical or mental damage." The many syndicated dailies repeated the message all over the country. In doing so they were all echoing the conclusions of one of the conference chairmen, Dr. Max Fink who had stated, "concerns that long term cannabis use is associated with individual or social toxicity are not confirmed."

Dr. Fink might have tempered his statement had he carefully considered the study of Dr. Coggins of Florida, presented to the conference on the subject of chronic marijuana smokers in Costa Rica. The results showed that 9 percent of the sample showed an atrophy of the testis and 25 percent a positive blood test for syphilis. The non-smoking control group showed an incidence of only 1.3 and 9 percent (respectively) of these symptoms. The atrophy of the testis found in this study corroborates our observations at Columbia University of a decrease in spermatogenesis after prolonged cannabis intoxication. The increase in syphilis might be explained by a deficiency in the smokers' immunological system. The Costa Rican marijuana smokers also had a decrease in their immunoglobulin level comparable to what we had observed in our study. Even in Jamaica, the incidence of a positive blood test for another disease, yaws, is higher among ganja smokers (57 percent) than among non-smokers (37 percent).

Unfortunately, no attention was paid to these negative observations either at the conference or in the newspaper accounts that followed. Only those sections of the reports favorable to the notion that marijuana is a harmless drug were emphasized by those who, like Dr. Fink, predicted that "national re-legalization would probably become public policy within the decade".

As an antidote to the widely circulated, but misleading conclusions of the New York Academy of Science Conference, I was eagerly awaiting publication of the Proceedings of the Helsinki Symposium on Marijuana which would clearly demonstrate that this drug produces damage to human cells. Since such information was largely unknown to the American public, Dr. William D. M. Paton, co-editor of the monograph, and I decided to hold a press conference in New York for science editors of the major US journals and newspapers as well as the radio and TV networks.

When on April 1, 1976 at 10 a.m. Dr. Paton, who had flown in from Oxford for the occasion, and I gathered at the site of the press conference, the oak-paneled room at the University Club in downtown New York, only one science writer was seated. This lone curious reporter was Brian Sullivan of the A P wire service. Spread out before us on the long table were the striking blue-covered copies of the new publication: *Marihuana: Chemistry, Biochemistry and Cellular Effects*, 500 pages containing 43 reports from the international symposium of the VI International Congress of Pharmacology.

Undaunted by our miniscule audience, Paton proceeded to comment on the press release we had carefully drafted. He stressed the damaging effects of *all* marijuana products (not only the psychoactive chemical THC) on cell division and the formation of DNA that had been observed by eight scientists reporting at Helsinki. He noted that experimental doses used in the *in vitro* experiments were carefully calculated to simulate those reached in chronic human consumption. Results of the proceedings point to the two major targets for alteration by chronic cannabis use: the cells of the immunity system and the testis. Then Paton concluded: "The significance of these effects must be sought long-term, so far as human use goes, in the fields of immunology, endocrinology and testicular function, teratology, and genetic effects. It needs to be stressed that this *will* be long term. One is only too familiar with the lag between exposure to a drug and appearance of effect (e.g. cigarette smoking); but one must also recognize a *lag in capacity to recognise an effect*. As far as I know there is no machinery set up (which must surely be prospective) to test this for marijuana."

The next speaker, through the use of a "conference phone" was Professor Robert Heath from Tulane, who discussed with us his latest experiments on rhesus monkeys. These indicated that primates exposed to marijuana smoke had permanent alterations in their brain wave patterns recorded from the limbic area (that part of the brain which controls emotional behavior).

Following the press conference, Brian Sullivan released an Associated Press wire describing the book and summarizing its contents to 110 countries. He included a comparison between the results of the Helsinki conference and those of the New York Academy of Sciences. His story was not picked up by a single publication in the United States.

Although disappointed, I was not surprised at the "silent treatment" from the media. Experience had led me to realize that the media amplifies and conveys to the public at large "new" ideas and opinions of some of the leading articulate intellectuals of the day. The more provocative an idea, the more it challenges the established order, the greater its chance to be aired.

At Columbia our studies were proceeding with the collaboration of a host of colleagues: Hembree, Osserman, Morishima and Zeidenberg.

Our first observation, reporting a decrease in cellular mediated immunity of chronic marijuana users, had not been duplicated by other investigators. In our own subsequent studies of marijuana smokers, in a hospital environment, we were not able to show a decrease in "cellular mediated immunity" when we used the same test of mitogen stimulated lymphocytes, earlier described. However, other tests showed a decrease in the number of actively functioning lymphocytes when compared to a group of control subjects. We also noted that marijuana smokers have lower immunoglobulin blood levels. These are substances produced by the lymphocytes to protect the organism against toxic proteins secreted by invading germs. There was still evidence of decreased immunity caused by marijuana.

Such observations were not very impressive to a practicing physician since they were not accompanied by any disease reflecting a breakdown of the immunity system. They could be interpreted only as danger signals for the future. We decided, therefore, to concentrate our efforts on the study of gonadal function and sperm formation of marijuana smokers. At the same time, in the Research Laboratory, Bernard Desoize was investigating the mechanisms by which THC and other cannibinoids prevent normal cell division and DNA synthesis, our basic original finding.

Shortly after the abortive news conference, I had the opportunity to present the results of our Columbia University studies on the spermatogenesis of marijuana smokers before the French National Academy of Medicine, in Paris. This distinguished assembly included some of my mentors in medicine such as Professors Bugnard, Wolff, and Lamy. As on another occasion, my talk was followed by penetrating questions from physicians and scientists with a deep and long-standing human experience.

Professor Lépine, former director of the Pasteur Institute, spoke with alarm against "the increase of cannabis intoxication" and called for this problem to be examined "with due attention by the medical profession in view of its actual danger for our youth". These negative aspects of marijuana use were picked up by a Parisian evening newspaper with a wide circulation and the sensational aspects of my presentation were exaggerated and headlined in a front page article, "Hashish: sterility ... disabled children". Another example, this time on the opposite side, of how the media sometimes has difficulty understanding the scientific subtleties of a research report!

Other French newspapers, however, were more hesitant about conveying even the danger signals of pot to their readers. After all, the abuse of drugs in France was not on the same scale as it was in the United States, and a policy of silence seemed justified. But in other European countries, such as Holland, where use of pot had been decriminalized, its consumption had increased among young people. Amsterdam had become the European capital of the traffic of hashish and opiates.

The first evidence of the development in France of a more serious drug problem appeared in the leftist paper *Liberation*. On June 18, 1976, it devoted a whole page to an article, "The appeal of Joint 18" which was a pun on the date of 18 *Juin* made to sound like "18 joint". The reference was famous to the French because it was the date of DeGaulle's appeal to them to continue to resist the Germans after Petain's capitulation in 1940 during World War II.

The article quoted American studies that claimed that cannabis had none of the harmful effects of alcohol and tobacco. The example of the United States was used to point out that marijuana was smoked by "thousands of people in press, government, and business offices, in secondary schools, universities, factories and the armed services". To put an end to this legal ambiguity, *Liberation* demanded a total decriminalization of cannabis usage, cultivation, and importation into France. This manifesto was signed by more than 150 people: journalists, doctors, lawyers, musicians, actors, writers, film-makers, all declaring that they had smoked marijuana and would continue to do so.

Ever the one to try to set the facts straight, I wrote to the editor to inform him of the recent studies that showed that there are medical hazards linked to the consumption of cannabis and to urge him to consider the social problems which would arise if such a drug were in general use. True to form, *Liberation* never published nor even answered my letter!

The controversy was continued some time later by *Le Monde* (France's even more erudite journalistic equivalent to the *New York Times*) in an article entitled "Drug usage stabilized". Although cannabis was referred to as the "softest of the illicit drugs", young people were warned against its use since for some of them it could lead to an escalation to harder drugs. *Le Monde* approached the decriminalization problems with extreme reserve. Still, I detected in this article a leaning toward re-evaluation of the question of the controls of marijuana usage which had so far not been at issue for the French public.

The influence of publicity (in the media) is well understood by the French sociologist, Emile Durkheim. In his classic book *Le Suicide* he analyzes this influence as it relates to his subject: "In reality, what can contribute to the rise of murder or suicide is not so much the fact of talking about them as the way they are talked about. Wherever these practices are abhorrent, the reactions they elicit are reflected in the manner in which they are reported, which neutralizes rather than excites individual propensities. But, conversely, if a society is in a state of moral disarray, its uncertainty reveals itself when, faced with immoral acts, it treats them with an involuntary indulgence which tones down their very immorality. Then does example become a threat, not so much as an example, but because social tolerance and indifference decrease the awe it should inspire."

Substitute "the use of drugs" for the words murder and

suicide in this passage, and how perfectly these lines apply to the permissive reaction of many American and European journalists and commentators today.

The London *Times* offers an early example of a permissive attitude towards the use of cannabis. In 1967, *The Times* carried a full page ad. claiming that cannabis was a harmless, leisure drug. "Its use should therefore be tolerated by society just as is the use of tobacco or alcohol, whose dangers are unquestionable." Signatures of the famous from the world of Arts, Letters and Sciences, from the Beatles to a Nobel Prize winner appeared at the end of this appeal. Nine years later this article, which also had received considerable attention in the United States at the time, was echoed in France by the "Appeal of Joint 18". But certainly it would be unfair to place the entire blame on the press when in reality, it is expressing the social trend, spearheaded by an increasing number of intellectuals, toward a more liberal attitude about drug use.

How pervasive this trend had become was very clearly demonstrated during an International Colloquium on the Prevention and the Treatment of Drug Abuse, sponsored by the International Council on the Problems of Alcohol and Drug Abuse and held in the summer of 1976 in Hamburg. Although one group presided over by Professor Soueif of Cairo was devoted to a thorough study of all the scientific ramifications of the use of cannabis, most of the other participants, trained in the disciplines of the social sciences, were interested only mildly in the psychometric studies of Soueif or in my studies of the alterations of DNA formation among marijuana smokers. But they were very interested in the report of Dr. Arnao of Rome who described the effect of marijuana on the "cultural deconditioning" of certain members of the Roman aristocracy. He interpreted such "deconditioning" as a beneficial factor for a society in search of authenticity.

I wondered if, as Dr. Arnao claimed, the use of pot favors the frittering away of middle-class social norms, is not American society a prime example of such a phenomenon? Along with the use of pot and the seeking of instant pleasure, there has been a dramatic increase in the divorce rate, juvenile delinquency, overt homosexuality, and promiscuity. This of course could be only a coincidence.

As the year continued, I noticed in the United States a more generalized acceptance of the use of pot and its commercial exploitation as a new industry. Thus, on the occasion of a debate on marijuana, I had the opportunity of meeting Mr. Thomas Dryer, a young man of 23, who obligingly offered me a copy of the magazine he edits, *High Times*. This magazine, already a year old, was devoted entirely to the use of "leisure" drugs, especially pot, but also betel, coca and cocaine. Interspersed with articles describing the heavenly paradises created by the use of these drugs were advertisements describing the numerous accessories needed for their proper consumption: pipes of all kinds, chillum, narghiles, roach clips, precision scales, cutters. There were discounts for bulk orders. Also offered were tiny silver, gold-filled or solid gold spoons to sniff cocaine, along with snuff boxes, coke screens. Some ads invited the reader to join the beautiful people who get "bonged". The numerous ads for cigarette rolling papers, *Job* and others, in a double wide size especially designed for marijuana, reminded me of an article in the *Wall Street Journal* reporting that the sale of cigarette paper had leaped in 10 years from 2 to 50 million dollars!

Mr. Dryer was obviously very proud of his enterprise—its circulation of 400,000 a month and its financial success. Above all, he said, it performed a service to a large segment of the population by providing support for their program of emancipation from "puritanism" and offering objective information on leisure drugs. "Besides", he added, "the market potential is 2 to 3 billion dollars in this field. A minimum of a quarter of a billion dollars comes from accessories known as paraphernalia."

Mr. Dryer was highly sceptical, however, when it came to my statements about the medical hazards of pot. "You are in the minority. Most doctors I have consulted are of the opposite opinion. I am convinced that pot is harmless." He smiled courteously. "Decriminalization of pot is a *fait accompli*, and the same should necessarily follow for cocaine. NORML, the lobby for the repeal of repressive laws on marijuana, has helped us very much." In turn, I noted in the current issue, *High Times* had expressed its thanks to NORML by sending a check for 25 thousand dollars.

A few months later, 40 thousand copies of *High Times* destined for Canada were seized on the border by Canadian authorities because they believed the publication "encouraged the public to use illegal drugs". Such was not the case in the United States where *High Times* continues to prosper, increase its circulation and attract the notice of established publications. In 1978, the Sunday editorial section of the *New York Times* carried a full page ad. extolling *High Times* which was claiming a readership of 4 millions. Two other magazines, *Head* and *Stone Age* devoted entirely to marijuana and other illegal drugs, are also available.

But no one, not from academia, not from the press, not from the church, or the scientific world, has protested this massive propaganda that entices young people to experiment with drugs. Why have they all given up? Have they joined the bandwagon in favor of social acceptance of mind-altering drugs that organizations like NORML and the Drug Abuse Council have led by flooding pressrooms, libraries, schools, legislative bodies with their pamphlets and publications?

The Drug Abuse Council, unlike NORML, is not a "lobby", but a non-profit organization established in 1972 by prestigious American Foundations, like Ford and Carnegie, who endowed it with 8 million dollars. The mission of the Drug Abuse Council is to research "new solutions to drug use and abuse, in a non-biased manner and without government interference." Its board is made up of well-known American personalities. Its president, a man I have met several times, is Dr. Thomas Bryant, an extremely urbane psychiatrist who is also on the Board of NORML.

The Drug Abuse Council, with an annual budget of 2 million dollars, has financed surveys to define the sociological components of the use of illegal mind-altering drugs in American society. Conducted primarily by psychologists, sociologists, psychiatrists, these surveys are an attempt to find out why individuals, especially young people, turn to drugs. "After having identified the causes that lead an individual to drug abuse", Dr. Bryant once told me, "it should be possible to find remedies. Above all, it is important not to treat drug users as criminals. In any case, repression does not work in a democracy." The Drug Abuse Council thus proposed the decriminalization of marijuana as one of the first solutions to the drug use problem among juveniles. Its reports were sent to the highest policy-making levels in government.

The basis for Dr. Bryant's advocacy of decriminalization of marijuana was his belief that marijuana usage has no harmful effects on health or behavior. That is where, in my opinion, he made a fundamental error.

But not all the surveys sponsored by the Drug Abuse Council concerned themselves with marijuana. Other studies of heroin and cocaine use indicated that a large number of Americans (millions, we were told) are able to use these drugs without abusing them or being adversely affected in their social adjustment. They had learned how to control the use of these "leisure" drugs, just as many control their use of alcohol. One survey in particular caught my attention. It was entitled "The Availability of Heroin", and advocated making heroin available to heroin addicts to allow them to function in society. Such a program, it was proposed, would eliminate the criminality associated with the illegal traffic of that drug and allow the social readjustment of the user, like the English model already in operation. It was noted that the substitution of methadone in the treatment of heroin addicts is only a subterfuge, since it replaces one drug with another, no less dangerous.

I found a flaw common to these surveys. They ignored a fundamental pharmacological law—the use of any drug bears a price which may, in certain cases, be paid by a child who did not ask to be born. A more immediate and serious consequence of these studies was the escalation of the social acceptance of drugs. After having advocated, and obtained the decriminalization of marijuana in many states, this group was now pushing for the same measure for *all* illegal drugs. According to this philosophy, the only way society could defend itself from so-called dangerous drugs, whose source could not be controlled, was to educate each citizen in the means of self-control. The availability of drugs was to be accompanied by a massive educational program to warn against their use, or if need be, to teach how to use them in moderation. In a country fond of a belief in easy and fast solutions to complex problems, such ideas were gaining ground. Decriminalize the use and cultivation of marijuana for personal use, provide heroin to the heroin addict, these were the headlines in press, radio and television. How difficult it is to counter such a well-orchestrated campaign, and what will happen if such opinions eventually prevail in the whole of the United States?

At the highest level of government a young psychiatrist, Dr. Peter Bourne, the appointed personal advisor to President Carter on Drug Abuse, declared to *US News and World Report*: "The present trend seems to be in favor of decriminalization and even legalization of drugs, including heroin. This proposal is not politically acceptable at the present time, but we are going to have to consider a move towards the decriminalization of heroin on a world-wide scale." His colleague, Dr. Robert Dupont, Director of the National Institute on Drug Abuse (NIDA), echoed his statements: "The penalties inflicted for possession of illegal drugs will have to be lowered and eventually eliminated."

In his new book on cocaine, Professor Lester Grinspoon added his voice to this attitude. Just as he once championed the decriminalization of marijuana, Grinspoon was now taking a new look at cocaine, a recreational drug which is "non addictive" and in most cases "well tolerated." He thought that users were unfairly penalized by arbitrary laws. The favorable reviews of his book appearing in the *New York Times* assured it of wide distribution in the United States.

Aided by the media, reinforced by government officials, given legitimacy by "scholarly" publications, the "escalation" of the social acceptance of recreational drug use was in full swing in the States. Added to marijuana, the use of cocaine had become fashionable among the affluent who do not shrink from paying two thousand dollars an ounce (more precious than gold at a mere 200 dollars the ounce).

Because of the growing social acceptance of drug use and the failure to control its spread through a strict policy of enforcement, the American government was impelled to re-examine its stand. Should a new policy be adopted in order to tolerate the use of mind-altering drugs, heretofore considered dangerous? Should the responsibility and the control of their use be transferred from society to the individual who would be taught how not to use them? In the first step, the use of all mind-altering drugs would be decriminalized, in the second, their sale would be made legal. To me this attitude was like the old simplistic saw: "To protect yourself from the rain, jump in the river!"

But at the same time this new attitude towards drugs was gaining converts, our cannabis research, patiently pursued, was yielding tangible results. In the laboratory, Bernard Desoize had succeeded in showing the intimate mechanism of how cannabis derivatives exert their toxic effect on cells in penetrating the cell membrane and preventing the renewal of protein reserves and nucleic acids. And at the New York State Psychiatric Institute where we had completed a study of sixteen volunteer heavy marijuana smokers, our earlier observations were confirmed: after one month of heavy cannabis use, all subjects showed a decrease in sperm formation and also, what was more serious, a considerable increase in abnormal forms of sperm. We had a definitive study in hand: it was a distinct possibility that there could be a genetic danger linked to the regular consumption of cannabis.

In other parts of the country, other scientists were uncovering serious consequences of marijuana use. A team led by Dr. Ethel Sassenrath in California reported on a three year study of the effect of daily administration of THC to a colony of monkeys. They observed that the drugged animals had a larger number of miscarriages and of still-born infants. Those monkey infants who survived behaved abnormally—they were hyperactive and responded in an exaggerated way to external stimuli.

Before the dangers of the use of this drug were denounced, will it be necessary to wait for the day when behavioral abnormalities, similar to those in Sassenrath's monkeys, will show up in the children born from marijuana smoking parents?

The same country whose Food and Drug Administration has established rigorous regulations for therapeutic drugs seems ready to tolerate the generalized usage of mind-altering drugs, along with their sequel of addiction, of social, psychological and genetic dangers. Where are the courageous intellectuals to speak out against this attitude? Why this abdication of intellectual leadership?

Abraham Lincoln's words, pronounced in 1838 during an address before the Young Men's Lyceum in Springfield, Illinois, are prophetic today, "If destruction be our lot, we ourselves must be its author and the finisher. As a nation of free men, we must live through all times, or die by suicide."

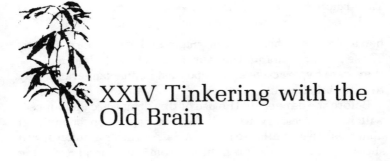

XXIV Tinkering with the Old Brain

Those intellectuals who openly advocate the right of the individual to use his "recreational drug of choice", or who by their silence appear to condone such use, ignore the significance of a growing body of scientific knowledge of the neurophysiological basis of man's behavior.

In the past 20 years, research has revealed that man's brain is formed of two different parts, each with its own distinctive function and evolutionary history. The first, the paleocortex or "old brain" (also called the limbic system) is located at the core of our brain. In animals, this is the greatest portion of the brain. It was also the most important part of the brain of primitive man. But the structure of his brain has evolved over the millions of years through the addition of successive layers that make up the second part, the neocortex or "new brain". Whereas our intellectual faculties—language, symbolic expression, analytical ability, consciousness of the self—derive from the new brain, our old brain is the control center of memory storage, our emotions, our instincts and our subconscious.

"The old structure", says French Nobel prize-winning geneticist Francois Jacob, "which in lower animals is in total command, in man has been relegated to the department of the emotions." The totality of human behavior is the result of the close interaction of the activities of the old and the new brains. And yet, as noted by Jacob, integration between the two brains is imperfect because of the very nature of this divided structure: a dominating neo-cortex is coupled to a primitive nervous and hormonal system that can never be totally subjugated. "It is somewhat like adding a jet engine to an old horse cart. It is not surprising in either case that accidents, difficulties and conflicts do occur."

Our brain chemistry acts to maintain a "delicate balance" between these two parts of the brain. When drugs are used to fight mental illness, such as depression or schizophrenia, they are given to combat a specific imbalance. But because drugs are not absolutely selective, they can have an effect on sites other than the target areas meant to be treated. Hence the all-importance of the physician's expertise: he must weigh the expected benefits against the possible side effects before he prescribes any drug. When healthy individuals take drugs for pleasure rather than to correct some chemical malfunction, they run the risk of disrupting the extremely delicate chemical equilibrium of their brain. The chemical linkages controlling the relationship between the old and new brains can be upset, if tampered with, in such a way as to make the brain's ability to function dependent on a chemical source of stimulation and thereby to lose its ability to respond normally without it.

Neurochemists have discovered that psychotropic drugs used in minute amounts concentrate in certain areas of the brain which contain a certain specific "receptor". This was first found to be true of the opiates, and has now been discovered for the tranquillizers (like Valium) which localize in certain areas of the old brain associated with the control of anxiety. The drug may be compared to a key which "locks" on the receptor. In contrast to psychotropic drugs, a substance like alcohol affects the brain in a non-specific way, and in gram rather than milligram amounts.

The scientist's ability to study and gain information about these effects is due to the fact that the brain, like the heart, generates very small currents of electricity that can be recorded by a machine called an electroencephalograph (similar to an electrocardiograph). Recorded from sensors, or electrodes, that are placed directly on the scalp, these currents show primarily the activity of the *new* brain. But in 1953 effects resulting from direct electrical stimulation of the *old* brain were discovered at the Montreal Neurological Institute. Two scientists, Penfield and Jasper, gained access to the limbic area during brain surgery and discovered that electrical stimulation of the limbic area in their awake patients caused a loss of identity, feelings of fear, paranoia, distortions of perception, and alterations in time sense.

The observations of Penfield and Jasper led to more advanced experiments on animals. Olds and Milner from McGill University, using rats, inserted tiny metal rods (electrodes) well past the surface of the brain into the limbic area. By this means they were able to localize an area that the rats learned to stimulate themselves. As soon as the animals were able to associate pushing a lever with pleasurable stimulation of a specific part of the limbic area, the hypothalamus, they established a pattern of frequent self-stimulation that continued until the animals were completely exhausted—they pressed the lever as many as 3000 times in one hour! The fact that this newly learned activity took precedence over all other drives, including sexual and appetite led the researchers to conclude that there is a special area in the old brain which when stimulated induces in the animal a type of behavior associated with reward and pleasure.

Then similar observations were reported by Professor Robert Heath, Chairman of the Department of Neurology and Psychiatry of Tulane University, who studied rhesus monkeys and mental patients. In his published reports he has concluded that electrical stimulation of the hypothalamic part of the old brain in both primates and in man produces sensations of well being and euphoria. Furthermore, these sensations spread through the entire nervous system and their prolonged effects can escape completely any control by the "new brain".

Marijuana, like other psychoactive drugs, has been found to act on the old brain and alter its functioning. This has been demonstrated by the animal studies of Dr. McIsaac (University of Texas) and Dr. Heath. Dr. McIsaac injected radioactive THC into the blood stream of monkeys. With instruments sensitive to radioactivity he studied the distribution of THC in the brains and was able to observe that the highest concentration of the drug had accumulated in the limbic area, and that it had remained there for up to 4 hours. Dr. Heath experimented with rhesus monkeys who were made to inhale marijuana. By using electrodes implanted deeply into the monkeys' brains, he was able to observe bursts of abnormal electrical activity, or "spiking" caused by marijuana in the septal area of the brain, a focal point for pleasure and reward. The more common type of *scalp* electroencephalogram is unable to record these changes in the limbic area; only a delicate experiment involving deeply implanted electrodes can register brain wave changes in this area.

In another series of experiments performed by Dr. Heath, monkeys "smoked" marijuana daily for six months followed by a six month period of abstinence. The abnormal brain waves in the limbic area recorded by the electrodes persisted throughout *both* periods—smoking and abstinence. Thus there is a danger that chronic use of marijuana could cause longterm alterations in brain function of the limbic area in man as well. To acquire further information, Dr. Heath sacrificed some of the monkeys and examined portions of their old brain under an electron microscope. He was able to see actual damage in the synapses of the limbic tissues. Synapses are the "switches" that regulate the nervous system's communication between the brain cells.

These experiments strongly indicate the possibility that delta-9-THC and its metabolites interfere with the normal functioning of the limbic system and with the relationship between the old brain area and the new brain and thereby disrupt the mechanisms that control our emotional life. Of crucial importance is this: there appears to be an interruption of the free and natural flow of signals between the two main structures of the brain which can prevent the regular duplication of patterns of coherent behavior.

The manner in which THC effects the old brain can explain

some of the more common elements of the acute marijuana experience—personality changes, alterations in time sense, disruption of memory storage, pleasurable feelings. Perhaps this is also the key to "uncommon" elements such as flashbacks or cannabis-triggered mental illness. The flashback could be an indication that memory of the active experience has been stored in the limbic area of the brain. Even when smoking has ceased, the experience felt during intoxication can return with the vividness of the actual happening. As Heath's experiments have demonstrated, the abnormal electrical activity caused by THC in the limbic area of the brain persists for hours after administration of the drug.

It has been demonstrated that "pleasure" has a biological basis in the old brain; this included sexual pleasure. Marijuana's direct effect on this area relates to another element of the marijuana experience: the aphrodisiac properties of cannabis. Users everywhere claim that both sexual performance and enjoyment are enhanced by the use of marijuana.

Marijuana is known to slow down the passage of time, so the user can have a subjective impression of a very long-lasting orgasm. But as always, there is a catch. This effect occurs with *low dosage*; larger doses provoke the desire but diminish the performance; steady use may kill both together. In the words of Theophile Gautier, a wild young French Romantic poet of the late 19th Century, "After a good stiff dose of hashish, the smoker would not lift a finger for the most beautiful maiden in Venice."

Another catch is that different people react to the drug in different ways. Marijuana is known for its unpredictability, and the response to its effects varies with the mood of the user. Marijuana may thus magnify whatever may be the emotional state of the partners: when someone is feeling warm and romantic, marijuana intensifies the experience. On the other hand, it can increase feelings of suspicion and distrust. So even this drug cannot help people escape from the person to person "chemistry" necessary for true sexual enjoyment.

Although the use of marijuana is an undependable way of

increasing sexual pleasure, physically it can have some serious consequences. In man studies have shown that the drug affects both the quantity and quality of sperm. In women, marijuana impairs the production of hormones which regulate the menstrual cycle and ovarian function including egg maturation. Because of this risk, the United States government forbids the use of women as experimental subjects on projects studying the long term effects of marijuana.

Despite the fact that we know that marijuana can disrupt the close chemical interaction between the old and new brain, at present there is no satisfactory method for assessing damage to man's limbic system or the resulting changes in personality. This is why a discussion of the long term effects of marijuana on the central nervous system remains so controversial. One aspect of this problem, however, is now widely accepted by psychiatrists: patients prone to schizophrenia must not use marijuana. Case studies of patients suffering from this illness have shown that marijuana can trigger severe mental disturbances or cause a relapse.

Recent scientific studies suggest that marijuana causes biochemical alterations in the limbic part of the brain that controls our emotional balance and the sensations of well-being. In addition, chronic use of marijuana may leave a long-lasting mark on the "old brain".

Through the artificial stimulation of the pleasure center of the brain, the indiscriminant use of marijuana and other related "recreational" drugs allows the abuser to obtain immediate gratification without requiring him to exert any sustained or disciplined effort of his own mental faculties. While this is a problem at any age, the adolescent is particularly susceptible to deleterious effects. Chemical stimulation of the pleasure centers endangers the adolescent's chance to develop his own natural resources for joy and emotional stability. Fooled by the effects of a drug, he is unable to judge either the extent or the consequences of his "habit". When tolerance develops, and the same degree of pleasure is no longer provided, young people may seek more potent drugs. Once the old brain is saturated by the effects of drug abuse, it may become incapable of responding to the pleasures of *normal* physical and intellectual stimulation.

In order to test the motivation of marijuana users, Professor Jack Mendelson from Harvard, designed a study reminiscent of the famous experiment of Olds on rodents which preferentially pressed on a lever to stimulate their pleasure center. In the Harvard study the marijuana users could press a button to accumulate points which would enable them to obtain marijuana cigarettes. As one could have expected, the subjects kept smoking marijuana and pushing the button in order to obtain the drug. But Mendelson interprets the results of his study as an indication that marijuana smoking does not inhibit motivation in general. ... In doing so, he confuses motivation directed towards a satisfaction resulting from the chemical activation of the brain reward system, and motivation directed towards a reward resulting from achievement. These two motivations are mutually exclusive, though the physiological end result of the final reward might be similar, as noted by Moreau 140 years ago:

"It is really happiness that hashish gives, and by that I mean mental not sensual joy. ... and one can draw a strange conclusion, that all joy even though its cause is strictly mental and highly idealistic could well be a purely physical sensation developed physiologically, exactly like that produced by hashish."

The late Professor Hardin Jones has pointed out that the cumulative effect of marijuana on the brain might lead to a state of "sensory deprivation", a condition in which the "blunted" pleasure center may not respond to activities which could otherwise bring natural gratification.

How can any society afford the cost of letting any of its members, particularly its youth, "tinker with the old brain"?

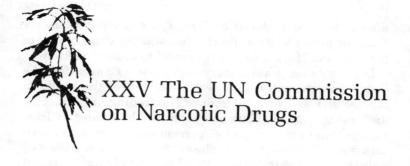

XXV The UN Commission on Narcotic Drugs

When I arrived in Geneva at the end of February, 1977, the annual meeting of the UN Commission on Narcotic Drugs had been in session for two weeks with another eight days remaining. A rather dull and lackluster meeting it was, because the subject was not one to inspire the participants. The role of the commission is to watch over the enforcement of the terms of the various international conventions sponsored by the United Nations and to establish, on a world scale, a control of narcotic and dangerous drugs. To the bans established by the Single Convention of 1961 had been added those of the Convention on mind-altering drugs of 1973. But, it appeared that the more the legal bans against dangerous drugs increased, the more their consumption spread throughout the world.

At this 1977 meeting, therefore, the delegates were forced to admit to themselves that the recommendations of previous years for controlling drug traffic had not been followed. Indeed, traffic in opiates, the major concern of the Commission, was on the upswing. The only difference was a change in the production centers and the distribution networks. Although Turkey was no longer a major center of production, other countries like Pakistan, Afghanistan, and especially the "Golden Triangle"—Burma, Laos, Thailand—were now steady suppliers, supplemented by a new producer, Mexico. The traditional "connections" that linked the Middle East with the Mediterranean ports of Istanbul and Marseilles had been

195

dismantled and replaced by Bangkok and Amsterdam via Rome or Moscow. Now, Amsterdam was the drug capital of the Common Market Countries for all to see and to know.

Despite its being a signatory of the Single Convention, the Dutch government was powerless to control the traffic in opiates and was very tolerant of the trading of hash. This distressing state of affairs was confirmed by a delegate from Interpol who reported that 45 percent more heroin had been seized in 1977 than in 1976. The amounts seized represented only the tip of the iceberg, or 10–20 percent of total trade and consumption. Other banned drugs were also being intercepted in increasing quantities, cocaine and hashish particularly—its consumption was on the rise in all countries of the world.

I spoke with a Norwegian journalist who told me about the situation in his country which up to now had been spared a serious drug problem. In Oslo there were an identified several thousand heroin addicts, and it was common for many school children to smoke pot, considering it a harmless "soft" drug.

"But they are wrong!" I could not help exclaiming.

"I don't wish to question your word, Professor, but many of your colleagues have assured me, just as strongly, that the use of hashish is not seriously dangerous. They are the ones that our young people prefer to listen to."

Once more, I described the harmful effects of cannabis. And then I asked the journalist what he thought was the cause of the sudden explosion of drug abuse among Norwegian youth.

"Our country has become an oil producer with a very solid currency—it has one of the highest standards of living in the world," he answered.

Dr. Olav Braenden, who had joined our conversation, added, "The upsurge of drug addiction that we are now observing comes from an increasing demand for drugs from the citizens of wealthy industrialized countries. This increase in standard of living is an important factor in the use of narcotics among youth. Would the proper solution then be to decrease our standard of living?" None of us was ready to answer this question.

I discovered a little later, in a conversation with a delegate from Iran, another big oil-producing country, that a problem similar to Norway's existed there, too. "The use of opium and of hashish", he confided, "goes back to ancient times. When the Shah came to power, however, he took extremely repressive measures, including giving the death penalty to pushers. As a result, the consumption of those drugs decreased except among the peasantry. But in the last few years the picture has changed again due to the great influx of capital from the sale of oil and the resulting accelerated industrialization of the country. A new and alarmingly large wave of drug addiction is afflicting the urban neoproletariat and students."

"Where do the drugs come from?" I asked.

"From Pakistan and Afghanistan, growers of both hashish and opium and with whom we have common frontiers. Our greatest concern is heroin, which in our country is inhaled, not injected in the veins as in the United States or in Europe."

"And what measures are you planning to combat this problem?"

"First," he said, "we will attempt to wipe out the source of narcotics. This can be done only with concerted cooperation between nations such as is possible with this particular Commission. But we also have the task of educating and rehabilitating all our young people who have already been exposed. Here the American experience can be extremely useful to us."

I shook my head without answering.

A Lebanese doctor added his country to the growing list of those with a considerable drug abuse problem. Beirut, a city half destroyed by civil war was also experiencing a drug crisis. In the course of the fighting, many soldiers had taken amphetamines and other stimulants. Even after the end of hostilities, they had continued to use drugs and some were now shooting heroin.

"We would like to start on a rehabilitation program", my Lebanese colleague told me "to save these unexpected vic-

tims of the civil war. But our country cannot afford it. So I
have come to the UN Commission on Narcotics to seek help."

I encouraged him in his efforts, hoping that with the recon-
struction of Lebanon, the situation would be corrected. But
my surprises were not at an end: along came the delegate
from Senegal to introduce a resolution asking the Commission to turn its attention to the African populations south of
the Sahara. It appeared that in the Third World countries,
drug abuse was spreading at an alarming rate. Countries of
the Arab League requested that any drug information published by the Commission be translated into Arabic.

But the largest question still nagged, how could all these
appeals, all these recommendations, always unanimously approved by the delegates, stop the proliferation of drug usage
in the world? I could sense among the delegates a vague
uncertainty; they were not quite clear about the exact nature
of their mission. And there was a distinct aura of gloom
among those organizations dependent on the work of a committee whose inefficiency was only too apparent.

What could be done to hold back this movement that was
affecting more and more youth between the ages of 15 and 25,
namely the future of mankind?

I asked one of the veterans of the permanent Secretariat of
the Commission who had followed its progress over 15 years.
"What we need", he said, "is a spokesman capable of instill-
ing enthusiasm in the men of goodwill who are now gathered
in the Palace of Nations in Geneva to help humanity fight the
degradation caused by drug abuse. But, as you have found
out in America, it seems that there is no one who wants to be
the standard bearer of this rather unpopular cause."

"But", I objected "the United States does not represent the
whole world."

"Certainly not", he replied "but it is the only country
which can effectively support this great cause. Once, after
the passage of the Single Convention in 1961, the United
States had such a man, Mr. Harry Anslinger."

"Anslinger ... his name is now cursed in his country."

Now this was true, but in Geneva in 1961, this had not been

the case when Anslinger had headed the American delegation. Then his jovial and dynamic personality animated the Commission's work and moved it towards the goal set by the United Nations: the gradual elimination of illicit drugs from the world. Towards this end he had consulted well-known pharmacologists, such as Dr. Nathan Eddy and Dr. Harris Isbell. All the delegations, from the East, the West and the Third World highly respected him.

"Wasn't this goal somewhat amibitious?" I asked.

"Perhaps, but I don't have to tell you that today we have fallen to the opposite extreme." He shook his head and added: "What a change!" There was no need for him to elaborate further.

In 1977, 16 years later, the American delegation was led by Dr. Peter Bourne and the former head of Public Relations for the Drug Abuse Council, Mrs. Falco. In the States they had advocated decriminalization of the use of illegal drugs and were not alarmed by the increasing availability of these drugs in American society. Because their position was in conflict with the one advocated by the United Nations, the United States no longer was in the forefront of the world effort to combat the generalized use of narcotics as it had been in the time of Harry Anslinger.

But there were encouraging signs to show that the battle could still be fought. Thanks to the United Nations Fund for the Control of Narcotics, the Commission had been able to organize a pilot program in Thailand. Its goal was to aid the Thais to replace the poppy crops, so sought after for opium production, with crops of edible food products.

I paid a visit to one of the moving spirits of the last four years behind the coordination of this program, Mrs. Waldheim-Natural. Even her home betrayed her dedication to this cause for inscribed over the entrance was a quote by Buddha, "You will abstain from all substances which could intoxicate your mind."

This young woman told me of the very encouraging results obtained by the program in 25 villages in Thailand where the poppy fields had been replaced by coffee, fruit and vegetable plantations. "We have also been able to establish schools, craft centers, and medical dispensaries that have transformed the life of the villagers" she related. When they grew poppies, they lived in destitution because they had no share in the immense profits of the opium trade. They needed to be rehabilitated. The UN Program was successful, she told me, but it cost 4 million dollars. And, she added, all this is only a start. There are more than 800 villages in the same region which must be rehabilitated. If they are not, all our efforts will have been in vain. And then, this experience should be extended to Burma, the leading world producer of opium with 400 tons a year.

Perhaps there were reasons to be hopeful, since this was the first time that an international experiment of this kind had been successful. People would not forget such a precedent that could be used as an example for other countries to follow.

"This experience could be followed in Morocco and Lebanon with plans to find a substitute economy for the cannabis crops" Mrs. Waldheim-Natural said. "The great lesson of the Thai program is that when the cultivation of harmful substances is eliminated and replaced by traditional food crops, a true rehabilitation of the farmers and their villages follows."

I could not help but think of the totally different attitude that prevailed in the United States concerning cannabis cultivation: A senior spokesman for the National Institute on Drug Abuse had just advocated decriminalization of the cultivation of cannabis for personal use! Hard on the heels of this recommendation was a bill to implement it in the State of California, supported by both political parties, NORML, and vendors of supplies necessary for such cultivation.

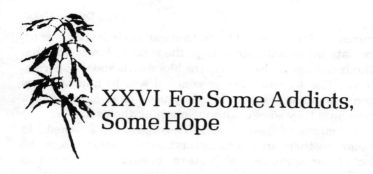

XXVI For Some Addicts, Some Hope

Eight years after the Englewood High School PTA meeting that first sparked my interest in marijuana, the Chapaqua School invited me to participate in a debate, "Should cannabis be legalized?" I accepted, but having just returned from Geneva and still suffering from jet lag, I enlisted the services of my wife as chauffeur for the thirty mile drive into the heart of wealthy Westchester County.

Upon our arrival we were taken to the comfortable auditorium of that magnificent school already filled with parents, students and teachers. Sharing the podium with me were a young lawyer, representing NORML, and the school psychologist, both of whom favored decriminalization of marijuana, the "soft drug". As usual, my presentation pointed out the dangers linked to the regular use of cannabis by adolescents and was illustrated with slides and tables. Minimizing these effects, that my opponents claimed had not been really proven, they insisted on stressing the legal inequities of New York State's repressive laws against the use of marijuana. The psychologist justified the use of cannabis among the young, who, after all, were merely following the example of their parents who smoked tobacco and drank alcohol. He added that it was necessary to find out why young people smoked pot in order to help them. Enthusiastic student applause greeted my two adversaries, but most of the questions were addressed to me. What they revealed was a considerable

ignorance of the medical facts: that cannabis derivatives accumulate in the brain, the lungs, the sexual glands; and that
cellular damage is observed in the blood cells and the sperma-
tozoids. The students' major concern was to find out how
much marijuana they could safely use—how many times a
week could they smoke without harming themselves!

In the middle of the debate, the Headmaster intervened. "In
my opinion, there are too many unknown questions about the
effect of marijuana on health. As the person in charge of this
school, I believe that the use of marijuana is incompatible
both with our mission as pedagogues and with an orderly
system of education." Immediately the NORML representative challenged this outspoken individual. "Sir," he said,
"do you want to send a young person to prison for smoking
one joint?"

How many times before had I seen such debates end in
confusion? My wife had already given up and had earlier left
the auditorium. She was exasperated, "I couldn't stand what
your opponents were saying! They were speaking in bad
faith. Obviously, they don't care if young people smoke this
'harmless' marijuana, but instead of admitting it, they seek
the support of youth by denouncing the prison sentences
exceptionally inflicted on a few pot smokers." Marilyn rarely
lost her temper. She added, "These people pretend that they
want to discourage the use of marijuana, but they offer no
program to accomplish this goal. It is clear that what they
want is the free sale of marijuana. I was so indignant, that I
couldn't listen to them any more."

And then Marilyn told me that while waiting for the end of
the debate, she had spoken with some students who had
joined her. Most of them said they smoked marijuana, some of
them smoked every day. One girl of fourteen claimed to have
been a regular smoker since she was ten—an unhappy confirmation of official statistics. A 1976 survey of 17,000 high
school seniors by the National Institute on Drug Abuse indicated that 53% smoked marijuana regularly.

"But what concerns me most," said my wife, "is how ignorant these students are of studies describing the damage

cannabis can cause. They don't know about cellular damage—the girls don't know that marijuana accumulates in the ovaries. I asked them the question suggested by the psychologist, 'Why do you smoke marijuana?' Their answers were vague. 'I don't know . . . I can't tell you exactly . . . It's done . . . I like the feeling I get . . .' It seems to me that these young people are drifting. They are jaded—they lack enthusiasm. They don't have the feeling of their power, or their worth, or their integrity. Their studies don't seem to be enough to fill their lives. Their energy isn't channeled, they withdraw into themselves. They need an ideal!"

On the return trip home I was overcome by a deep weariness combined with a profound discouragement at the vision of my efforts of so many years spent in vain. But as if reading my thoughts, Marilyn interrupted the silence, "We are so lucky; we have healthy children." How could I not be cheered by her intuitive observation? "We are lucky", I replied, "and so are they". In my thoughts I was glad that they had spent their formative years in French schools at a time when there did not exist a drug problem, for I believe that this absence of an early exposure to the "drug culture" had a very positive effect on their development.

Marilyn continued, "Our children have experienced joy in their lives."

"But how," I asked, "can they communicate this experience to their young friends? This is a problem that is neither scientific nor intellectual."

"No", said Marilyn, "to communicate joy is a spiritual problem, a religious one, even. Isn't that what de Felice says in that book you like so much?"

She was referring to a book I discovered by chance several years ago in a Paris bookstore. The title had piqued my curiosity, *Poisons sacres, Ivresses divines* (Sacred poisons, divine intoxications). This work, published in 1935, was the only one which for me had succeeded in providing a general explanation for the complex problem of drug addiction.

De Felice's theory was simple. As old as recorded history, drug addiction is a result of man's desire to surpass himself and reach happiness. Here are his own words,

> Man is constantly laboring to surpass himself. This feature explains what he does to increase his power, extend his knowledge, reach beauty, fill himself with a richer, more intense life that he believes to be divine in nature. He feels he is not mistaken when he thus attempts to rise above himself because of the happiness he experiences each time he is conscious of succeeding. Happiness is inseparable from a feeling of growth and progress. It exists only when one can record a gain, a victory, a conquest, it is the reward of a risk incurred, the inner confirmation of the value and the success of the effort accomplished. Drug usage, with its physiological and psychological consequences, has been for man a way to obtain, if not the reality, at least the illusion of this surpassing of the self and its accompanying happiness.

Although these intoxications are an obvious cause of deterioration for the human being, they are still witnesses in their way to his innate need for an escape towards a superior life. They may even have contributed to reinforce his belief in the possibility to surpass himself, as he dreams he can, and the ambition to reach this goal by varied means.

It is true that these practises can move man away from the goal that he should reach, since they degrade him instead of elevating him. But, in the meanwhile, they allow him the momentary exaltation to which he is so strongly attracted and which, in order to enjoy, he will seek by exposing himself to undisputed dangers. Should it not be appropriate to take into account, for all those who use drugs, the aspirations which move them and the risks they take? Maybe there is more vitality in their souls than in those of their accusers who ignore their anxieties and condemn them without trying to understand them. As for a way to redress the error of those whose very desire to become free has turned them into slaves of drugs and poisons, would it not be to direct their ambitions towards satisfactions of a superior mystical order?

What remains unquestionable, however, is the deep disturbance caused in our civilized world by the extensive use of intoxicating beverages, or narcotics and stupefying drugs. Modern man does not escape any better than did his predecessors the permanent and fundamental law of his being which forces him to seek himself beyond what he is. However, our contemporaries, when they wish to satisfy their need for escape, are turning more and more, through a strange aberration, towards the old mystical customs which have been in constant use among primitive cultures. Drug use is one.

If such means to carry man beyond himself give him the illusion he is surpassing himself, they also result in bringing him down to a level notably inferior to the one where our western culture seems to have established him. No one, indeed, would deny that a state of semi-hypnosis hampers the free function of the mental faculties. Everyone also knows that addiction to alcohol or drugs degrades physically, intellectually, and morally.

Thus, by returning day by day towards these inferior forms of mystique that will unavoidably cause a regression, civilized humankind is working unwittingly towards its own decline. The progress realized in the technological field cannot compensate the degradation of souls, which it condones if it does not help correct. The fall might be hastened if these means supply human beings in the process of regression with ways of decreasing their personal value, and thus could precipitate a general ruin.

The heart of the matter lies there and the stakes are the future of our civilization . . .

These themes expressed by Philippe de Felice more than forty years ago had a striking accuracy considering that the problem of drug addiction was barely detected in the western world, let alone France. Marijuana, nowadays so easily

available in our society provides an answer to a fundamental
human need that cannot be satisfied in a distraught society.
As a pharmacologist and a physiologist, my regret is that the
pleasure centers buried deeply in the brain cannot distinguish between the profound joys of great human achieve-
ments and the ephemeral exaltations derived from intoxication on drugs or alcohol. But nature has not endowed us
with this power of discrimination, which the believer calls
"grace". Therefore it is the job of society to preserve our
youth from substances that may be associated, even fleet-
ingly, with the chemical induction of happiness." Marijuana
smokers I have observed appear happy and content when
under the influence of this drug. But another author, Doctor
Olivenstein, gives such "happiness" its full dimension by
entitling his book, *There Are No Happy Drug Addicts*.

But how can one protect the young against the deception of
marijuana which places its imprint on their brain, alters the
course of their emotional life, and precludes truly joyful
experiences? What other rational solution can there be than
abstinence?

By the time we reached home, close to midnight, I could
still not escape my central problem of how to communicate to
young people, and their elders as well, that the use of marijuana can be harmful to their bodies in the long run, and
heavy use can ruin their lives. For the past ten years, in my
trips all over the United States, the solution so important for
future generations has eluded me.

Several months later, vacationing in the South of France
near Toulouse, I found a possible answer at a nearby rehabilitation center for confirmed heroin addicts. The inspi-
ration of its founder and "Patriarch", Lucien Engelmajer,
this center was located in the country-side. We visited him
and his entourage—family, assistants, and young people—
one afternoon. We stayed and talked with them all until one
o'clock in the morning. The group was working feverishly to
make their Chateau de la Mothe ready for a UNESCO conference. Room by room, they were restoring the delapidated
building. Their enthusiasm was such that the Chateau was

well on its way to renovation on my return fifteen days later.

Engelmajer is a very impressive man of husky build who radiates conviction from within. In his book, "The Patriarch", he describes the long, hard battle he and his wife have fought to establish a therapeutic community unique in the world. He details methods he uses to rehabilitate young drug addicts. At the Chateau de la Mothe his methods could be seen in action.

The seventy former addicts who live there arise early in the morning to work in the fields or workshop, their meals are served at regular hours, and they participate in some form of exercise of sport. There is only one taboo : no drugs—even during withdrawal from heroin—and no alcohol. Tobacco cigarettes are permitted. In a way, the program resembles an adult scout camp where everyone is totally committed to the events of each day.

What a comfort it was to observe these young people who were happy, busy and self-satisfied! Where only months before they had been completely under the stultifying influence of drugs, now they were actively working and full of appreciation for the beauty of their natural surroundings. All this thanks to the presence, will and application of one good man who has understood how to combine love with common sense and discipline. It was an 18 year old girl, a former heroin addict of 5 years, said to me, "Here I have found renewed hope!"

On the subject of marijuana the Patriarch is unequivocal, "Of course it is a dangerous drug. Everyone of our young people without exception began by taking marijuana—and then escalated to harder drugs. I am ignorant of what marijuana can do to your cells, but I do know it disconnects something in the brain. Here our young people need to be alert, with all their mental faculties able to respond to the call of their consciences and to the needs of others in the group. They must be awake and aware—that is why there is no marijuana or hashish allowed."

I hope that this message of the Patriarch will be heard by other young people. I hope that his methods of rehabilitation will spread to help prevent or cure others who have been seduced by drugs. The problems of drug abuse are a menace to the future of modern society. As for the older generations, they should recall that the survival of our civilization has always been dependent on the observance of certain taboos, and the taboo against drugs is one of them!

On my return to the United States, I became acquainted with "thereapeutic communities" similar to those of the Patriarch. The drug-free rehabilitation programs organized and led by Father O'Brien at Day Top Village, and by Mitchell Rosenthal in Phoenix House, are other heartening examples of what can be done; they have enabled scores of young people addicted to heroin and cocaine to restore their health and recover a drug free, creative and satisfying life. Most of the youth I met in these centers acknowledged having started drug tripping, with marijuana, often before age twelve.

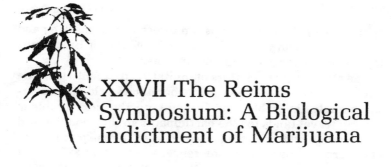

XXVII The Reims Symposium: A Biological Indictment of Marijuana

As marijuana gained more and more acceptance in the United States, scientists were patiently pursuing their studies of the biological effects of the drug. At the meetings of the American Pharmacological Society, new reports described the damaging effects of marijuana on cells and reproductive function. Publications of these studies were scattered in specialized journals and slipped into oblivion. The time had come to organize a new international symposium where all the researchers could present and discuss their latest findings which would then be published in a single volume. My colleagues William Paton of Oxford and Monique Braude of the National Institute on Drug Abuse were very favorable to the idea and agreed to co-organize the symposium.

The date of the VIIth International Congress of Pharmacology to be held in Paris in July of 1978, three years after the Helsinki meeting, appeared most suitable. The Program Committee of the International Congress approved our suggested title and program: "Marijuana: Detection in body fluids, cellular responses, effects on reproductive function and brain."

While looking for a suitable location to hold our symposium, preferably out of crowded and distracting Paris, I thought of Reims. One hundred miles from Paris, this capital of the Champagne country has a fine University where Bernard Desoize had returned after his stay in my laboratory at Columbia. The officials of the University of Reims welcomed the opportunity to host an international meeting and selected Dr. Jean-Claude Jardillier, professor of Biochemistry, to be in charge of local arrangements.

The response to my letters of invitation to scientists in the United States—as well as those around the world—was overwhelmingly favorable, and brought up the next problem: getting travel funds for the participants so they could afford to attend! In addition, money was needed for the publication of the proceedings of the conference. My goal was $25,000—a relatively modest sum for such a conference. It was soon evident, however, that the difficulties involved in raising money for such a "lost cause"—informing the public about the dangers of marijuana through an international gathering of prominent scientists—were overwhelming.

From out of dozens of letters sent to Foundations, individuals and major corporations, I received only three positive replies and a total contribution of $4,500. The negative answers to my request were frustratingly similar: "We approve of your objectives and goals, but we are unable to help you at this time." In a country where four to five billion dollars are spent on the consumption of marijuana and the purchase of its accompanying paraphernalia, it is impossible to raise a few thousand dollars for a scientific assessment of this drug which is used by millions!

From France, luckily, I obtained a more positive response. The Ministry of Health, the French National Institute for Medical Research and the University of Reims agreed to contribute $12,000 to the local organizing committee of Professor Jardillier. The expenses of the participants would be covered while they were in Reims as well as all of the other costs of organizing the meeting. Even the United States government came through at the last minute with approval and funding of my conference grant application to the National Institute on Drug Abuse. This gave me about $8,000 to pay part of the organizing expenses and defray the travel costs of some of the 20 American lecturers.

The preliminary program changed and grew up to the final deadline when on a bright sunny day about 100 scientists

from fourteen different countries filed into the great auditorium of the University of Reims Medical School to begin
their two-day meeting. Many veteran marijuana researchers were in attendance: Agurell from Sweden; Mechoulam,
the discoverer of THC from Jerusalem; Zimmerman and Jacubovic from Canada; Kaymakcalan from Turkey; Waller, from
the University of Mississippi "Marijuana Farm"; Leo Hollister from California; and Monroe Wall from the Research
Triangle Institute in North Carolina. There were also
younger scientists in biochemistry, pharmacology and cell
biology eager to present their latest findings to the aging
experts.

The first session, even for biologists, was forbidding, dominated as it was by organic chemists. The projection screen
recorded a dazzling array of pictures of the many formulas of
the different cannabinoids—fifty-eight of them identified so
far. The expert "pharmacokineticists" described the complicated curves tracing the storage of the cannabinoids in the
body and their slow elimination over several days. These are
the scientists who specialize in the study of the absorption,
transformation and elimination of drugs, and more particularly for this conference, of cannabinoids from the
organism.

Dr. Edward Garrett, Graduate Professor of Chemistry at
the University of Florida at Gainesville, stated that in his
experiments with dogs it took thirty days for a single dose of
THC whether large or small, to be eliminated from the body.
After five days Garrett could detect that 40 percent of the
administered dose was still present in the organism, 20 percent as THC and 20 percent as "metabolites" (by-products).
He described how THC is transformed by the liver into other
compounds which are eliminated via the bile into the intestine and then reabsorbed into the "portal circulation",
that is the blood vessels which go back to the liver. This
process of "entero hepatic recirculation" contributes to the
lingering of THC by-products in the body. Since no THC is
eliminated by the kidney, it must be transformed by the liver
before being excreted. This explains, said Garrett, the great

difference between THC administered by mouth and by in-halation. In the former case, THC after absorption by the intestine passes through the liver where much is eliminated before it reaches the tissues where it is stored. When THC is smoked, it first goes into the tissues where more is stored because it has not yet entered the liver.

Garrett's experimental considerations were fully confir-med by Professor Agurell from Uppsala University in his work with human volunteers. During a period of several days, alternate doses of marijuana containing 20 milligrams of THC were given to the volunteers to either smoke or take by mouth. An examination of their blood levels after each type of administration showed that the concentration of the THC entering the body appears to be 10 to 20 times greater when smoked than when ingested. To translate this into practical terms, what has appeared to be abnormally high doses of marijuana used in animal experiments, in reality is similar to human consumption. When absorption in body fluids is compared, animals must be administered large doses of marijuana by mouth or by injection in order to end up with the same amount that might result when marijuana is *smoked* by an individual.

Other chemists have tried to come to terms with the pro-blem of identification and measurement of different canna-binoids in body fluids. This is not an easy task and one that requires the most complex and expensive equipment. Of all the cannabinoids, THC is the most elusive. Accurate measurement of marijuana in the blood stream has become a high priority because of the need to establish liability in the case of accidents, particularly automobile, that might have been caused by someone "high on pot".

Professor Marks from Birmingham, England reported at Reims that his group has developed an "immuno assay tech-nique" that makes it possible to measure the by-products of marijuana in blood and urine. Although this technique is not specific for THC alone, it can indicate whether or not a subject has used marijuana in the previous twenty-four hours. When this test was used in England to analyze the body fluids of drivers killed in motor accidents, 19 percent of the tests were positive – indicating the presence of marijuana. Unfortunately this screening test is not as simple as the "alcohol test", and it requires a specialized laboratory.

The chemists are still trying to discover a rapid method of determining whether or not THC is present among the other cannabinoids that can be detected. Picture the smoke from a marijuana cigarette: half of the cannabinoids (THC and non-active ones) are absorbed by the blood streams in the lungs. THC leaves the blood within minutes and is trapped by fatty tissues, is slowly released and partially eliminated only when it has been transformed into metabolites by the liver. One hour after smoking a joint, the blood contains a mixture of non-psychoactive by-products of marijuana, but very low levels of THC.

Dr. Wall offered an example of the problem of detection of THC in recalling the case of the Chicago motorman who was driving an elevated train that left the tracks, killing or injuring forty people. Wall had been called in to examine the blood and urine of the injured motorman; the tests were positive, but he was able to conclude only that "This man could have been sober or as high as a kite." Cannabinoids had been found in his body fluids, but hardly any evidence of THC.

Any scientist or legal expert who wants a fool-proof test faces a dilemma: A person detected to have a high level of cannabinoids in the hours following intoxication can be assumed to have consumed marijuana containing a good percentage of THC, but this cannot be *proved* scientifically, and there is always the possibility that the cigarette contained no THC!

After the "complicated chemists" the next session, "Biochemical and cellular effects" was familiar territory. This was the area in which I had specialized ever since our first observation that indicated that human lymphocytes did not divide properly when minute amounts of cannabinoids were added to cell cultures. With my associates Dr. Desoize, Dr. Banchereau and Dr. Leger I had attempted to pinpoint the mechanism of this effect. Our most recent work presented at Reims by Dr. Desoize showed that the cannabinoids act primarily on the membrane surrounding the cell, preventing the cells from picking up the building blocks essential for the proper formation of proteins and nucleic acids.

Proud as I was of our explanation, it was soon evident by the papers that followed, of Dr. Stein of the University of Florida and Dr. Carchman of the University of Virginia, that our research was incomplete. These two scientists arrived independently at similar conclusions. They did confirm that the cannabinoids prevent protein synthesis by their action on the cellular membrane, but they showed that in addition, these substances also alter the machinery of the cell in a more fundamental way by reacting with membranes inside the cell, including that of the nucleus.

Understanding the implications of this effect necessitates an explanation of the function of the cell membrane. This acts as a "selective barrier"—made of fat—that allows the desired protein or nucleic acid "building block" such as leucine, uridine and thymidine to pass through into the interior of the cell. Thus in our experiments, we found that fat soluble cannabinoids lodged in one part of the membrane prevented the transport of these building blocks into that area.

Stein and Carchman's studies elaborated on this concept because they were able to show a similar effect on membranes within the cell itself, that surround the cell organelles and most important the cell nucleus. The nucleus acts as a "command post" that sends messages to different parts of the cell telling them to perform certain functions. For example, telling the ribosomes to produce enzymes (or proteins). When cannabinoids lodge in the nuclear membrane, they cause its "messages" to become garbled. The ribosomes might be ordered to produce too much or too little of a particular enzyme, and this in turn will change the ability of the cell to perform certain functions. A fundamental principal of cell biology is that form and function are closely related—any change in structure, such as is caused by the cannabinoids, will alter function.

Dr. Stein in his reported experiments used biochemical techniques to *measure* the ability of the cell nucleus to perform certain functions. Dr. Carchman, on the other hand, through the use of the electron microscope was able to *see* changes in the nucleus. His evaluation of nuclei from cells treated with THC and cultivated *in vitro* showed that the THC produces a dramatic "condensation"—or compacting—of nuclear material. His observations were confirmed by Dr. Issidorides of the University of Athens who analyzed white blood cells from chronic hasish users and found the same abnormal condensation of the nucleus.

As one scientist after another presented his results, the detrimental effect of the cannabinoids on cellular function became more and more evident. Such fundamental observations, made in the test tube should alert biologists to the potential effects of marijuana products on the living organism. Unfortunately, many today discard all of these "*in vitro* experiments" as unrelated to what may happen in the human body. What they forget is that most of the major discoveries in medicine were initiated in the test tube: from Pasteur's observations of bacteria to Flemming's discovery of penicillin.

The presentations at Reims continued to provide confirmation of earlier studies in every area of marijuana research. This was true of the investigation of the effect of marijuana on cells that have the fastest rate of multiplication: those of the testis, the gland that produces millions of cells every day. Dr. Zimmerman from Toronto, experimenting with mice, injected them five days in a row with different cannabinoids: THC (the psychoactive compound) and CBN which is not psychoactive. After 35 days, animals treated with THC had a three-fold increase in abnormal forms of sperm and a five-fold increase in those treated with CBN. Five years earlier, I had reported at the US Senate hearings that CBN was from 3 to 5 times more toxic to cells than THC. At the Helsinki meeting, Dr. Bram from the Pasteur Institute reported that five times more THC than CBN is required to inhibit the division of cells. But again, all these early studies were in the test tube.

Further observations by Dr. Zimmerman indicated that mice treated with THC had abnormal chromosomes in the germ cells from which the spermatozoa is formed. This experiment raises a fundamental question which as yet remains unanswered: are cannabinoids "mutagenic"? Are they able, like X-rays, to change the character of a gene that will be perpetuated in subsequent divisions of the cell in which it occurs? Because of Zimmerman's observations, such a possibility cannot be discarded.

There is also a risk of an increased incidence of cancer cells in subjects who use marijuana regularly. Cecil Leuchtenberger of the Swiss Cancer Institute has hinted at this possibility in her observation of the malignant transformation of lung tissue by marijuana smoke. Another veteran cell biologist, Dr. Szepsenwol of Florida International University, reported a troublesome finding in his presentation at Reims. He observed that 4 out of 200 mice treated with weekly THC injections in the shoulder developed "fibrosarcomas" or cancer of the muscle, something that is a rare occurrence in mice. Control mice who received placebo "shots" were not affected. While these experiments were preliminary, they still represent one more potential danger of marijuana, especially when they are considered in the light of Zimmerman's observation. Szepsenwol also worked with female mice given 2–5 mg of THC once a week until maturity. Once mated, the mice had a high incidence of reproductive mortality—deaths of offspring were due to the inability of the mothers to lactate, an indication that THC decreases in mice the production of prolactin, a pituitary hormone that is essential for proper lactation. (A decrease in prolactin blood concentration was since reported by Dr. Kolodny, in young women smoking marijuana.)

Marijuana's profound effect on the cells of living animals was also evident in experiments on the lungs of rats exposed to marijuana smoke. At one time or another, everyone has heard stated by a friend "Why marijuana is less dangerous than tobacco", an affirmation repeated innumerable times by the media. Reports at the Reims symposium did not support such a claim, in fact, quite the opposite was true. Dr. Rosenkrantz of the Mason Research Institute in Massachusetts used a smoking machine (designed to deliver "puffs" of smoke of a given duration and frequency) to expose rats to daily doses of marijuana for a 3 to 12 month period. THC blood levels measured in the animals indicated that such exposure approximated those reached by a man smoking 1 to 6 "joints" a day. When the exposure time of the rats exceeded three months, lesions of the lung tissues began to appear. After one year of smoking, they were most striking, consisting of areas of chronic inflammation and tissue breakdown intermingled with healthy tissue. The presence of chloresterol in these lesions is indicative of tissue destruction. Some animals who were left to recover for thirty days without smoking before being sacrificed also had the same pulmonary lesions, showing that these lesions are not readily reversible. Exposure of the control animals to placebo or tobacco smoke for the same period did not produce similar lesions.

Dr. Gary Huber, chief of the pulmonary division at Harvard Medical School presented additional evidence proving the damaging effect of marijuana smoke on the lung. He used very sophisticated techniques to compare the effects of marijuana and tobacco smoke on the pulmonary defense system which protects the lung against bacteria and foreign particles. His conclusion: "It has been implied that marijuana may be considerably more toxic to the lung than tobacco. Our data would support that hypothesis."

These recent studies, documenting the damaging effect of marijuana on the lungs confirm earlier reports. The Leuchtenbergers for example, who found that marijuana smoke evokes in human lung cultures atypical growth and malignant transformation similar to that produced by tobacco cigarettes, "Marijuana smoke, however, produces more severe alterations in DNA and chromosomes of the lung cells." And Chari-Bitron who reported at the Helsinki conference that pulmonary macrophages are paralyzed and destroyed by minute amounts of THC. And Tennant five years earlier who found a damaging effect of hashish smoking on the structure and function of the lungs of American soldiers.

And at the University of California, studies by Dr. Tashkin show that "chronic marijuana smoking causes narrowing of both the large and smaller airways leading to 'airway obstruction'". His subjects were 17 hospitalized volunteers who smoked an average of 5 cigarettes of marijuana for 74 days. After 48 days, a series of pulmonary function tests revealed a 25–75 percent drop in normal readings.

On the East Coast, Dr. Mendelson of Harvard Medical School found similar abnormalities of pulmonary function in 15 out of 28 casual to heavy marijuana smokers studied over a period of 3–4 weeks of smoking in a hospital ward. He reports "Six marijuana smokers with significant impairment of vital capacity had no history of prior use of tobacco cigarettes. It is clearly necessary to conduct further extensive studies of the effects of long-term marijuana smoking on the lung because our preliminary data is highly suggestive of potentially deleterious effects. Failure to find abnormalities in routine chest X-rays or in clinical examinations to show evidence of pulmonary disease indicates that the changes produced by marijuana are insidious and not easily detected. If further studies confirm these findings, the population at risk should certainly be informed of this potential hazard!"

All of these positive findings presented at Reims and elsewhere call into question the *Jamaican Report*, so acclaimed by the media, which could not find any adverse effects on pulmonary function of 30 ganja users who had smoked for thirty years this cannabis preparation that is far more potent than marijuana. In reviewing the published data I noted that the comparison of controls and ganja smokers was presented in such a way that it could not be properly evaluated statistically.

Another study of chronic hashish users in Greece, by Fink and Stefanis, had also claimed not to find abnormal physical symptoms. But they had not performed any pulmonary function studies! Nonetheless, it is these two studies that are referred to in the press to bolster the thesis that even heavy marijuana smoking is less harmful than tobacco. Some reappraisal of this claim is now in order.

The session on the effects of marijuana on reproductive function highlighted the Reims meeting. It was chaired by a world recognized expert, Dr. Tuchman-Duplessis, Professor of Embryology at the University of Paris and by Dr. Monique Braude of NIDA, the coorganizer of the Symposium. In addition to Dr. Zimmerman, three other scientists: Professor Fujimoto of Albert Einstein College of Medicine, Professor Harclerode from Bucknell and Dr. Huang from Columbia University, reported an impairment of spermatogenesis in rats and mice treated with marijuana smoke, marijuana extract, of THC. By whatever method, after two or three months, a dose related atrophy of the testis, the seminal vessicles and the prostate occurred. Sperm count decreased and histological sectioning of the testis showed a dose related degeneration of the tubules where sperm cells are formed. Dr. Fujimoto, as had previous investigators before him, observed that all of these changes were reversible if the treatment with marijuana products was stopped after three months.

There was no common agreement concerning the mechanism by which marijuana impairs testicular function and sperm formation. For Harclerode, these changes are brought about by an action of the drug on the pituitary gland: he recorded a decrease in FSH and LH (pituitary hormones that control testicular function) during THC treatment. As a result there is a decrease in testosterone, which might account for the impairment of spermatogenesis. Because Dr. Huang did not observe changes in sexual hormones, he suggested that the decrease in spermatogenesis might be due to a direct action of the drug on the "germinal epithelium"—the layer of cells in the testis that produces sperm.

Studies on man reported by Dr. Hembree confirmed the observations made over the past three years which were first reported at Helsinki. Sixteen subjects had been studied following the protocol previously described. After a period of one month, studies of the subjects' semen samples showed decreased spermatogenesis, decreased sperm motility and increased number of abnormal forms of sperm. But, all these changes occurred without any measurable change in pituitary hormone or testosterone, indicating that marijuana has a possible direct effect on the testis. Dr. Wall, who gave injected doses of THC to his volunteer subjects, reported finding a transient decrease in testosterone measured within the six hours *following* injection. In the Columbia studies, testosterone was measured in the morning before the subjects began smoking. This was because, under the influence of marijuana there is an increase in pain sensation and we wanted to spare our subjects the extra discomfort of a venous puncture once they began smoking. This way, we might have missed the changes in testosterone observed by others who measured it after administering THC.

It was evident from the Reims reports that more research is required to clarify the exact mechanism of the action of marijuana on testicular function. The drug might act by two mechanisms: first, THC through its immediate action on the old brain and the pituitary could cause a decrease in the "gonadotropins", FSH and LH which would cause a fall in testosterone; second, the many metabolites of THC and other cannabinoids as they accumulate in tissues would directly impair cellular division of the sperm cells.

But women are not immune from the effects of marijuana— female sexual function is equally disturbed by the drug and through very similar mechanisms as in the male. Dr. Fujimoto reported that female rats exposed to injections of THC or marijuana extract for three months showed a dose related decrease in ovarian and uterine weight, which is reversible when treatment is stopped. Reversibility has not been tested for longer periods of exposure, however.

The short term effects of THC on reproductive function of primates were illustrated by Dr. Carol Smith, a lovely young lady from the Uniformed Services Medical School in Bethesda, Maryland. Doses in these experiments could be compared with those used by the occasional smoker (one or two "joints" a week). Dr. Smith directs a group of doctors who are studying hormonal control of the menstrual cycle.

The rhesus monkey is the experimental animal of choice

because, like humans, the female of the species has a 28 day menstrual cycle. Furthermore, when studying the effect of marijuana, monkeys have to be used instead of female human volunteers because until recently the Food and Drug Administration has not allowed controlled studies using women as subjects.

Dr. Smith reported that a single injection of THC roughly equivalent to a marijuana cigarette containing 10 mg THC will lower for several hours two of the basic hormones, FSH and LH which control the function of the ovary. In another study, Dr. Smith administered daily doses of THC to the primates at the beginning of their menstrual cycle for a period of twelve days. As a result, there was no ovulation at the end of this cycle. All control animals who received an injection without THC did ovulate. Dr. Smith also showed that the effect of THC on female reproductive function is not exerted in the same way as contraceptive estrogen pills, because it does not attach to "receptors" in the uterus. Marijuana cannot, therefore, be considered to be a dependable substitute for "the pill".

Never had such fundamental implications been so clearly demonstrated: when THC reaches infinitesimal concentrations in the old brain (a billionth of a gram) it will disrupt the basic hormonal mechanisms that regulate female reproductive function. These mechanisms are located in the pituitary – the master endocrine gland which secretes the hormones FSH and LH that regulate the production of estrogens secreted by the ovary. It is well established that the release of FSH and LH by the pituitary is controlled by "polypeptides" or chemical messengers produced by the "hypothalamus" portion of the old brain. The effects of marijuana on the primitive brain and how such effects can influence man's emotional behavior have been discussed in a previous chapter. Now Dr. Smith was illustrating how this "tinkering with the old brain" also disrupts female endocrine function which controls reproduction! She expressed her "extreme concern about the effects of this drug on the developing reproductive system of female teenagers. This phase of development is particularly vulnerable to disruption by drugs. It might take as little as 2 joints a day to inhibit sex hormones." (This prediction was confirmed a few months later by Kolodny who reputed the interference of marijuana with menstrual cycle in women.)

Dr. Ethel Sassenrath of the University of California also studied the effects of marijuana on rhesus monkeys. She fed a group of 19 a daily chocolate cookie laced with 2.4 to 4.8 mg/kg of THC for a period of five years. This experiment resulted in a five-fold increase in reproductive failure in the treated females (42 percent failure versus 8 percent in the control group). Losses occurred throughout pregnancy and parturition: abortions, fetal death, still birth and neonatal deaths. When male monkeys fed THC were mated with undrugged females, there was no such significant increase in reproductive failure.

Those infants of THC treated females that survived appeared normal. However, male offspring were significantly smaller than the controls and their behavior suggestive of hyperactivity and increased responsiveness to environmental stimuli such as sound and light. Sassenrath concludes, "The patterns of reproductive failure in female primates treated with THC indicates that this drug is toxic to the embryo and fetus. This toxicity, however, is not characterized by any highly *specific* birth defect such as a stunting of limb as was the case with thalidomide."

Sassenrath's observations on monkeys agree with those of Dr. Rosenkrantz's on rodents. This embryo toxicity could be caused by impairment of the "maternal support system", the supply of blood and nourishment from mother to offspring through placental circulation. In conclusion of the session, Professor Tuchmann Duplessis said, "Experimental investigations as well as clinical observations demonstrate the harmful effect of cannabis on the testis, the ovary and the 'hypothalamic-pituitary axis' (the part of the brain which controls endocrine function). Considered by some as a 'soft' drug, if not innocuous, cannabis is undoubtedly harmful to man."

By the last session of the Symposium chaired by the veteran researcher Leo Hollister of California, most of the scientists were close to mental exhaustion. And yet this final session, dealing with the effects of marijuana on the brain, deserved their undivided attention. Because of the limits of time, some papers could not be presented. The two first communications, by Professor McGeer of Vancouver and Dr. Luthra from Washington, D.C., described the biochemical changes in the brains of new-born rodents whose mothers had been treated with delta-9-THC. The most striking alteration was a decrease in nucleic acid and protein concentration. McGeer showed that these biochemical changes were associated with morphological—structural—changes in the brain of the offspring. The changes were located in the "ribosomes", those parts of the cell where proteins and RNA are manufactured. Dr. Luthra concluded his paper by stating, "This effect of delta-9-THC on the neonate macromolecules could be a determinant factor in producing behavioral aberrations in the developing organism."

Several investigators discussed the effects of marijuana on the limbic system of the old brain, describing how it altered the responses of the deep-seated structures that control emotional life, endocrine function, and memory storage. The specific alteration by marijuana of the "septal area", where the reward center of the brain is located, was described by Dr. Pradhan of Howard University in Washington, D.C. He studied rats fitted with metal rods inserted into the septal area of the "old brain". They were then easily taught to self-stimulate their brains by pushing a lever that sent an electric current into the "pleasure center". This behavior soon took precedence over all other, that is until the rats are fed THC. Dr. Pradhan observed that THC, like morphine, decreases the need for self stimulation behavior—the drug gave them the pleasure they sought, and they were less likely to press the lever. After repeated administration of the drug, however, tolerance developed—the animals no longer received the same pleasurable reward and went back to pushing the lever!

In order to place in perspective the effects of marijuana on the reward center of the brain, the two poles of human satisfaction must be understood. Brain reward, or self-satisfaction can be associated with a sequence of events that increase drive and act as an incentive, or, on the other hand to a sequence of events that reduce drive and act as a "satisfier". Thus reward may be triggered either by "drive induction" or "drive reduction". Cocaine and amphetamines reward the brain in the former manner, whereas marijuana rewards in the latter. This also explains why the real drug "connaisseur" goes from one type of drug to another according to his mood.

A challenge to the belief of many psychologists that the mind expanding property of cannabis, even when frequently experienced, will not be associated with long lasting structural alterations of the brain was presented at Reims by Professor Heath of Tulane. He is a pioneer in brain research who for the past thirty years has studied the function and structure of the limbic area in man and primates. His latest findings corroborated earlier observations: that marijuana smoke, in amounts reached in human consumption, causes structural alterations in the limbic area of the brains of primates where Heath had previously recorded persistent abnormal brain wave patterns. These cellular brain alterations, clearly identifiable under the electron microscope include: (1) widening of the synaptic cleft, (2) abnormal deposits of dense material in the synaptic cleft, (3) clumping of synaptic vesicles—an early sign of nerve degeneration, (4) fragmentation and disorientation of the rough endoplasmic reticulum structure within the cell which is involved with protein synthesis, (5) in the nucleus of the cell a significant increase in "inclusion bodies", structures not normally present. According to Heath, all these changes occur at the sites of the brain where activity is correlated with emotion and behavior.

Changes in the brain are not readily reversible: they can be seen five to six months after cessation of the animals' exposure to marijuana smoke (which had been for a period of three to six months). Because in the past critics have said that the doses of marijuana used in Heath's experiments were abnormally high, he also showed incontrovertible evidence that the dose of marijuana given to the experimental animals was similar to that reached in human consumption—he compared blood levels of the animals and of humans after one dose and one joint respectively, and found the amount of cannabinoids to be the same.

Impairment of brain function in the rat after being fed THC or ethanol for six months was next reported by Dr. Kalant of the University of Toronto. One month after the end of treatment, both groups displayed a significant impairment of learning a specific motor skill as well as abnormal brain wave patterns in the hippocampus, a structure in the old brain. Such abnormalities were similar and in the same location as those observed by Heath in monkeys. When tested one or two months after the end of drug treatment, the rats treated with marijuana or alcohol also displayed an aggressive behavior toward mice, assaulting and killing them.

Dr. Chapman, Chairman of the Department of Behavioral Biology at the University of California and colleague of Dr. Sassenrath reported abnormal individual and group behavior of rhesus monkeys. They had studied the behavior of monkeys fed THC over several years (the impairment of reproductive function in these animals that they discovered was an unexpected "spin-off" of a behavioral experiment). After an initial period of withdrawal and indifference, the drugged animals displayed increased irritability and aggressiveness, especially marked in monkeys exposed to social stress. Unable to adapt or cope, they hit, bit and chased the other monkeys. Some became so fierce that they killed other more placid cagemates, an unusual occurrence in a colony of "normal monkeys". "This type of behavior", concluded Chapman, "lends credence to the concept of direct neuropharmacological effect of THC on the brain centers controlling behavior." Dr. Sassenrath added that video tape studies of the female monkeys treated with THC showed that they were very indifferent to their offspring—grooming, hugging or playing with their infants much less.

Will these facts constitute enough of a warning to all the young women who are smoking marijuana today, or shall we have to wait until the abnormalities observed in the THC-fed monkeys of Chapman and Sassenrath are documented in females and offspring of the human species?

One paper did carry a ray of hope for a useful application of a substance derived from marijuana. Dr. Ralph Karler, a neurophysiologist from the University of Utah Medical School, reported that cannabidiol (CBD), a non-psychoactive cannabinoid, had proved to be a potent anticonvulsant agent, as effective in animal preparations as drugs commonly used for epilepsy. Doses administered were rather high, 100 mg/kg, and on a prolonged usage would be associated with the impairment of cell division in the sex organs. However, when one is treating a disease with potent medications to alleviate life-threatening conditions, side effects may have to be accepted. Mechoulam reported that three out of four patients treated with daily doses of 300–400 mg of CBD during three weeks had been relieved from their epileptic seizures.

By contrast, THC in the same proportions used by Karler did trigger certain forms of epileptic tracings. And he pointed out that it was "street knowledge to avoid smoking marijuana if one is epileptic", a statement seconded by Dr. Fehne from Albuquerque, New Mexico who reported similar studies.

The media, while ignoring the reports of the damaging effects of "pot", have dramatized the potential therapeutic applications of the weed. Marijuana extracts were indeed used in the prescientific era for a wide range of ailments ... from tetanus to menstrual cramps. However, when modern pharmacology developed specific medications for specific ailments cannabis preparations were no longer prescribed. More recently marijuana and THC have been advocated for the treatment of high pressure in the eyeball (glaucoma) and for the relief of nausea in cancer patients being treated with chemical substances which, while destroying the tumor, induce vomiting. But for such specific applications THC has to be proven more effective than currently used drugs: the phenothiazines for nausea, pilocarpine and beta blockers for glaucoma. Furthermore, in line with modern pharmacology, organic chemists have been able to modify the chemical structure of THC so as to increase the therapeutic action of the drug and eliminate its mind-altering side effects. This method has resulted in the synthesis of a new compound "nabilone" which is being tested according to the scientific standards of the Food and Drug Administration. On a dose basis in the preliminary trials Nabilone has proven to be more effective than THC in lowering intra-occular pressure and relieving nausea without producing the side effects of THC. It seems, therefore, that modern pharmacology has not found a use for THC which could not be more effectively produced by other drugs ... including the new synthetic cannibinoid, Nabilone.

After all the reports were in, the Reims Symposium, unlike that of Helsinki, received better treatment from the press. In France all major newspapers reported the main findings—*Le Monde* stated that the scientists assembled at Reims had delivered a "severe indictment" against cannabis. This was tempered somewhat by the medical editor of the same paper in order to placate the growing numbers of intellectuals in Paris who were starting to smoke pot. He took the organizers of the meeting to task for not having stressed the dangers of tobacco smoking and of alcohol!

In the United States, the *New York Times*, as well as other publications which had been informed about the Reims meeting, remained silent.

But a few days after the meeting, the *Washington Post* published a full page article in its Sunday editorial section entitled, "The Case against Marijuana". Written by Peggy Mann, a seasoned author and journalist, the article was a straight forward account of the proceedings of the Reims conference. It was also syndicated in other newspapers across the country.

The message was clear, and it was coming primarily from America where most of the current marijuana research had been performed. The country which had introduced the Western World to the "innocuous delight" of the ancient marijuana habit, was now in its own laboratories accumulating compelling scientific facts which proved that there are grave dangers associated with the use of this drug. But were the facts coming too late? Would the knowledge of the harmful effects of marijuana be powerful enough to offset the urge of the "old brain" to continue its insatiable quest for pleasure, so easily satisfied by puffing on the weed? I had my doubts. And these doubts were sustained by three articles that appeared in the same issue of the *Washington Post* describing the drug scene in America.

The first was entitled, "Drug Use on the Increase, Millions Ignore Doctors Warnings". It stated in its opening sentence "many young Americans (12 million between the ages of 12 and 15) live, work or play beneath a mushrooming cloud of marijuana smoke. Almost one out of five Americans say they've tried it: about one out of 14 regularly smokes it." The increased use of cocaine was also noted, and the expert opinion of Dr. Lester Grinspoon was quoted, "Cocaine was adopted as the champagne of illicit drugs."

The second article was devoted to the Drug Set and headlined, "Drug Culture Members Find They're in the Seat of Power". It described the routine use of cocaine and marijuana among the younger generation of Washington D.C. lawyers, administrative experts, business men and consultants. Some who were interviewed reported how they had contracted the habit of "better living through chemistry" in college and had to keep using their favorite chemical in their Washington professional career. One member of this new swinging crowd was the Drug Administration advisor to President Carter, Dr. Peter Bourne whose dismissal (at about the same time as the Reims Symposium) had become the talk of the town. He had withheld the real name of a patient—a secretary in his office—on a prescription for the narcotic qualude, a widely abused drug. A member of the press also revealed that the President's drug advisor had been seen sniffing cocaine in their presence at the most recent party given by NORML.

After being fired, Bourne, in his parting remarks, denied any wrong doing and claimed that many other staffers in the White House used "recreational" drugs—as if it were the most innocuous pastime. The first public acknowledgement of widespread use of drugs in official Washington came from the "horse's mouth." President Carter reacted sharply and informed his staff "You will obey the law or seek employment elsewhere."

The third article of the *Post* summarized the situation with the headline: "Revolution: Drugs' Acceptance Rises and Spreads," and went on to say, "Only one percent of the people now cite drug abuse as a major national problem. The drug revolution clearly has come of age, accepted as a matter of course everywhere in the country. Usage of some kind of illegal drug has become part of our culture."

"Prohibition was doomed when the trend-setters, the 'élites' if you will, the lawyers, judges, editors, writers, public officials and other professionals ignored the law. Something of the same has been happening today with illegal drugs, particularly the use of marijuana and, now, cocaine. . . . There is the implicit message, like it or not, coming out of that swish cocaine party for public officials, journalists and others in this self-important capital city: that younger group, the sub-culture of a culture, will soon be moving into leadership positions in America."

If this was so, my feeling was that such a leadership would be short-lived, or else the nation would be faced in the years ahead with a major public health problem.

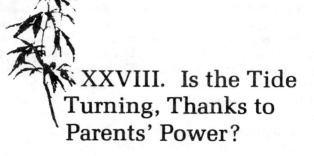

XXVIII. Is the Tide Turning, Thanks to Parents' Power?

As scientists pursued experimental and clinical studies to learn more about the damaging biological effects of marijuana, or argued over the significance of such studies, a more powerful movement was at work in America to counter the drug culture in general, and marijuana in particular: the parents' movement. For years, nearly daily, I had received letters or phone calls from distraught parents. They bore the same message: "My child smokes pot regularly, we see that it is harming him, but he does not want to stop, claiming that it is not harmful. What can we do?" But what could I answer, except to give these mothers or fathers or grandparents words of encouragement and hope, which sounded quite bland and of little practical help. In the past year, however, things have changed, and I can tell my callers with a confident voice, "Get in touch and work with your local Parents' Movement for Drug Free Youth!"

The movement began in 1976 in Atlanta when a group of parents attending a backyard birthday party made a shocking discovery: their children—sixth through eighth grade—were smoking marijuana regularly and drinking occasionally.

After going through the painful process of denial, guilt,

and accusation, the parents decided to join together in an effort to understand why their children were routinely "getting high", what consequences this practice might have, and finally, what they as parents should do about it.

In their primary investigation, the parents learned several lessons:

—First, the illegal use of drugs, especially marijuana and alcohol, had become accepted, expected, and "normal" behavior for a majority of adolescents in their community.

—Second, youngsters fervently believed in the myth of "harmless marijuana." They went further and viewed the herb as a wonder drug for curing cancer, preventing nearsightedness, and clearing tobacco smoke from the lungs.

—Third, children had absorbed from the prevailing culture much superficial rhetoric concerning their "rights" to make their own decisions about everything from illegal drug use to choice of school curriculum.

—Finally, young people chorused that "everybody smokes pot," that drugs are everywhere, and that "partying" is synonymous with "getting high."

The need to counter powerful peer and cultural forces was obvious if parents hoped to regain drug-free children and prevent more children from becoming involved with drugs.

Despite the consensus prevailing in 1976 among drug counselors, psychiatrists, and the media that marijuana was a relatively benign substance and that parents should not "hassle" their youngsters for using it, the Atlanta parents trusted their own instincts that their children were gradually deteriorating in personality, intellectual functioning, and physical health because of pot-smoking.

Rejecting outdated drug pamphlets then available (and which described marijuana as less harmful than alcohol and tobacco), the parents went to medical libraries to seek out the latest scientific research on marijuana and prepared their own informational materials. *Keep Off the Grass* became recommended reading!

Within their families they decided to take a strict antidrug position based on the argument that marijuana is a health hazard and that parents have the right and the responsibility to protect their children's health.

The parents then devised a common behavioral code for age-appropriate privileges to include limits and responsibilities for children of junior high age. Making a mutual commitment to keep in touch, share information, and back one another, the parents implemented their plan to counter drug-oriented adolescent peer pressure with stronger and better-informed parental peer pressure.

Much to everyone's surprise, it worked! The task was not easy; more often it was tedious, frightening, and "embarrassing" (the universal reaction of the young people). But within six months the parents knew they were once again raising drug free children—truly "normal" in their high spirits, open communication, and eager participation in family and school activities.

But the parents also knew that many other parents would soon be learning the hard way about widespread adolescent drug use if they, newly educated "do-it-yourself" drug experts, just sat back and did not share their hard-won knowledge. So the original parent group turned to local parent-teacher organizations and religious institutions for help with meetings to create widespread parent awareness.

While they slowly made progress combatting the use of marijuana at the local level, the parents became increasingly concerned about the apparent apathy and ignorance at governmental levels. Thus, in March 1977, one member of the group, Dr. Marsha Manatt, wrote to Dr. Robert Dupont, then Director of the National Institute on Drug Abuse (NIDA), to express the parents' concerns about the confusing messages coming to young people from the legislative hearings on marijuana decriminalization. Dr. Manatt pointed out that the hearings did not consider the adolescent's particular vulnerability to any kind of psychoactive drug use.

Proving that even in the federal bureaucracy a concerned professional can respond quickly, Dr. Dupont soon visited the children and their parents in Atlanta. He became excited about what he saw—the pragmatic effectiveness of a "parent peer group" in reversing negative peer pressure on adolescents. He commissioned Dr. Manatt to write about the Atlanta story, including the important new medical findings, so that other parents could be helped to form their own groups (the resulting booklet, "Parents, Peers, and Pot"—published by NIDA in 1979—has been requested by more than 700,000 parents!).

Dr. Dupont also instructed Tom Adams of NIDA's Pyramid Prevention Project, to lend technical and travel assistance in order to send effective parent group leaders to more communities.

Hoping to expand the project, Adams in turn put Marsha Manatt in touch with Dr. Thomas Gleaton, a professor of health education at Georgia State University in Atlanta. Despite ten years of teaching drug education courses in the schools, Gleaton had been frustrated by the acceleration of drug use. He also sponsored an annual Southeast Drug Conference to help professionals and teachers deal with drug abuse, and after hearing about the effectiveness of the Atlanta parents' group (and trying out their program in Dublin, Georgia), decided to target the spring 1978 conference toward parents. He recognized that alerted, informed parents had been the missing ingredient in previous drug prevention efforts.

At a seminar entitled "The Family Versus the Drug Culture," many more Georgia parents learned about the latest research on marijuana and other drugs, about the changing cultural trends that influenced their children, and about the effective steps two parent groups were taking to counter the drug culture.

Just how powerful and commercialized that drug culture had become was vividly demonstrated at the conference by an exhibit of "kiddie drug paraphernalia" gathered by a new community action group, DeKalb Families in Action, organized in November, 1977 to deal with the sudden appearance of drug toys and comic books in neighborhood head shops and malls.

Working with their elected officials and PTA leaders, the DeKalb group introduced legislation in Georgia to ban the sale of drug paraphernalia, and they mounted community awareness programs about the commercialized drug culture that glamorized drugs to children. The continuing efforts of president Sue Rusche and other members have encouraged similar legislative efforts in many states.

One group of five parents who had attended the 1978 conference went back to their PTA and initiated a summer-long project of drug education seminars for the parents of Northside High School (a large, urban school with a 50:50 black-white mixture and a wide range of family incomes). Under the leadership of Judy Kiely and Rosellen Amisano, they developed small clusters of parent peer groups, based on teenagers' friendship circles, within a broader framework of parent education. Their community action group, "Unified Parents", issued a set of suggested social guidelines—concerning parties, curfews, chaperoning, and rules on alcohol and drugs—that were received enthusiastically by parents.

The group also solicited the involvement of local physicians, juvenile court judges, and police officers in developing strict, but constructive, ways of dealing with juvenile drug and alcohol offenses.

The unprecedented series of parent-sponsored seminars convinced Northside principal Bill Rudolph that with a strong parental support organization he could take the difficult and initially painful steps necessary to tighten school discipline and raise educational standards at the school.

By working closely together and maintaining a non-judgemental attitude, Principal Rudolph and "Unified Parents" can point proudly to a complete turnaround in attitudes and behavior. Within three years there has been a dramatic reduction in drug and alcohol use, and along with the reduction, a dramatic rise in SAT scores, math and reading skills, enrollment in advanced science and foreign language courses, and participation in athletic and extracurricular activities.

Northside High School, once called "Fantasy Island" by its critics, is an all-American "normal" school again—filled with a majority of drug-free teenagers who try to make the most of the opportunities a good public school can offer. Most importantly, the students are again proud of themselves and their school.

When parents in Naples, Florida heard of the parent groups forming in Atlanta, they decided to mount a communitywide parent education project in the summer of 1978. They utilized important new articles on marijuana research written by Bruce Frazer for *Patient Care* magazine and by Peggy Mann for the *Washington Post*. "Naples Informed Parents" (NIP) continues to prove that parent power can indeed nip the marijuana epidemic in the bud by urging parents to become informed and contact the parents of their children's friends.

Bruce Frazer became executive director of "Citizens for Informed Choices on Marijuana," a Connecticut-based organization that publishes pamphlets on marijuana research and on parent peer groups.

Peggy Mann, a concerned mother and a tireless writer, went on to publish a steady stream of excellent articles on marijuana and the parents' movement, including a series for *Reader's Digest* that provoked an unprecedented 3,500,000 requests for reprints.

By the fall of 1978 the media began to pay attention to the marijuana problem. NBC consulted with concerned scientists and with parents in Georgia, Florida and Ohio (including a pediatrician, Ingrid Lantner and a schoolmaster, Richard Hawley, from Cleveland) and produced an excellent documentary, "Reading, Writing, and Reefers," which alerted a mass audience to the health hazards of marijuana and the epidemic nature of its use among young children.

Meanwhile, in Atlanta, as requests for drug information poured in from parents all over the country, Dr. Gleaton opened the PRIDE (Parent Resources and Information for Drug Education) office at Georgia State University to serve as a resource center and net-working mechanism for parents.

The March, 1979 PRIDE conference was entitled "Parents, Peers, and Pot." I, along with other scientists, policymakers, physicians, and educators, was invited to exchange ideas, goals, and action plans with parents from many states.

The parents' movement had mushroomed into a powerful national force, backed enthusiastically by Lee Dogoloff, White House advisor on drug abuse policy; Peter Bensinger, director of the Drug Enforcement Administration; the House Select Committee on Narcotics Abuse; and top NIDA officials. By the April 1980 PRIDE conference, there were more than 300 known parent groups. Dr. Gleaton then initiated the formation of the "National Federation of Parents for Drug Free Youth." With the strong leadership of president Bill Barton, a founder of Naples Informed Parents, and the financial support of a Texas foundation, the National Federation now speaks for nearly 700 parent groups as it calls for a stronger national policy on drug trafficking and for all-out commitment by American parents to reduce adolescent drug use. I was asked to become the chairman of the scientific committee of the Federation.

To make sure the parents' message gets to state and federal legislators, Otto and Connie Moulton, a magnificent husband and wife team from Danvers, Massachusetts, founded the Committees of Correspondence, which urges citizens to write to their elected officials about critical issues involving drug abuse. Their motto is, "Write Makes Might!"

How far the parents' movement has progressed from that summer night of shocked discovery in 1976 was demonstrated at the April, 1981 PRIDE conference entitled, 'The National Parents' Movement for Drug-Free Youth." Representatives from hundreds of parents' groups from 34 states and two foreign countries (Sweden and England) assembled in Atlanta. I shared the podium with Dr. Robert Dupont, now president of the American Council on Marijuana; H. Ross Perot, the Dallas businessman who heads the Texans' War on Drugs Committee; Robert Heath, Carlton Turner and Peggy Mann.

Parents heard from the nation's top drug policymakers

about the critical need for stronger antidrug legislation and international action. They visited workshops given by other parents who had become "do-it-yourself" drug experts in order to protect the youngsters in their neighborhoods.

The principal message was that ordinary parents working in their homes, neighborhoods, and schools are the key to the national antidrug effort. When one mother calls the parents of her child's best friend, when six parents get together, when two hundred parents gather at a PTA meeting—when they make a mutual commitment to help one another raise drug-free children—then positive parent power can indeed overcome negative peer power and destructive drug power. By rebuilding networks of neighbors to act as extended families to provide consistent protection, guidance, and affection from home to home, parents can prove that they are not helpless in the face of the biggest drug epidemic in history. By showing the courage and commitment to act as strong parents, they can also provide a healthy model for adolescents to emulate.

Already there was no more talk of decriminalization, and still less of legalization. The pro-pot advocates of NORML were less vocal. But the battle was far from won. Marijuana was still widely used by 40 million Americans. In the country 60 tons were consumed daily, creating an illegal trade of 25 billion dollars a year. Cannabis had become a major cash crop in Colombia, Jamaica, and California, evaluated in billions of dollars. So there were many reasons for parents and their allies to stand steadfast.

I was convinced that only a grassroots parents' movement had the power to stop the marijuana roller coaster in the United States. The scientists may provide sound arguments for keeping away from pot, but this is not enough. Only parents can create and maintain a challenging and warm milieu in which their children may grow up drug-free. A united parents' group may also influence legislators and create with them a national sense of purpose which has always been part of the American dream.

This sense of purpose was evident at the First National Convention of the National Federation of Parents for a Drug Free Youth which I attended in October, 1982. The motto of the meeting: "Drugs and Youth: an American Crisis" inscribed under a frayed American flag was most appropriate. Over 500 parents from nearly every state of the union assembled in Washington, and crowded workshops, plenary sessions, and seminars under the vigilant leadership of Bill Barton, Mary Jacobson and Gill Gerstenfeld. The presence of First Lady Nancy Reagan highlighted the meeting. Nancy, as many parents addressed her with affectionate respect, has devoted most of her time to helping parents and families concerned with drug abuse since moving to the White House.

A most sensitive, soft-spoken person, she stressed at the convention the importance of proper parenting in the home and drug-abuse prevention education in the schools. Before the press corps and the TV cameras she delivered the basic message of the parents' movement for every home in the country to hear. Her warning was clear: "Drug abuse is tearing our children and our families apart. Unless we act now, we may lose our whole next generation to drugs."

Dr. Carlton Turner echoed Nancy Reagan's words. As senior policy advisor to President Reagan on drug abuse prevention, Dr. Turner coordinates the administration's top priority efforts in the field. Dr. Turner is a dynamic young chemist who has isolated and measured many of the different chemicals contained in marijuana. He has served as director of the University of Mississippi marijuana project where the marijuana used for scientific and medical purposes is grown, and was one of the first scientists to warn against the potential damaging effect of this plant.

In a forceful and articulate address, Dr. Turner reviewed the measures taken by the administration in the area of law enforcement, namely, legislation to allow military intelligence to aid civilian authorities in signalling incoming aircrafts or ships and enactment of programs in the United States to eradicate marijuana cultivation by spraying herbicide as well as initiation of legislation aimed at seizing assets of traffickers, thereby attacking them where it hurts the most—their pocketbooks. According to Dr. Turner, thanks to the support from a solid group of parents striving to decrease the demand for drugs in their families and communities, the administration could now undertake these measures aimed at curtailing drug supplies.

Dr. Harold Voth, a leading psychiatrist from the Menninger Clinic and a Rear Admiral in the U.S. Navy who formulated an effective prevention and rehabilitation program to curtail drug use in the Navy, also spoke at the conference. In a calm, compassionate voice, Dr. Voth described the steps for a parent to take should he find his child using drugs. The infinite patience, affection and firmness required in such instances are qualities most often found in the family milieu.

When my turn to speak came, I discussed the historical aspects of drug abuse, summarizing the conclusions of my latest writing effort, "The Escape of the Genie", a history of hashish use throughout the ages. My slide map of the world was flashed on the screen to illustrate the spread of marijuana use to the four corners of the world over the past millenia. Only in the last years of that time span did the drug catch up with the Western World, and more particularly the United States, in a major way. The only countries which have rejected the use of cannabis are the U.S.S.R. and its satellites for ideological imperatives, and China and Japan for cultural reasons. Those countries which have used hashish the longest—India, Pakistan, Afghanistan, Iran, and the Islamic nations—are underdeveloped and in the throes of political instability. Historically, widespread use of hashish can be said to be associated with national decline and fragmentation.

The damage caused by marijuana will be reflected first in its detrimental effect on society. Only later will such damage manifest itself in physical disabilities in the individual. Moreover, an assessment of social damage is out of the scientist's realm, and no "biological markers" (measurements in body fluids) exist for analysing the disruptive effect of marijuana on individual and social behavior. So by asking physicians and scientists for a ruling on the health hazards of marijuana, is not our society shirking its responsibility to set standards for responsible behavior?

Today, the United States is the greatest consumer of marijuana in the world. Can we turn the tide, as the Chinese did in their campaign against opium at the turn of the century? Then, China was in the throes of an unprecedented opium-smoking epidemic. Two wars waged by the British, whose trade depended on exchanging Indian-grown opium for tea and silk, forced the drug on the Chinese. By the end of the 19th century there were tens of millions of addicts on every level of Chinese society, and the country was threatened with fragmentation. But this dismantling did not occur thanks to a national revival program stressing the traditional Chinese values. The program's first objective was to stem opium addiction, a goal achieved with the help of President Theodore Roosevelt, who was instrumental in stopping the Indian opium trade.

What China did to stop opium addiction, the United States can do in the case of marijuana. Such a policy would be in keeping with the liberal reform movement begun at the turn of the century, led by Theodore Roosevelt. This movement, dedicated to the protection of the individual against private interests, initiated national and international drug legislation that still prevails today. This legislation is based on the premise that addictive drugs with high abuse potential must be strictly controlled and used only for scientific or medical purposes. To this premise, as American as apple pie, the Parents' Movement is dedicated.

I was followed on the podium by Dr. Hans Hartelius from Sweden. Hartelius is one of the leading Swedish psychiatrists who has spent a lifetime studying the effects of alcohol and drug abuse on the Swedish population. The Swedes, more than any other people in the world, are followed by medical professionals from cradle to grave through a most elaborate system of social security which maintains a health record of every citizen.

Drug abuse in Sweden, said Hartelius, constitutes a major threat to the health, maturation, and social adjustment of young people. The epidemic of drug abuse began after World War II and reached alarming proportions in the early seventies as a result of a permissive attitude of government and of certain physicians who were allowed to prescribe drugs of abuse (amphetamines, opiates) to drug addicts. It was also a time when those who advocated the "decriminalization" of marijuana, then being used on an ever increasing scale, were most vocal. This "permissive" drug policy in Sweden was associated with a major increase in mortality resulting from alcohol and drug abuse, especially among the young: the abuse of cannabis was associated with the occurrence of acute and chronic mental illness, such as cannabis "psychoses." Lack of motivation, poor academic performance, memory deficiencies were also reported among school children and young people smoking hashish. The spread of the drug abuse epidemic in Sweden was carefully monitored by Professor N. Bejerot, of the famed Karolinska Institute.

Finally in 1975, the Swedish government decided to end their permissive and most expensive experiment in drug abuse and reverted to a strict drug control policy based on prevention through education about the dangers of drug abuse (which in Sweden is defined as the non-medical use of legally controlled substances). In addition, drug enforcement efforts were increased and drug addicts were committed to rehabilitation centers. The Swedish government also in 1976 declared that it would oppose any suggestion aimed at decriminalizing or legalizing the private possession of marijuana.

In summary, in Sweden, after a most harrowing experience, there is today a broad political consensus that drug abuse is to be eliminated, and that only a very strict drug abuse control policy will be able to roll back the drug epidemic.

Hartelius ended his speech with a note which went to the heart of those in attendence, "Keeping its population, and in particular its young generations, healthy and drug free is one of the best investments a nation can make for its own future."

At the conference banquet, the Surgeon General, C. Everett Koop spoke. He reiterated his warning about the harmful effects of marijuana and emphasized that the prevention efforts of the Parents' Movement had the full support of the United States Public Health Service.

Their resolve reaffirmed, the parents spent an afternoon on Capitol Hill, visiting their senators, congressmen and legislative assistants. Now that Congress is aware of parent power, it will be more likely to enact the legislation required to roll back the tide of drug abuse.

When the three-day conference was over and the parents went home to their families and jobs, they were weary but pleased.

However, such a grassroots movements of parents, to have long-lasting effects, must create a national consensus on the social refusal of marijuana and other addictive drugs. Early in the 1990's this consensus was far from established. A strong movement for relegalization of all addictive drugs, including cocaine and heroin, flourished. The Drug Policy Foundation, based in Washington, led by Kevin Zeese and Lester Grinspoon of NORML and lawyers, judges, police officers and professors from the United States and abroad, initiated a campaign against drug prohibition. Widely publicized, it bred debates country-wide. The relegalizers are dividing public opinion, enhancing the confusion and misinformation about addictive drugs, preventing a consensus of social refusal. They are projecting abroad the image of the United States as a drug-consuming society incapable of controlling the plague that is eroding the nation. It will take continued efforts of the parents of America and their allies, to roll back the tide and their children will in turn have to participate to win this battle for survival.

XXIX. A Medical Indictment of Marijuana by the Surgeon General of the United States (1982)

During the seventies, the Research Institute of the University of Mississippi, Pharmacological Sciences, under the direction of Dr. Coy Waller and Dr. Carlton Turner, undertook the monumental task of collating and annotating all research papers on marijuana published between 1964 and 1979. They assembled 5,715 entries in two dictionary-sized volumes. Three independent scientific bodies made a general evaluation of these findings: the Scientific Council of the American Medical Association (A.M.A., 1981), a task force from both the World Health Organization and the Addiction Research Foundation of Toronto (WHO-ARF, 1981), and the Institute of Medicine, National Academy of Sciences, 1982.

All three groups expressed their great concern about the extensive use of marijuana, especially among the young, but they reached somewhat different conclusions from the documents examined. The most forceful statement came from the Council of the A.M.A.: "Marijuana is a dangerous drug. A growing body of evidence from both animal and human studies and from clinical observations attests to its deleterious effects on behavior, performance and functioning of

243

various organ systems (lung, heart, brain, reproductive organs)."

The WHO-ARF report noted in man the respiratory toxicity of cannabis, the development of tolerance to and dependence on the drug, the vulnerability of adolescents "undergoing rapid developmental changes" and of patients with a variety of diseases such as "various forms of mental illness, cardiovascular disease and epilepsy". The same report stated that the cannabis effects on the hormonal, reproductive and immunological states of the users is unclear, but it added, "The results of experimental studies in animals have consistently demonstrated toxicity at doses comparable to those consumed by man smoking cannabis several times a day. Respiratory Toxicity, CNS (brain) dysfunction, endocrine disturbances, reproductive defects and suppression of immunity have all been observed after treatment with THC or cannabinoids."

The report of the Institute of Medicine, the most prestigeous medical organization in the United States, associated with the National Academy of Sciences, was much more qualified. It stated: "Marijuana has a broad range of psychological and biological effects, some of which (at least under certain conditions) are harmful to human health. Unfortunately, the available information does not tell us how serious this risk may be."

The chairman of the I.O.M. Committee, Dr. Arnold Relman, editor of one of the most well-known medical journals in the world, *The New England Journal of Medicine*, went one step further. In a special editorial for the journal he wrote, "The verdict of the experts is—that there is no verdict. Marijuana cannot be exonerated as harmless, but neither can it be convicted of being as dangerous as some have claimed."

Indeed, when it came to specifics, the I.O.M. Report was non-committal. For example: "Although effects on female hormonal function have been reported, the committee says the evidence is not convincing ... Marijuana crosses the placental barrier, but there is no evidence as yet of deleterious effects on the foetus . . . THC appears to have a suppressive effect on the number and motility of human sperm, but there is no proof that it effects male fertility; . . . The drug may have a mild immuno-suppressant effect but apparently not enough to be of clinical importance; . . . Case reports suggest that it may exacerbate pre-existing mental illness; patients with a history of schizophrenia may be particularly at risk, although there are no controlled studies (this last statement overlooks the fact that since the second century A.D., the use of cannabis has been associated with an increased incidence of mental illness as described in scores of publications from all over the world. Interestingly enough, the opiates, also in widespread use throughout history, have not been linked with mental disorders); . . . Longterm heavy use may be associated with an 'amotivational syndrome', but the data does not establish whether use of the drug is a cause or a result of this condition."

The I.O.M. formulated these qualifications because it required a most rigorous standard of evidence to establish the existence of marijuana health hazards, namely: measurable pathological changes in man (similar to cancer of the lung found in tobacco smokers or cirrhosis of the liver in alcoholics). Such changes have not been observed yet. The I.O.M. gave little weight to experimental studies not performed on man or clinical observations which modern science cannot measure with objective tests, for example, lack of motivation or mental illness.

By contrast the Scientific Council of the A.M.A. gave greater credence to such evidence. For the Council, one indication of a health hazard was the detrimental effect of marijuana on adolescent development, even though the physicians who reported this effect lacked specific measurements. WHO-ARF also considered clinical evidence important. They took into account the relatively high incidence of cannabis related psychosis, especially in the developing countries (two members of the task force were from Africa and India).

Both the A.M.A. Committee and the WHO-ARF experts

took into account the animal experimental studies in their general assessment of the health hazards of the drug.

The three scientific groups were in agreement that more research was required to document health hazards of marijuana use in man, mainly in the form of long term "epidemiological" studies similar to those performed on tobacco smokers. But recommendations for long term "controlled" research, especially if on adolescents, raise an ethical dilemma because they imply that cannabis will continue to be used (illegally) at its present rate by millions of young people, and that a significant fraction of them will develop the pathologic lesions necessary for documenting (to the satisfaction of the I.O.M.'s criteria, that is) the damaging effects of the drug. Surely modern science might have designed a less arduous task to prove damaging effects in humans of a foreign substance!

As far as the therapeutic potential of marijuana is concerned, the three groups of experts recognized the use of cannabinoids (marijuana chemicals) in the treatment of glaucoma, nausea caused by cancer chemotherapy, and convulsive disorders, but they agreed that a final appraisal of therapeutic usefulness would require more investigation.

Because of the I.O.M.'s ambiguous position, therefore, the three groups could not speak with one voice on the main issue of marijuana's health hazards. Their conflict raises a crucial question: Is the I.O.M.'s required standard of evidence the most appropriate one? Should one discard as anecdotal all historical and clinical evidence which has in the past led groups such as the League of Nations and the United Nations to recommend the banning of marijuana from general consumption? Should one overlook the studies on animals and primates that demonstrate toxicity? Certainly, the FDA has banned scores of drugs, cosmetics, and food additives on the basis of far less experimental evidence!

The scientific controversy could go on for years because the human pathology of marijuana cannot be written before two or three decades of systematic research: it took sixty years to establish the pathology of tobacco smoking, and only in 1968 was the damaging effect of alcohol on foetal growth established scientifically by Professor Lemoine of the University of Paris who merely confirmed observations made since recorded history. Taking the tobacco story as a precedent, what would happen if and when actual pathological proof of damage ends the scientific controversy over marijuana? Will such scientific proof also end the social controversy that has raged since the dawn of mankind, pitting as it does the desires of the individual against the rules of society? One may doubt that it will.

The National Organization for the Reform of Marijuana Laws (NORML) gave the Institute of Medicine Report high marks for its usefulness and objectivity, but many practicing physicians, educators, and parents were disappointed. An important warning in the report's conclusion is, however, a redeeming factor: "What little we know for certain about the effects of marijuana on human health, and all that we have reason to suspect, justifies serious national concern."

Dust had barely settled on the controversy created by the I.O.M.'s report when an additional document was released by the Committee on "substance abuse and habitual behavior" of the National Research Council, an advisory body to the National Academy of Sciences. This committee was heavily weighted with sociologists and legal experts (like Professor John Kaplan, also a member of the advisory committee of NORML), adepts at the Lindesmith philosophy of free access to drugs. Not surprisingly, their report, coming after four years' deliberation, recommended the "decriminalization" of marijuana, based on the "social and law enforcement costs" created by total prohibition, and on the assumption that "decriminalization" would not increase consumption. And yet the Committee's own report indicates that during the decade when 11 states formally decriminalized marijuana, and others adopted a policy of de facto decriminalization, regular marijuana use tripled among adolescents and doubled among young adults. Although careful to analyze the policy costs of law enforcement to prevent marijuana use, the Committee neglected to assess the health costs resulting from marijuana use by millions of adolescents and adults.

After analyzing this report, the President of the National Academy of Sciences, Dr. Frank Press, took the unusual step of publicly stating his personal disagreement.

Dr. Press wrote:

> "My own view is that the data available to the Committee were insufficient to justify on scientific or analytical grounds changes in current policies dealing with the use of marijuana ... I am concerned that the committee may have gone beyond its charge in stating a judgement so value laden that it should have been left to the political process."

Dr. William Pollin, the director of the National Institute on Drug Abuse was equally critical of the report, and such criticism blunted its general impact on the public, though the media did give it wide coverage.

In the midst of these claims and counter-claims, the Surgeon General of the United States Public Health Service, C. Everett Koop, spoke out.

The Surgeon General is the chief medical officer in the nation. One of his responsibilities is to monitor outbreaks of infectious diseases in order to take measures necessary to stop their spread. Besides the control of infectious diseases, he is also concerned about the use of any substance which might be damaging to public health. At his desk "the buck stops" for health-related matters.

For this reason, in 1963 the Surgeon General issued the first warning about the damaging effects of chronic tobacco smoking on the lung and emphasized the risk that smokers had of developing lung cancer. His historical pronouncement ended decades of "scientific" controversy and paved the way for a vast campaign that has underscored the health hazards of tobacco smoking.

Thus, in the summer of 1982, after reviewing the evidence concerning marijuana, the Surgeon General issued the following warning:

"As Surgeon General, I urge other physicians and professionals to advise parents and patients about the harmful effects of using marijuana and to urge discontinuation of its use.

"The health consequences of marijuana use have been the subject of scientific and public debate for almost 20 years. Based on scientific evidence published to date, the Public Health Service has concluded that marijuana has a broad range of psychological and biological effects, many of which are dangerous and harmful to health.

"Marijuana use is a major public health problem in the United States. In the past 20 years, there has been a 30-fold increase in the drug's use among youth. More than one-quarter of the American population has used the drug. The age at which people first use marijuana has been getting consistently lower and now is most often in the junior high school years. In 1978, nearly 11 percent of high school seniors used the drug daily, and although this figure declined to 7 percent in 1981, daily use of marijuana is still greater among this age group than that of alcohol. More high school seniors smoke marijuana than smoke cigarettes. The current use (during the previous 30 days) of marijuana is 32 percent: 29 percent smoke tobacco.

"On March 24, Secretary Schweiker transmitted to the U.S. Congress a report reviewing the health consequences of marijuana use. *Marijuana and Health: 1982*, the ninth in a series, is primarily based on two recently-conducted comprehensive scientific reviews on the subject: one by the Institute of Medicine of the National Academy of Sciences, and the other by the Canadian Addiction Research Foundation for the World Health Organization. Both independent reviews corroborate the Public Health Service's prior findings of health hazards associated with marijuana use: acute intoxication with marijuana interferes with many aspects of mental functioning and has serious acute effects on perception and skilled performance, such as driving and other complex tasks involving judgment or fine motor skills.

Among the known or suspected chronic effects of marijuana use are:

—Impaired short-term memory and slowed learning;

—Impaired lung function similar to that found in cigarette smokers. Indications are that more serious effects may ensue following extended use;

—Decreased sperm count and sperm motility;

—Interference with ovulation and prenatal development;

—Impaired immune response;

—Possible adverse effects on heart function; and

—By-products of marijuana remaining in body fat for several weeks with unknown consequences. The storage of these by-products increases the possibilities for chronic effects as well as residual effects on performance even after the acute reaction to the drug has worn off.

"I am especially concerned about the long-term developmental effects of marijuana use on children and adolescents, who are particularly vulnerable to the drug's behavioral and physiological effects. The "amotivational syndrome" has been attributed by some to prolonged use of marijuana by youth. The syndrome is characterized by a pattern of loss of energy, diminished school performance, harmed parental relationships, and other behavioral disruptions. Though more research is required to clarify the course and extent, in recent national surveys, up to 40 percent of heavy users report that they observe some or all of these symptoms in themselves.

"The Public Health Service review of the health consequences of marijuana supports the major conclusion of the National Academy of Sciences' Institute of Medicine

'What little we know for certain about the effects of marijuana on human health—and all that we have reason to suspect—justifies serious national concern.' "

Koop's broad statement summarizes and underscores the contents of *Keep Off The Grass,* and echoes the conclusion reached by one of the scientists of the Reims Symposium, "Undoubtedly, cannabis is harmful to man." It was the first medical warning from the administration which clearly spelled out the health hazards of marijuana. A warning long overdue to parents, but which the National Institute on Drug Abuse had failed to give in its ten reports, *Marijuana and Health,* summarizing studies that cost NIDA tens of millions of dollars a year. Their conclusions, ambiguous and bland, declared "the significance of the biological and behavioral changes caused by marijuana in man is uncertain." There was no distinct indictment of the drug.

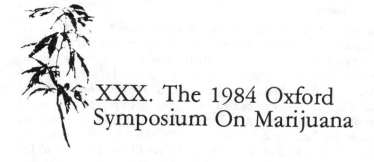

XXX. The 1984 Oxford Symposium On Marijuana

Nine years had passed since the First International Symposium on Marijuana of Helsinki and six years had elapsed since the one held in Reims. In spite of the large number of research reports presented at these meetings which documented the biological and medical damaging effects of the drug, many intellectuals and educators were not convinced, and elected to ignore the new evidence. Not to be discouraged, I teamed again with Dr. William Paton as twice previously, to organize the Third International Symposium on Marijuana of the IXth International Congress of Pharmacology which was holding its meeting in London.

Dr. Paton, or rather Sir William, since he had been knighted by the Queen in 1980, but still Bill to his friends, was retiring from the chair of Pharmacology at Oxford. This third symposium was to be held in his honor on the campus of his prestigious unversity. Dr. David Harvey, a pupil of Paton, assisted in the scientific and logistic preparation of the gathering which was held from the 6th to the 8th of August, 1984. One hundred scientists from twelve countries gathered around the veteran marijuana researchers of previous meetings: Stig Agurell from Sweden, Raphael Mechoulam from Israel, Gregory Chesher from Australia, Michel Paris and Bernard Desoize from France, Harris Rosenkrantz, Louis Lemberger, Reese Jones, Carlton Turner and Monroe Wall from the United States.

The papers presented at the Symposium extended the experimental and clinical observations reported at the previous meetings on the biological and medical damaging effects of marijuana. As could have been expected, impairment of brain and

251

reproductive functions were the principal health hazards of this drug described at this meeting. Dr. Ralph Hingson from Boston University reported that mothers smoking marijuana during pregnancy deliver infants 100 to 300 grams lighter, and with smaller head and brain than the infants of mothers who did not use the drug. Infants exposed to marijuana during their life in the womb were five times more likely to be disfigured and appear like babies born to alcoholic mothers with the "fetal alcoholic syndrome." The studies of Hingson were confirmed by those of Dr. Qutub Quazi and Dr. Doris Milman, pediatricians of the Downstate Medical Center in Brooklyn. In a paper published at the time of the meeting, Qutub and Milman describe abnormalities in five newborn babies associated with prenatal marijuana exposure: the babies displayed symptoms of intrauterine-growth retardation, low birth weight, small head circumference, abnormal facial features, slower growth and neurological problems.

These clinical observations confirmed the many experimental studies on animals which had described the damaging effects of marijuana on the development of the fetus. Unfortunately, such studies had not convinced some scientists and physicians who claimed that men are different from other animals. However, now that the evidence of damage to the human newborn was finally surfacing, these same scientists were still arguing about some shortcomings of the methods used by Dr. Hingson in his survey...and yet as reported at the Oxford Conference by Harris Rosenkrantz, the experimental scientific evidence of the damaging effect of marijuana on reproductive functions is overwhelming:

"Despite disagreements between and within human and animal studies, respectively, definitive evidence exists as to aberrations of sexual behavior, hormone imbalances, cycle derangements, inhibition of ovulation, interference with spermatogenesis, embryotoxicity, weak teratogen signs, delayed postnatal development, alterations of receptor and synthetic processes in the reproductive organs, and chromosomal anomalies."

In plain English: available evidence indicates that cannabis exerts significant damaging effects in all phases of reproduction and members of both sexes and in all species which have been studied.

These include fish, birds, rodents, mice, rats, hamsters, rabbits, dogs, monkeys, and last but not least, man. Rosenkrantz ended his imposing review by suggesting that THC caused such far-reaching damaging effects in all phases of reproduction because it interferes with Vitamin E, the so-called fertility vitamin, an intriguing hypothesis which will elicit a great deal of research.

Throughout recorded history of the past 2000 years, the use of marijuana has been associated with mental disturbances ranging from distorted perceptions to hallucinations and plain madness.

Reports from the recent American psychiatric literature indicated that subjects prone to mental illness were specially vulnerable to the disrupting effects of marijuana on brain mechanisms. In Oxford, Dr. Juan Negrete, from McGill University, documented these earlier reports in studying 137 schizophrenics of Montreal General Hospital:

> "The results indicate that schizophrenics who admitted to using cannabis during the study period, or who were found to have positive urine tests for THC, required more therapeutic intervention and showed twice the amount of delusional and hallucinatory activity than those who did not use cannabis at all."

Dr. Ulf Rydberg from Sweden reported that in his country, 100 patients a year are treated as in-patients in psychiatric clinics for cannabis-related diagnoses: amotivational syndrome, acute and chronic psychotic state.

Other experimental studies made by Dr. Guy Cabral and Dr. Albert Munson documented the impairing effect of THC on the immunity system of guinea pigs infected with herpes simplex virus which causes genital herpes: animals treated with moderate doses of THC and infected with the herpes virus had much more extensive lesions, and a mortality more than double that of the controls. This study raised a question which may not be answered yet: to what extent has marijuana contributed to the spread and persistence of the major epidemic of genital herpes which has been reported in the United States over the past ten years, concurrently with the widespread use of marijuana?

Unlike the meetings at Helsinki or Reims, the Oxford symposium received very scant press coverage. The controversial topic of the health hazards of marijuana, bandied around for so many years, was not newsworthy any more. The hot medical reporting was about AIDS and cocaine.

And yet, the public should have been informed about the results reported in Oxford, especially those pertaining to the damaging effect of the drug to the human fetus. Indeed, on the basis of current surveys, it may be estimated that close to one million women of childbearing age are current users of marijuana. Such a figure might seem high, but to my dismay, I discovered, a few months after the Oxford meeting, that the use of marijuana was not confined to the pregnant women of the large cities of Boston or New York but was also smoked by expectant mothers in Denver, Colorado. In the correspondence of the *New England Journal of Medicine* I read a letter from Dr. Carol Blackard who reported the presence of THC or of its metabolite in maternal plasma and umbilical-cord blood sampled from ten women who delivered their babies in two Denver general hospitals and admitted having smoked marijuana daily during the third trimester of their pregnancy.

All of this information was very distressing. It seemed that the pursuit of scientific knowledge and its dissemination may not be sufficient to curtail the widespread consumption of destructive pleasurable substances. A generation ago it was common folklore practice and knowledge that pregnant women should avoid taking drugs for the sake of the unborn child. This taboo no longer exists today. It can only be restored by a national consensus which will require a wide dissemination by the media of the damaging effects of marijuana and other dependence-producing drugs on fetal growth and development.

The damaging effects of maternal marijuana exposure to the newborn was illustrated by the experimental studies of Professor Susan Dalterio from San Antonio, Texas. Dalterio reported at the Oxford meeting that maternal exposure to a single dose of cannabinoids resulted in long-term alterations in the development of the reproductive system in both male and female offspring.

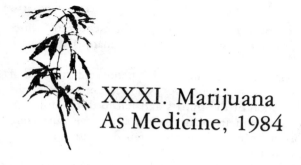

XXXI. Marijuana
As Medicine, 1984

A session of the Oxford meeting, held in conjunction with the World Health Organization, was devoted to the medical applications of cannabis.

Marijuana as medicine regained popularity and favor in the wake of the widespread use of marijuana as an intoxicant in the United States during the second part of the twentieth century.

To the old claims, new applications widely heralded by the medical and lay press were found for the old drug, in the treatment of glaucoma and of nausea and vomiting induced by cancer chemotherapy.

A powerful lobby, the Alliance for Cannabis Therapeutics, having close ties with NORML, the National Organization for the Reform of Marijuana Laws was formed in Washington, D.C. Its stated purpose was to "end the federal prohibition of cannabis in medicine and construct a medically meaningful, ethically correct and compassionate system of regulation which permits the seriously ill to legally obtain cannabis." This lobby was able to form an alliance of patients and their families, concerned citizens, humanitarians, public officials and elected officials.

In response to such political and public pressure, twenty-four states passed legislation which authorized the prescription of cannabis crude-drug preparations for the management of nausea and vomiting related to cancer chemotherapy. A bill (H.R. 4498) was presented in the U.S. Congress "to provide for the therapeutic use

of marijuana in situations involving life-threatening or sense-
threatening illness and to provide supplies of marijuana for such
use.''

It would appear that some confusion has permeated the mind of
the public, and of its representatives, who are not aware of the
therapeutic revolution of the thirties and fail to distinguish between a crude drug and its pharmacologically active pure components, in this instance, too many have failed to distinguish between marijuana and THC.

Dr. Carlton Turner pointed out that while crude-cannabis
preparations containing delta-9-THC display similar pharmacological properties as their main psychoactive compound, their
overall effect is different. The other cannabinoids (61 identified so
far) present in the crude material interact with the absorption,
availability and transformation of delta-9-THC in the body. The
other chemicals contained in the plant material (360 identified)
also possess some specific biological activity. Furthermore, the
respective amounts of chemicals contained in each preparation will
vary over a wide range: no two samples of crude marijuana, drawn
from two different batches of plants, will have the same composition: they are therefore two different drugs, and this holds true for
their THC content. Marijuana, the crude drug obtained from a
single cannabis plant harvested at 8:00 A.M. will be different from
the marijuana obtained from the *same plant* harvested at 10:00
A.M. the same day. When the crude drug is smoked, it contains
toxic substances such as benzopyrene, a cancer-causing chemical
produced by the burning process: it is 70% more abundant in
marijuana smoke than in tobacco smoke. Crude-drug marijuana
(cannabis preparations) used for smoking in the United States can
also be contaminated with salmonella bacteria which gives diarrhea, and with a fungus aspergillus, which may cause severe bron-
chopneumonia. (It has been recommended that the crude-drug
marijuana given to patients be sterilized.) It would be practically
impossible for a crude drug like marijuana therefore to comply with
the Pure Food and Drug Act which requires that all medicines be
labelled with the exact amount of chemicals they contain.

The ''bioavailability'' of delta-9-THC (the amount which
reaches the blood stream after its ingestion or inhalation), is by

itself quite limited (5-12% when given orally, 15-30% when inhaled). When THC is administered in the form of the crude drug (inhaled or ingested), its bioavailability will become still more uncertain. This is especially true when the crude drug is smoked. In the smoking process many chemical compounds are destroyed by the heat of the burning cigarette and new chemical classes are produced, depending on combustion temperatures of cigarette, pH of the plant material, moisture content, particle size and chemicals contained in the plant; puff frequency and volume inhaled are also to be taken into account. All of these chemicals will alter the pharmacological activity of THC, increasing or decreasing it according to the final mixture. "Bioavailability" of the pharmacologically active substances contained in the crude-drug marijuana is unpredictable.

Marijuana, the crude drug (with 421 different chemicals), also lacks specificity as was demonstrated by its historical usage for a wide array of ailments. One of the purposes of pharmaceutical science is to extract therapeutically useful compounds from crude material and to make them available in pure form to pharmacologists for systematic investigation: penicillin from the mold penicillium notatum, and digitoxin from the foxglove plant, are two of the most striking examples of such a scientific approach which has benefited all mankind.

There is no pharmacological or medical justification for the use of marijuana, the crude drug, in the treatment of specific ailments. Such use may be compared to the administration of a cocktail of unknown composition with resulting unpredictable effects — akin to the practice of voodoo medicine. Most of the therapeutic applications attributed to cannabis the crude drug have been traced down to the effect of its main psychoactive ingredient delta-9-THC and to a lesser extent to the nonpsychoactive cannabidol (CBD).

Many of the medical indications suggested for THC — against pain, convulsions, depression, anxiety, asthma, as a sedative and hypnotic and a tranquillizer — did not go beyond self-limiting clinical trials. However, two new indications were found: to treat the vomiting associated with cancer chemotherapy and glaucoma. Dr. Richard Gralla from the Sloane Kettering Cancer Institute of New York reported at Oxford a study which compared THC and metoclopramide in the treatment of nausea and vomiting induced by cisplatin. Cisplatin is a powerful anti-cancer drug which causes a great deal of vomiting. Gralla concluded that THC was less effective in controlling vomiting than metoclopramide administered in high dose by the intravenous route. I reported in turn that at Columbia Presbyterian Hospital in New York metoclopramide was the drug of choice to prevent the vomiting in cancer chemotherapy; and, recent studies carried out in collaboration with Dr. Henri Roche and Dr. George Hyman indicated that an old drug, compazine, when given intravenously, was more effective than metoclopramide.

The use of THC in the treatment of glaucoma was reported by Dr. John Merritt of Chapel Hill University, North Carolina. The lack of a THC preparation which could be applied directly on the eye, the hypotension and side effects of THC administered orally, limited its clinical trials. Louis Lemberger of Indianapolis reported the use of a synthetic derivative of THC, Nabilone, to control vomiting in patients receiving cancer chemotherapy. Its effectiveness must still be compared with that of compazine and metoclopramide which, associated with corticosteroids, were the drugs of choice.

Dr. J. Trounce, from Guy's Hospital in London, who chaired this part of the meeting, concluded "Unless a new and more scientific indication for cannabis and its derivatives emerges it seems unlikely that this group of drugs will play a major role in therapeutics."

The reasons for the failure of THC as a remedy are inherent to the drug: the diversity and variability of its actions, its limited and inconsistent absorption into the body and its undesirable side effects.

And today, for every ailment which THC might have mitigated in the past, there exist safer, more specific and much more effective drugs. A new specific compound, ondansetron, a serotonin antagonist has proven to be the best antiemetic in the treatment of chemotherapy induced vomiting (Grunberg, S.M. Making Chemotherapy Easier. *New England J. of Medicine.* 322, 846. 1990).

XXXII. The Classification of Marijuana Among the Dependence-Producing Drugs (Addictive)

The fact that THC containing marijuana possesses numerous pharmacological properties makes it difficult to classify in a specific class of drugs: it produces depressant and stimulant effects on the brain and in sufficient dosage may induce hallucinations. Marijuana and compounds containing THC should be classified in a category by themselves, among the dependence-producing drugs with a high abuse potential.

The popular classification of cannabis as a "soft drug" is incorrect and greatly misleading in view of the acute and chronic adverse effects associated with its use. Another misleading classification describes cannabis as a substance which produces "psychic dependence" in the absence of physical dependence! This classification was formulated at one time by the Committee on Drug Dependence of WHO which was also careful to emphasize that "psychic" dependence was paramount in drug-seeking behavior. The confusion created by this distinction was compounded by the claim that both cocaine and cannabis produced mild to marked "psychic" dependence and little, if any, physical dependence. This distinction between "physical and psychic" dependence was subsequently interpreted by many as indicating that truly addictive drugs were those which caused a physical dependence characterized by withdrawal symptoms of the opiate type. This misconception, which is still found in many publications dealing with drug dependence, led to the erroneous assumption that cocaine, cannabis and tobacco are not truly addictive and do not create "physical dependence" because cessation of their use is not accompanied by a full-blown withdrawal syndrome. One more step was to claim next that the use of cannabis and cocaine may be readily and promptly terminated if the user exerts enough "psychic" resolution. This clear-cut distinction between psychic and physical dependence illustrates the old dichotomy between mind and body which modern neurophysiology and psychopharmacology no longer justify since soma and psyche are inextricably interwoven. A classification of dependence-producing drugs should be based on "markers" which reflect the biochemical (therefore physical) alterations that they primarily induce in the central nervous system. We have therefore suggested that the following characteristics be utilized to identify addictive dependence-producing drugs:

1. **Primary pleasurable reward.**
2. **Neuropsychological impairment (reversible).**
3. **Abstinence syndrome.**
4. **Tolerance.**
5. **Reinforcement.**

1. They produce a primary pleasurable reward. We have described the pleasant effects of marijuana caused by its action on the brain pleasure "centers" described by Heath. This drug will also dissipate unpleasant feelings, decrease anxiety and produce detachment from the world and the feeling that one has entered a new dimension. These pleasurable sensations induce what is called a "positive reinforcement" in the brain. That is to say, the desire to repeat the same experience. The other side of the coin is that the pleasurable sensations induced by marijuana and other addictive drugs are associated with a temporary impairment of brain function.

2. Reversible impairment of brain function (Neuropsychological toxicity.) The effects of marijuana on brain circuitry and its chemical switches will produce anomalies of behavior and thinking such as adverse effects on arousal, awareness and judgment. As a result psychological and psychomotor performance will be im-

paired. These symptoms are reversible and dissipate when the pharmacological action of the drug has ended. *(Some addictive drugs such as nicotine, caffeine [in moderate amounts] and alcohol [in small amounts] do not produce any measurable symptoms of neuropsychological toxicity.)*

3. *Abstinence syndrome.* Interruption of the regular use of marijuana is associated with an abstinence syndrome which is characterized by irritability, uneasiness and anxiety; nausea, diarrhea and sweating have also been reported. These symptoms are much less severe than those accompanying withdrawal from opiates which are quite unpleasant and anxiety laden resembling a very bad bout of flu. However, withdrawal symptoms from heroin ("cold turkey") are not life threatening. The most severe withdrawal symptoms are those from barbiturates and include convulsions which may be lethal. Convulsions may also occur following withdrawal from tranquilizers and alcohol. Abstinence from cocaine and amphetamines is not accompanied by a withdrawal symptom of the opiate type but produces marked after-effects: prolonged sleep, general fatigue, depression and sleep anomalies. These depressive after-effects of major psychostimulant abstinence may be considered as withdrawal symptoms of the stimulant type and may act as "reinforcers" in perpetuating drug use.

Withdrawal symptoms may occur independently of tolerance and should not be considered as the major reinforcement for continuing drug use. The occurrence of a withdrawal symptom of the opiate type is not a prerequisite to the addictive process; it is not the sole symptom of "drug dependence."

4. *Tolerance.* This is the necessity of increasing dosage in order to obtain the initial effect. The capacity of the human organism to tolerate elevated dosage of addictive drugs without displaying any permanent physical damage is high. Tolerance is a drug-related adaptive process that allows the brain to function in the presence of a foreign substance which does not occur naturally in the internal environment. The use of marijuana, which has a very low acute toxicity, is associated with a high degree of tolerance. Chronic inveterate smokers will use 100 times the amount they started with. For other drugs tolerance is lower: one to ten for opiates, alcohol and barbiturates; one to fifty for cocaine. The higher the acute tox-

icity of the drug, the lower its tolerance. Development of tolerance is closely linked to drug dependence. Before becoming dependent on these drugs, brain biochemical mechanisms have to adjust to their repetitive disrupting effects. Tolerance accentuates the problem of drug supply and the need for readministration. It is primarily a symptom of biochemical changes which have occurred in the brain.

5. *Reinforcement.* Dependence-producing drugs act as "powerful reinforcers" inducing a craving for the drug and compulsive drug-oriented behavior and frequent (daily) self-administration, characterized by major involvement in securing its use and a high tendency to relapse after discontinuing use. Self-administration of the major dependence-producing drugs (opiates, cocaine, barbiturates) is also displayed by the monkey. When given free access to cocaine or amphetamines, these animals will immediately self administer high daily doses resulting in severe convulsions and death within three weeks. *Unlike man,* the monkey will not self-administer nicotine, hallucinogens and cannabis. Therefore, dependency-producing drugs are damaging to the individual because he has little control over their intake once he has begun their use. This is particularly true when the individual is young, because his brain is not yet fully structured. To control the immediate fulfillment of desire for fun is more difficult. This vulnerability of the young to dependence-producing drugs is well documented. In the brain of the young person, the pleasure centers tend to be dominant. Only through proper training of the "new brain" (that is, the "neo-cortex" that covers the old brain) will reason become strong enough so that the individual will be able to forego immediate satisfaction in order to obtain long-lasting rewards.

This proposed classification of dependence-producing drugs indicates that marijuana presents the five major features of dependence-producing drugs summarized in Table 1. This classification also illustrates a crucial difference between drugs which induce "neuropsychological toxicity" (impairment of brain functions) and those which do not, like tobacco and caffeine. This major difference accounts for the fact that the consumption of tobacco and caffeine (contained in coffee, tea and cocoa) are social-

DRUGS	Positive Reinforcement (pleasure reward)	Neuropsychological impairment (reversible)	Withdrawal symptoms	Tolerance	Self-Administration Man	Self-Administration Monkey
Opiates						
Morphine	+	+	+	+	+	+
Heroin	+	+	+	+	+	+
Methadone	+	+	+	+	+	+
Synthetic agonists	+	+	+	+	+	+
Major Psychostimulants						
Cocaine	+	+	+	+	+	+
Amphetamine	+	+	+	+	+	+
Psychodepressants						
Alcohol*	+	+	+	+	+	(+)
Barbiturates	+	+	+	+	+	+
Benzodiazepines	+	+	+	+	+	+
Methaqualone	+	+	+	+	+	+
Cannabis						
Hashish	+	+	+	+	+	o
Marijuana, THC	+	+	+	+	+	o
Hallucinogens*						
LSD	+	+	o	+	+	o
Psilocybine	+	+	o	+	+	o
Mescaline	+	+	o	+	+	o
Anticholinergic (Datura, Belladona)	+	+	o	+	+	o
Phencyclidine (PCP)	+	+	o	+	+	+
Solvents						
Benzene, Toluene	+	+	o	+	+	o
Acetone	+	+	o	+	+	o
Trichloroethylene	+	+	o	+	+	o
Ether, N_2O, $CHCL_3$	+	+	o	+	+	o
Minor Psychostimulants						
Tobacco (Nicotine)	+	o	+	+	+	o
Cola	+	o	+	+	+	o
Khat	+	o	+	+	+	o
Caffeine	+	o	+	+	+	o

* Alcohol in small amounts does not induce psychological or physical impairment
* Hallucinogens may induce severe mental reactions/"bad trips."

Table 1. Psychopharmacological and Behavioral Features of Dependence-Producing Drugs

ly accepted in all societies of the world. Alcohol in small, infre-
quent amounts does not impair brain functions but still has a
serious potential for abuse, which resulted in the total ban of its
usage in the Islamic world. All other countries have enacted laws
which penalize intoxication with alcohol, while banning altogether
other dependence-producing drugs which impair brain
mechanisms and behavior. The use of these drugs is to be limited to
medical and scientific purposes only. Such laws imply that certain
dependence-producing drugs like the opiates, cocaine and marijuana have a higher potential to induce dependence (or daily intoxication) than alcohol. These restrictive laws are based on sound
scientific evidence.

Pharmacological studies indicate that opiates, cocaine and
cannabis in minute amounts cause much greater disturbance
in the brain mechanisms controlling behavior than does alcohol
in larger amounts, and a greater incidence of compulsive drug-
oriented behavior resulting in frequent daily intoxication.

That opiates, cocaine and marijuana have a greater dependence-producing potential (or addictive power) than alcohol, is
proved by surveys performed in countries where the drugs are
socially acceptable and easily available. In alcohol-consuming
populations six to eight percent of the consumers are excessive
drinkers, who will consume on the average a daily intoxicating
dose of the drug and be addicted to alcohol.

In Jamaican villages, where marijuana is freely available and
socially accepted, 50% of the villagers who smoke marijuana, consume it heavily every day (the equivalent of 10 joints).

In Peru, 90% of the miners of the Andes who chew coca leaves,
consume them every day in large amounts: thirty to fifty grams
which is equivalent to 300 to 500 milligrams of cocaine. And it is
common knowledge that 95% of heroin addicts consume their
favorite drug several times daily.

Can one therefore conclude that the abuse potential (the
possibility of inducing daily intoxication) of marijuana, cocaine and
heroin is greater than that of alcohol? Yes, because the frequency of
use of a drug is related to its addictive, dependence-producing property on the brain. The preceding examples indicate that the abuse
potential of marijuana may be seven times higher than that of

alcohol, and the abuse potential of heroin and cocaine may be fourteen times higher. (See Page 283)

This scientific classification of dependence-producing drugs illustrates the extraordinary ignorance of Dr. Andrew Weil who does not hesitate to lump all drugs together, enlarging their register to include sugar "which like heroin is a white powder."

This classification also illustrates the fallacy of the "responsible use" of dependence-producing drugs, also advocated by Andrew Weil. Such a concept is based on a fundamental contradiction: How can one exert judgment and responsibility by using a drug which by its intrinsic property abridges and curtails judgment and responsibility?

The physicians and psychologists who are probing the responsible use of drugs are also underestimating another inherent property of these drugs, which is to stimulate the pleasure-reward brain mechanisms. To advocate the responsible use of drugs is to incite kids to play with the fire that drugs light in their brains. It is a concept which has no scientific basis and is loaded with immense individual and social harm.

Marijuana, as do other dependence-producing drugs, impairs basic neurotransmission mechanisms in the brain. After repeated exposure to the drug, biochemical changes become installed, leading to a pattern of drug-seeking, drug-consuming behavior the individual is less and less able to control.

XXXIII. The Physicians and Dependence-Producing Drugs

When it comes to dependence-producing drugs, physicians should know better than to advocate their responsible use, which they themselves are not always able to achieve. In spite of their knowledge about the serious physical and health risks of these drugs, the medical profession has the highest reported use of dependence-producing drugs among the professions.

This simple fact clearly illustrates the addictive power of dependence-producing drugs which are able to trigger in the primitive brain overriding mechanisms which overrule reason and intelligence.

Physicians are compassionate by nature and wish to alleviate the sufferings of their patients. The United States and most other countries of the world restrict the use of opiates to the relief of pain resulting from diseases. Even for such treatment, physicians are very cautious about administering painkillers such as opiates over prolonged periods because of the risk of addicting their patients. But the administration of opiates or cocaine *to addicts* is forbidden by law. Great Britain is an exception to this rule. In 1920, a committee of British physicians, the Rolleston Committee, recommended that heroin, morphine and cocaine be prescribed to addicts "for prolonged withdrawal treatments with a view to cure, when it has been demonstrated that addicts could not lead a useful and relatively normal life when deprived of the drug, but could do so on regular administration of a 'certain minimum dose'." This practice, which has been dubbed "the British System," worked satisfactorily as long as addicts were few in number: 500 per year between 1930 and 1960. It became unmanageable after 1960 when heroin had to be dispensed to more than 1000 users of the drug. Indeed, each addict had to be provided with daily doses of heroin as well as the syringes and needles required for administration of the drug 4 to 6 times a day. Because of this logistic problem and of the many instances of diversion inherent in such a scheme, heroin began to be progressively replaced by methadone maintenance (methadone, a long lasting opiate, needs to be absorbed only once a day by mouth): in 1980, 6 percent of the 2,800 British addicts were treated with heroin compared to 31 percent of the 1,400 addicts in 1973.

Therefore, there has never been a "British System" of opiate control *per se*, only a limited medical practice based on the Rolleston Committee's recommendation of free heroin availability for a few hundred addicts.

This limited practice clearly failed to cope with the relatively moderate increase in heroin addiction which occurred in Britain in the sixties. And yet Lindesmith (1965) in his classic treatise, "The Addict and the Law" advocated the "British System" as a model for America at the very time it was breaking down in England because the number of addicts treated with heroin had increased from 500 to 1,000! What would have happened in the United States if heroin had been provided to hundreds of thousands of addicts? Despite these facts, the "British System" is still advocated in the United States (Lindesmith, 1981; Zinberg, 1981; Drug Abuse Council, 1981; *New York Times*, 1982).

The failure of the medical practice in providing heroin to large numbers of addicts is due to the profound addictive and reinforcing properties of this drug. Its use spreads as an epidemic. Heroin exerts an attraction on many because of its unique euphoriant qualities by its stimulation of the brain reward system. Many addicts are proselytes who will divert some of their freely obtained drug to initiate others to the pleasure of the heroin "rush."

The lack of a medical treatment of drug dependence limits the

role of the physician to the advocacy of preventive measures based
on abstinence from drug exposure. The best example the physician
may give should be his own. It is therefore disheartening to observe
the present trend reported in a survey performed at the 1984
American Medical Student Association Conference and reported in
the *New england Journal of Medicine* by Dr. Roberta Epstein.
"Nearly two-thirds of the students (65.2 percent) had tried marijuana, and 33 percent had tried cocaine. Stimulants and tranquilizers had been tried by 26.3 and 20.2 percent, respectively. The
percentages of students who classified themselves as drug "users"
were as follows: marijuana, 27.4; cocaine, 10.8; stimulants, 6.9;
and tranquilizers, 9.9." This data indicates that future American
physicians who will be practicing in the new millenium 2000 stand
a one in ten chance of being cocaine users, and a one in four chance
of smoking marijuana!

Furthermore, Dr. Epstein reported that no significant correlation
was found between the use of drugs and whether or not the student
had completed a course on drugs as part of the medical school curriculum.

If such attitudes toward dependence-producing drugs are found
today among some medical students, they just reflect the general
acceptance of these drugs in our society at large.

It is urgent therefore to create a consensus in the country to
restore a social refusal of the most addictive drugs which have been
so widely used in the United States during the past 20 years. Once
this consensus is reached, effective measures may be taken to
decrease further the supply of dependence-producing drugs as well
as their demand.

Meanwhile, the momentum of Parents for Drug Free Youth and
of PRIDE will be effective in protecting our children against the
temptation of marijuana and other dependence-producing drugs.

And if one of our kids starts using marijuana, we also know that
we can depend on physicians like Dr. Harold Voth to help the
youth get drug-free.

XXXIV. How to Get Your Child Off Marijuana

By Harold Voth, M.D.
Senior psychiatrist, the Menninger Clinic, Topeka, Kansas

Discovering that a child smokes marijuana is shocking for most parents. How can they end the child's use of the drug? That question has been studied for thirty years by psychiatrist Harold M. Voth of the Menninger Foundation in Topeka, Kan., who says that parents must be quite firm. His advice may seem harsh. But it is effective.

The advice I have will work for parents who are strong and committed to carrying out three principles to save their child from marijuana:

1) Determine for certain that your child is using marijuana.
2) Take responsibility for your child's life when he cannot adequately do so.
3) Find substitutes for marijuana for your child.

To find out whether your child is a user, ask him point-blank. You may get a straight-out yes. If he denies it, but your suspicions tell you otherwise, then you face the next very difficult step.

You simply must invade his privacy and carry out a thorough search of his room. And do it more than once. Also, look for these telltale signs:

• Youngsters who smoke marijuana sooner or later show some degree of estrangement from their family. They become less concerned for the other family members.

• With the chronic user, school grades may begin to slip. And there is less talk of future goals. A hostility toward "the establishment" frequently occurs.

• The user's appearance deteriorates. Hair gets longer and sometimes clothing gets "far-out".

• Check for eyedrops. Marijuana causes the eyes to be bloodshot and users will attempt to conceal this sign with eyedrops.

• If your child is out of money and is vague about it, he may be buying marijuana. If he has an unexplained ample supply of money, he may be selling drugs.

• Strange phone calls are cause for worry, as is vagueness about social activities.

• Frequent colds, boils or other kinds of infections are often signs of marijuana smokers, for users commonly have less resistance to infection. A chronic cough is often due to the irritating effects of the smoke.

Once you are certain that your child is using marijuana, you must get it out of his life by keeping him away from the substance.

You must take responsibility for your child's life, since he cannot adequately do so. If he could, he would not be damaging himself through the use of marijuana.

The time for an all-out confrontation has arrived. Explain what you plan to do and why. Make it unmistakably clear that you intend to win the battle and that one day he or she will love you more for having taking some decisive steps.

Halt all of your child's activities away from home, unless you or someone you trust accompanies him. The single exception can be school.

However, drugs can be obtained easily at schools and are even smoked during school hours. So take your child to school and pick him or her up immediately after.

All other activities should cease immediately. If you are indecisive or inconsistent, your child will almost surely use marijuana if given the opportunity. And if he does, your final victory will be set back.

At this point, the child's promise to quit smoking marijuana is usually an empty one. If he secretly has no intention of stopping but says he will, you have set him up to con you. This creates guilt and makes matters worse.

So if you discover he is continuing to use marijuana in school, take him out of school.

And begin making periodic searches. Listen in on phone calls and keep a close check on the money your child spends. You may have to take over his personal finances entirely.

In families where both parents work, arrangements will have to be made so the child is never home alone. This may require hiring someone to pick up your child after school and to stay with him until a parent comes home. The mother or father may even have to take a leave of absence from work.

Giving up your job or taking your child out of school may seem like too high a price to pay. But consider the alternative of losing your child.

Tell your employer what you are doing and why. Tell the school principal. Your child may lose a school year, but that is far less serious than allowing marijuana to continue to damage his mind and his body.

Sending your child for counseling when he is using marijuana will probably be a waste of time and money. Dry your child out first and then attend to emotional problems professionally, if it is necessary and if you can afford it.

Be prepared for your child to threaten to run away. Never call your child's bluff and point to the door.

Eventually the child will give up marijuana. Your child will then need a substitute—and the best is concerned and loving parents.

Also, consider meeting with other parents and their marijuana-troubled children. Such meetings provide a place to "sound off" thereby draining away some of the anger and frustration that would otherwise be expressed at home.

I further recommend an information clearinghouse be set up in your group. Several members should make it their responsibility to collect and report on the old and newer evidence of the effects of marijuana on man and society. All evidence converges to indicate the eroding role of this drug on the growing child and adolescent.

Epilogue

When reflecting upon the rapid and widespread usage of marijuana in our society in the past two decades, I am reminded of the old Arabian story in *The Thousand and One Nights*. A Genie escapes from its bottle and it is impossible to put it back inside. Ever since it has been floating hither and thither, creating mischief wherever it goes. I have been told that, for the poet who wrote the story, the Genie represents Hashish.

The damage done by the widespread use of hashish in the Moslem world is clearly documented by the Arabic historians of the 12th to the 16th century. A scholarly account of their voluminous writings has been compiled for the English reader by Dr. Franz Rosenthal, Sterling Professor of Near Eastern Languages at Yale University. His book *The Herb: Hashish Versus Moslem Medieval Society* had to be published in Holland in 1972 and it has been ignored ever since by the media in spite of its timeliness.

In reading *The Herb*, one learns that a similar controversy as the one raging today divided the ancient Islamic world. For several centuries the partisans of "the grass which gives joy and repose" battled the detractors of "the weed which impairs body and mind, and damages society". At one time, in the first years of the 15th century, restrictions against hashish were set aside, resulting in general availability, acceptance and abuse. The historian of the era, Al Magrizy, wrote that as a result, a general debasement of the people was apparent. Finally all the scholars and religious leaders of the time condemned the weed . . . not from religious fervor, but because of the harm it had done to their society.

It was too late. Says Rosenthal: "The conflict between what was felt to be right and socially good and what human nature craved in its search for play and diversion went on" . . . until this day.

Will history repeat itself? If it does, *Homo sapiens* of the 20th century will have to ignore the scientific facts that were not available 800 years ago: Cannabis is a drug which impairs the structure and function of cells in the blood, the lungs, the reproductive organs and in the brain.

In the seventies, scientific findings failed to convince a number of vocal social scientists and psychiatrists, whose tolerant and uninformed views dominated the media. The ensuing social acceptance of "recreational" drug use permeating many segments of American society resulted in a national disaster: the marijuana epidemic was compounded first by heroin, and then by cocaine and crack.

Today the tide may be turning, thanks to the unflagging efforts of grass-roots America in its desire to know the truth, exert its good sense and protect its children.

In the coming century, I believe that the American people, having learned the hard way, will once again give the world the example of a progressive society where children may grow up happy and drug free.

Appendices

General Clinical Effects of Dependence-Producing Drugs

The use of dependence-producing drugs will induce acute and chronic symptoms described in Table 2. Acute symptoms will vary with each drug, but they are not very specific and are often common to all of these different drugs. The diagnosis of an intoxication requires, therefore, the identification of the causative agent in blood or urine. Special kits are now available for such purposes.*

Dependence-producing drugs which have the most profound effects on the brain (opiates, major psychostimulants, barbiturates) especially when administered intravenously may induce acute cardiac or respiratory arrest and sudden death. Unlike these drugs, cannabis does not kill instantly by overdose, which accounts for its reputation of "soft" drug and its widespread usage and popularity. Chronic daily intoxication induces a general condition of mental and physical deterioration which is comparable in all dependence-producing drugs which induce "neuropsychotoxicity." The long-term damaging physical effects caused by the use of alcohol, tobacco, opiates, cocaine and amphetamines are well documented. People abusing cocaine, amphetamines, alcohol and marijuana are prone to mental disorders. By contrast the chronic user of opiates has not been associated with severe psychiatric problems.

*Emit Cannabinoid Assay Syva, Palo Alto, California.
Roche Abuscreen for Cannabinoids, Roche Diagnostic, Hoffman La Roche, Nutley, N.J.

As mentioned in the Preface to this new edition, the chronic use of marijuana is associated today with cancer of head, neck and lung, and increased vulnerability to viral infections. It also causes persistent memory deficits in adolescents, and is prospectively associated with the development of schizophrenia. The more foreboding report shows an increased incidence of a deadly form of child leukemia in the offspring of women who smoked marijuana during pregnancy. So scientists are starting to observe on human subjects all of the damaging effects of cannabis which could have been predicted from the experimental studies described in these pages. And yet these investigations were ignored by those who claimed, like Professor Lester Grinspoon in 1971 and again in 1977, that "no amount of research is likely to prove that cannabis is as dangerous as alcohol and tobacco."

GENERAL EFFECTS OF DEPENDENCE-PRODUCING DRUGS

Type of Drug	Acute Subjective Effects	Symptoms (outward signs of use)	Effects of an Overdose	Some Long-Term Effects
Opiates opium morphine heroin methadone	euphoria, relieves mental and physical pain.	myosis, lethargy, sweating, slurred speech.	respiratory depression, cardio-respiratory collapse and death.	loss of appetite and weight, malnutrition, amenorrhea, impotence, susceptibility to infections, feto and genotoxicity
Stimulants "uppers" cocaine "coke or snow" amphetamines anorectics "diet pills"	elevates mood, stimulates alertness and mental processes, heightens perception, feeling of power.	dilated pupils, rapid pulse, increased blood pressure, insomnia, loss of weight and appetite, over-excitability, tremors.	hallucinations, paranoia, lethal convulsions, cardiac damage, stroke and death.	loss of weight, ulceration of nasal septum (when sniffed), impotence, paranoid psychoses, myocarditis fetal toxicity.
Depressants alcohol	depressed cottical control and awareness.	slurred speech, poor equilibrium (ataxia), obtundness, aberrant and violent behavior, nausea, thirst, increased diuresis.	loss of consciousness, coma and death.	mental and physical deterioration, cirrhosis, dementia, malnutrition, convulsions after withdrawal.
barbiturates "downers"	tranquility, disorientation.	dilated pupils, respiratory depression, rapid pulse, loss of coordination and balance.	loss of consciousness, coma and death, low margin of security – the drug of suicide (associated with alcohol)	disruption of normal sleeping pattern, double vision, convulsions after withdrawal.
minor tranquilizers benzodiazepines	relieve anxiety.	disorientation, lethargy.	loss of consciousness, but does not cause death when taken alone.	possible convulsions after withdrawal.

Cannabis marijuana (pot, grass) hashish (hash)	euphoria and tranquility, distorts and heightens perception, hilarity, mood swings.	red eyes, rapid pulse, lack of coordination, impaired psycho-motor performance for 24 hours.	panic reaction, acute toxic psychosis. Does not cause death.	Cancer of lung, head and neck, increased viral infection, abnormal sperm fetotoxicity, persistent memory deficits, schizophrenia.
Hallucinogens (psychedelic drugs) LSD "acid" mescaline "Mexican peyote" psilocybine phencyclidine anticholinergics (datura, belladona)	(in very small dose (unpredictable effects, (usually visual hallucination – very pleasant or frightening.	dilated pupils, sweating, trembling, loss of judgment, incoherence, some times panic state.	severe mental disturbance, acute psychosis leading to suicide or assault or homocide (phencyclidine).	flashback, prolonged psychosis.
Volatile Substances gasoline, ether trichloroethylone N$_2$O, CCe$_4$ solvents in glue and cleaning fluids	(euphoria, lightheadedness, possible hallucinations.	dilated pupils flushed face, general confusion.	loss of consciousness, possible suffocation, coma and death.	risk of pulmonary kidney and brain damage.
Minor Psycho-Stimulants tobacco (Nicotine)	(stimulates awareness (and mental acuity)	heart rate increases	none reported	increases risk of cancer of the lung and bladder, cardiac infarction, atherosclerosis, peptic ulcer.
caffeine	stimulates awareness	heart rate increases	none reported	?
khat	stimulates awareness	heart rate increases	none reported	?

TABLE 2

Experiments Performed by Dr. Akira Morishima of Columbia
University College of Physicians & Surgeons

Effect of Heavy Marijuana Smoking on Human Lymphocytes (White Blood Cells) Compared to Lymphocytes from Non-Marijuana Smokers

Heavy marijuana smokers have a marked increase in *micronuclei,* cells with less than the normal complement of forty-six chromosomes.

The pictures show:

A. Normal lymphocyte with forty-six chromosomes

B. Abnormal lymphocyte with twenty-four chromosomes—a micronucleus

Lymphocyte cells were allowed to grow in culture for three days.

Percentage of micronuclei

Cells from non-marijuana smokers:	Cells from marijuana smokers:
15%	36%

A   B

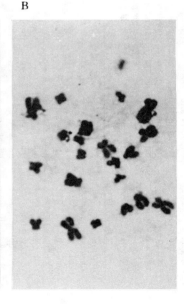

Photomicrographs by Dr. Wylie Hembree of Columbia University College of Physicians and Surgeons, New York.

A. Sperm cells from a twenty-five-year-old tobacco cigarette smoker. Normal ovoid cells.

B. Sperm cells from a twenty-three-year-old heavy marijuana smoker. Note high incidence of abnormal cells.

A

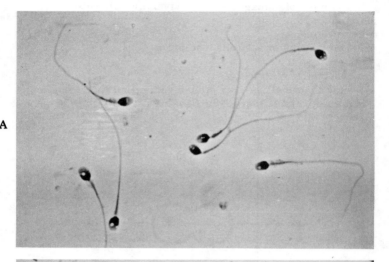

B

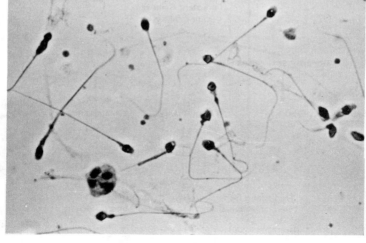

Damage to the genetic information contained in DNA has the following effects:

Extensive damage: cell death
Lesser damage: cell repair or
                      cell survival with abnormality (mutation)
                      (This is usually rare, due to protective mechanism of the system.)

If a number of damaged cells survive, this can cause:

malignancy

cellular aging

effect on gonadal or sex cells leading to:

    sterility

    abortion

    fetal abnormality—may jump a generation before appearing

Habitual, chronic marijuana smoking can be said to be genetic roulette.

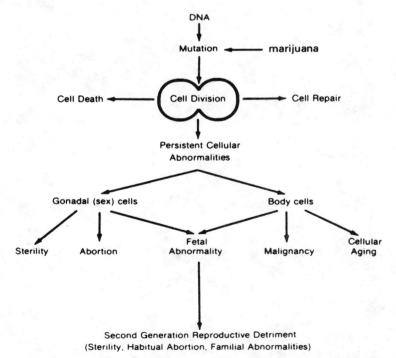

Schematic representation of the consequences of altered DNA.

In alcohol-consuming populations, 6 to 8% of the consumers will be excessive users, consuming a daily intoxicating dose and are addicted to alcohol. The higher the total consumption, the greater the number of users, and the greater the number of users, the greater the number of abusers.

Surveys of populations consuming cannabis, cocaine or heroin show that 50 and 90, to 95% of the consumers use these respective drugs in daily intoxicating doses when they are available. In conclusion, the abuse potential of cannabis, cocaine and heroin is 7 and 13, to 14 times greater than that of alcohol.

DAILY INTOXICATING DOSE

ALCOHOL
France 1956
Scotland 1983
U.S.A. 1984

MARIJUANA
U.S. Seniors 1978

MARIJUANA
Jamaican Farmers 1974

COCAINE-HEROIN
World Wide

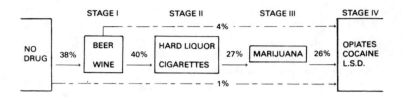

This diagram illustrates the successive stages in adolescent drug use observed in two follow-up surveys ("longitudinal") of 5,468 New York State High School students between fall 1971 and spring 1972, and of 985 seniors 5 months after graduation. Students start use of legal drugs, beer or wine, and go on to the smoking of cigarettes and drinking of hard liquor. While 27 percent of students who smoke and drink progress to marijuana within a 5 to 6 month follow-up period, only 2 percent of those who did not drink or smoke previously do so. *Marijuana in turn is a critical step on the way to other illicit drugs*: while 26 percent of marijuana users will experiment with L.S.D., amphetamines and opiates, only 1 percent of non-drug users and 4 percent of legal drug users do so. This sequence is found in each of the 4 years in high school and in the year after graduation (Kandel D. Stages in adolescent involvement in drug use. *Science*, 190: 912, 1975).

A 1980 study confirmed the statistical progression of marijuana to heroin and cocaine, "The linkage between marijuana use and later heroin or cocaine use is *ten times* greater than the evidence of linkage between cigarette smoking and lung cancer" (Clayton, R. and Voss, H. *U.S. Jour. of Drug and Alcohol Dependence*, Jan. 1982).

Marijuana Rescheduling Petition by NORML Denied by DEA

On December 29, 1989, the Federal Register published a ruling from the Drug Enforcement Administration which denied a petition presented by the National Organization for the Reform of Marijuana Law (NORML), to reschedule marijuana from Schedule I to Schedule II of the Controlled Substances Act. Controlled drugs in Schedule I have a high potential for abuse, and no currently accepted medical use in the United States. Examples of such drugs are: heroin, peyote, mescaline, marijuana, LSD, methaqualone and others. Controlled drugs in Schedule II have a high potential for abuse with severe liability to cause dependence. Examples of such drugs are opium, morphine and cocaine. These substances, which have unique therapeutic properties, may be dispensed by physicians on special order forms for patient care. The D.E.A., after an exhaustive analysis of the record, concluded that marijuana should remain in Schedule I.

The ruling by the Drug Enforcement Administration follows.

Taken from the Federal Register, Vol. 54, No. 249, December 29, 1989.

This is a final order of the Administrator of the Drug Enforcement Administration [DEA] denying the petition of the National Organization for Reform of Marijuana Laws [NORML] to reschedule the plant material marijuana from Schedule I to Schedule II of the Controlled Substances Act. This order follows a rulemaking on the record as prescribed by the Controlled Substances Act, 21 U.S.C. 801, *et seq.,* and the Administrative Procedures Act, 5 U.S.C. 551, *et seq.* There are seven parties in the rulemaking proceeding. Four parties, NORML, the Alliance for Cannabis Therapeutics [ACT], the Cannabis Corporation of America [CCA], and Carl Eric Olsen, comprised the pro-marijuana parties, those advocating the rescheduling of marijuana from Schedule I to Schedule II. The three remaining parties, who advocated that marijuana remain in Schedule I were DEA, the National Federation of Parents for a Drug-Free Youth, and the International Association of Chiefs of Police [IACP].

The two issues involved in a determination of whether marijuana should be rescheduled from Schedule I to Schedule II are whether marijuana plant material has a currently accepted medical use in treatment in the United States, or a currently accepted medical use with severe restrictions; and whether there is a lack of accepted safety for use of marijuana plant material under medical supervision. After a thorough review of the record in this matter, the Administrator rejects the recommendation of the administrative law judge to reschedule marijuana into Schedule II and finds that the evidence in the record mandates a finding that the marijuana plant material remain in Schedule I of the Controlled Substances Act.

The pro-marijuana parties advocate the placement of marijuana plant material into Schedule II for medical use in the treatment of a wide variety of ailments, including nausea and vomiting associated with chemotherapy, glaucoma, spasticity in amputees and those with multiple sclerosis, epilepsy, poor appetite, addiction to drugs and alcohol, pain and asthma. The evidence presented by the pro-marijuana parties includes outdated and limited scientific studies;

chronicles of individuals, their families and friends who have used marijuana; opinions from over a dozen psychiatrists and physicians; court opinions involving medical necessity as a defense to criminal charges for illegal possession of marijuana; state statutes which made marijuana available for research; newspaper articles; and the opinions of laypersons, including lawyers and associations of lawyers. The Administrator does not find such evidence convincing in light of the lack of reliable, credible, and relevant scientific studies documenting marijuana's medical utility; the opinions of highly respected, credentialed experts that marijuana does not have an accepted medical use; and statements from the American Medical Association, the American Cancer Society, the American Academy of Ophthalmology, the National Multiple Sclerosis Society, and the Federal Food and Drug Administration that marijuana has not been demonstrated as suitable for use as a medicine. Each of these areas will be discussed separately.

The record contains many research studies which have been published in scientific journals and many unpublished studies conducted by individual states. In order to evaluate the validity of any research study many factors must be considered. Certain scientific practices have been generally accepted by the scientific community which are designed to increase the validity of experimental studies. Studies or research projects which do not follow these accepted scientific practices have very limited, if any, credibility. A review of such studies must first examine the degree to which researchers control, or hold constant, all the variables which could affect the results, except that variable being studied. For example, if you wish to evaluate the effectiveness of marijuana on a group of glaucoma patients, you must control any other medication which the patient is taking. Otherwise, it is impossible to conclude that the results are attributable to the marijuana.

The second factor, or aspect of the design of a research project which must be evaluated, is the placebo effect. This is the tendency of research subjects to act and respond in a manner they believe is expected of them. To eliminate this factor, research subjects are usually "blinded," or not informed, of what drug they are receiving. Results of non-blind studies are questionable since they could be attributable, in large part, to psychological reactions of subjects rather than any real effects from the experimental drug. The next factor which must be minimized or eliminated for a research study to be valid is the expectation of the researcher. This is especially true where the effect being measured is subjective and not objective. For example, if the researcher is evaluating if the patient is nauseated, that is very subjective. If the researcher knows which patients are receiving the experimental drug, his perception of the results could be significantly altered.

Other factors to be considered when evaluating the validity of research include the number of subject in the study, how the subjects are selected for the study, the length of the study, or how many times the experimental drug is administered, and the measurement of results in quantifiable, objective terms. The fewer the subjects in a research study, the less valid the results. If the sample of subjects is not statistically significant, the chances of the same results being duplicated in other individuals is reduced. Subjects for a research study should be randomly selected and representative of the population that is targeted to use the drug. Testing of marijuana in cancer patients for relief of nausea and vomiting should not be limited to those who have previously used marijuana recreationally and request its use in the study. The length of a study is particularly significant when the drug is to be used to treat a chronic condition such as glaucoma or spasticity. Studies based upon acute or one-time administration of the drug must be viewed with caution when the goal is treatment of a chronic condition. The effectiveness of the drug for long-time administration and the existence of side effects resulting from chronic use will not be revealed in acute studies.

In addition to factors related to the design and execution of a research study, there are two other factors which must be reviewed in evaluation of a research study. Research results are always considered tentative or preliminary until they have been replicated or confirmed by another researcher. The research study must be reported in sufficient detail to permit others to repeat it. Finally, publication of a study in a scientific journal, especially a journal which subjects an article to review prior to publication, adds validity to a study. Journal publication subjects a study to review and scrutiny by the scientific community and opens the door to replication of the studies. Unpublished studies are inherently suspect.

While research studies with the limitations mentioned above may provide useful and preliminary data which will be valuable in designing further studies, research studies with substantial limitations are not sufficient to support a determination that a drug has an accepted medical use. Both the published and unpublished research studies submitted by the pro-marijuana parties in this proceeding to support marijuana's medical use suffer from many deficiencies. They are, in essence, preliminary studies. None of these studies has risen to the level of demonstrating that marijuana has an accepted medical use for treatment of any medical condition. The three medical conditions for which the majority of evidence in the record was presented are: [1] Nausea and vomiting associated with chemotherapy, [2] glaucoma, and [3] spasticity associated with amputation or multiple sclerosis. Evidence presented in each area will be discussed separately.

Nausea and Vomiting

Five studies were presented by the pro-marijuana parties to support the medical use of marijuana as an antiemetic. The first study by Sallan, et al., *Antiemetic Effect of Delta-9-Tetrahydrocannabinol in Patients Receiving Cancer Chemotherapy,* 293 New England Journal of Medicine, 796-797 [1975], utilize synthetic tetrahydrocannibinol [THC] and not the plant material marijuana. Although delta-9-THC is an active ingredient in the marijuana plant material, marijuana contains over 400 other chemicals. At least 61 of these chemicals are cannabinoids. All these chemicals could have some effect on the human body. Since THC is only one of the many active ingredients in marijuana, THC studies are of very limited value in evaluating the therapeutic utility of marijuana. The route of administration, smoking versus oral injection, is a significant difference between use of marijuana and THC. Therefore, the results of the Sallan study are of little or no benefit in evaluating the medical utility of marijuana for treatment of nausea and vomiting associated with chemotherapy.

The second study compared a combination of pure THC and marijuana to placebo cigarettes. This study by Chang, et al., *Delta-9-Tetrahydrocannibinol as an Antiemetic in Cancer Patients Receiving High-Dose Methotrexate,* 91 Annals of Internal Medicine, 819-824 [1979], was randomized, double-blind, and placebo controlled. The study concluded, "that a combination of oral and smoked THC is a highly effective antiemetic compared to placebo***" This study was limited to 15 subjects, some of whom received both marijuana and THC at the same time. The validity of the results of this study is severely limited by its small size and administration of the mixture of the two drugs, THC and marijuana. The study is not helpful in determining the therapeutic utility of marijuana alone in treating nausea and vomiting.

The third study conducted by Dr. Thomas J. Ungerleider, a psychiatrist, involved the administration of marijuana to 16 bone marrow transplant patients suffering from severe nausea and vomiting from radiation therapy. The results of this study are of little value due to the limited number of patients, the subjective nature of the data, and the fact that the results of the study were never published. The conclusion that there was less nausea and vomiting with use of marijuana was based upon the subjects' and researcher's subjective determination. There were no objective measurements, such as number of incidents or frequency of vomiting. During cross-examination, Dr. Ungerleider indicated that the results of the study were not published because there was not enough hard data.

The fourth study compared marijuana to THC as an anti-emetic. Levitt, et al., *Randomized Double Blind Comparison of Delta-9-Tetrahydrocannabinol (THC) and Marijuana As Chemotherapy Antiemetics.* [Meeting Abstract], 3 Proc. Annu. Meet. Am. Soc. Clin. Oncol. 91 [1984]. It concluded that THC is superior to marijuana in controlling nausea and vomiting. A specific formulation of synthetic THC has been approved for marketing and is available as a prescription drug for treatment of nausea and vomiting associated with cancer chemotherapy.

The fifth study presented by the pro-marijuana parties is actually a group of programs, collectively labeled "Controlled Substances Therapeutic Research Programs," conducted by six states in the 1970's and 1908's. These programs involved the use of both marijuana cigarettes and synthetic THC capsules. The programs were given Investigational New Drug [IND] approval by the Food and Drug Administration [FDA] and the marijuana and THC were supplied by the Federal Government. The protocols of these programs were very loosely constructed. There were no controls. That is, there were no individuals who did not take the experimental drug to compare with those who did. The studies were not blind or double-blind. Every research subject knew what drug they were receiving and, in many cases, were permitted to request either marijuana or THC. The studies were not randomized. In most instances, the results were measured by the subject's subjective evaluation of the drug's effectiveness. This is even more of a problem where the drug in question is a psychotropic or mind-altering substance like marijuana, which by its very nature makes some individuals feel "high," and may distort their perception of physical symptoms. There were no objectively measured results. The results were not published in scientific journals and, in some cases, data were lost or not recorded. The number of individual who actually smoke marijuana in these studies was relatively small. These state studies were born of compassion and frustration. They abandoned traditional scientific methods in favor of dispensing marijuana to as many individuals as possible on the chance that it might help them. Though well-intentioned, these studies have little scientific value.

The research studies presented by the pro-marijuana parties of this proceeding do not support a conclusion that marijuana has a therapeutic use for treatment of nausea and vomiting associated with the chemotherapy.

The pro-marijuana parties presented many testimonials from cancer patients, their families, and friends about the use of marijuana to alleviate nausea and vomiting associated with chemotherapy. These stories of individuals who treat themselves with a mind-altering drug, such as marijuana, must be viewed with great skepticism. There is no scientific merit to any of these accounts. In many cases, the individuals were taking a variety of other medications and were using anything which might help treat the cancer as well as the nausea. They were using marijuana purchased on the street, and were unaware of the strength of the drug. They were not using the drug under medical supervision. Many of these individuals had been recreational users of marijuana prior to becoming ill. These individuals' desire for the drug to relieve their symptoms, as well as a desire to rationalize their marijuana use, removes any scientific value from their accounts of marijuana use. There is no doubt that these individuals and their loved-ones believed that marijuana was beneficial. The accounts of these individuals' suffering and illnesses are very moving and tragic; they are not, however, reliable scientific evidence, nor do they provide a basis to conclude that marijuana has an accepted medical use as an antiemetic.

There were many physicians and other medical experts who testified in this proceeding. In reviewing the weight to be given to an expert's opinion, the facts relied upon to reach that opinion and the credentials and experience of the expert must be carefully examined. The experts presented by the pro-marijuana parties were unable to provide a strong scientific or factual basis to support their opinions. In addition, many of the experts presented by the pro-marijuana parties did not have any expertise in the area of research in the specific medical area being addressed. The pro-marijuana parties presented the testimony of five psychiatrists to support the use of marijuana as an antiemetic. None of these individuals is an oncologist, nor have they treated cancer patients. Three of the psychiatrists, Drs. Lester Grinspoon, Thomas Ungerleider and Norman Zinberg are current or former board members of NORML or ACT. All these physicians indicated that they relied on scientific studies which they had read, their experience with cancer patients, or stories from others, to reach their conclusions. When questioned on cross-examination as to which studies they relied upon, most were unable to list one study. A review of the available literature has already demonstrated the unreliability of the studies that exist. The testimonials upon which these psychiatrists relied are also scientifically suspect. The opinions of these psychiatrists are, therefore, of little value in determining whether marijuana is therapeutically useful as an antiemetic.

Two pharmacologists, Drs. John P. Morgan and Philip Jobe, presented testimony on behalf of the pro-marijuana parties. Dr. Morgan is a professor at the City College of New York. He does not treat patients, nor is he an oncologist. His opinions are based upon a review of scientific studies and stories told to him by others. He has ties to NORML and is in favor of legalizing marijuana. Dr. Jobe is a pharmacologist and psychiatrist. He testified that his knowledge of marijuana's effects as a drug as based upon a review of the literature and stories from individuals undergoing chemotherapy. On cross-examination, Dr. Jobe indicated that this anecdotal information came from approximately four or five individuals. He also indicated that his knowledge of marijuana was not current. The opinions of Drs. Morgan and Jobe are of little value in determining whether marijuana has a medical use.

Two general practitioners, Drs. Andrew Weil and Arthur Kaufman, also provided testimony on behalf of the pro-marijuana parties. Neither are oncologist, nor do they treat cancer patients. Dr. Weil is a wellness counselor at a health spa and Dr. Kaufman is an officer of a company that audits hospital quality control programs. Dr. Weil has written a number of books on drugs and admitted that he has person-ally used every mind-altering, illicit drug he has written about. Dr. Kaufman stopped practicing medicine in 1974, and was unable to provide any information on cross-exam-ination regarding the basis for his opinion that marijuana has an accepted medical use. Neither Dr. Weil nor Dr. Kauf-man has a credible basis for their opinions regarding mari-juana, and therefore, their testimony will be disregarded.

Four oncologists presented testimony on behalf of the pro-marijuana parties. They were Drs. Deborah Baron Gold-berg, Ivan Silverberg, John Bickers and Ronald Stephens. Dr. Goldberg is a board certified oncologist, but practices primarily internal medicine. She only administers chemo-therapy to one or two patients a year. In her career, she has administered chemotherapy to no more than ten patients whom she believed to be using marijuana. On cross-exam-ination, she could not recall any studies regarding mari-juana. Dr. Goldberg was a member and financial contributor to NORML. Dr. Silverberg has practiced oncology for 20 years. He is a Professor of Clinical Oncology at the Univer-sity of California at San Francisco, but is not a board certi-fied oncologist. In his testimony, Dr. Silverberg indicated that there was voluminous medical research regarding mar-ijuana's effectiveness in treating nausea and vomiting. On cross-examination, Dr. Silverberg could not identify any studies and was forced to admit that he had been incorrect and that there were, in fact, very few studies conducted using marijuana as an antiemetic. Although Dr. Silverberg has advised patients to use marijuana to control nausea and vomiting associated with chemotherapy, he has never been involved in any research nor has he documented any of the observations. Dr. Bickers is an oncologist in New Orleans and is a Professor of Medicine at the Louisiana University School of Medicine. Although Dr. Bickers claims that young patients have better control over nausea and vomiting after using marijuana, he has never documented this claim. Dr. Bickers was unable to identify any scientific information which he relied upon in reaching his conclusion regarding marijuana. Dr. Stephens, an oncologist, Professor of Medicine and Director of Clinical Oncology at the University of Kansas, characterized as a "highly effective, and in some cases, critical drug in the reduction of chemotherapeutically-induced emesis." During cross-examination, Dr. Stephens stated that he was unaware of any scientific studies which had been done with marijuana, and that he had never done research or treated patients with marijuana. He indicated that he received his information about the patient's use of marijuana from the nursing staff or the patient's family. None of these oncologists based their opinions about marijuana on scientific studies or their own research. Most did not base their opinions on their direct observations, but on the opinions of others. In light of lack of scientific basis for these opinions, they will be given little regard.

The agency presented the testimony of nationally recognized experts in oncology. Dr. David S. Ettinger, a Professor of Oncology at Johns Hopkins School of Medicine, is the author of over 100 published articles on cancer treatment. Dr. Ettinger testified:

"There is no indication that marijuana is effective in treating nausea and vomiting resulting from radiation treatment or other causes. No legitimate studies have been conducted which make such conclusions."

He continued by stating that:

"Although extensive research has been conducted using ***[THC]*** an antiemetic treatment for cancer chemotherapy patients, very little research has actually

been conducted using marijuana ***for the same
purpose. Most of the information concerning marijuana's effectiveness is anecdotal or comes from uncontrolled studies."

Dr. Richard J. Gralla, a Professor of Medicine at Cornell
University Medical College, and an Associate Attending
Physician at Sloan-Kettering Memorial Cancer Center, is
an oncologist who has spent his entire professional career
devoted to cancer research and treatment. Dr. Gralla has
conducted extensive research with antiemetic drugs and
testified that there are currently many new medicines that
control nausea and vomiting associated with chemotherapy
more effectively than marijuana. He also stated that most
physicians and oncologists have little interest in marijuana
because of its negative side effects and other problems associated with its use. In conclusion, Dr. Gralla stated that he
and his fellow cancer specialists at Sloan-Kettering do not
accept marijuana as being medically useful to treat nausea
and vomiting associated with chemotherapy.

Dr. John Laszlo, currently Vice President of Research for
the American Cancer Society, is an expert who has devoted
the majority of his over 30 years in medicine to the treatment of cancer. During his career, he spent eleven years as
the Director of Clinical Programs at the Duke University
Comprehensive Cancer Center. Dr. Laszlo has authored numerous scientific articles about cancer research and treatment and has written a book titled, *Antiemetics and Cancer
Chemotherapy*. In his testimony for this proceeding, Dr.
Laszlo stated that he does not advocate the use of marijuana
as an antiemetic, in part because there has not been sufficient treating of marijuana to show that it is a safe and
effective drug. He also indicated that because there are
other available, highly effective antiemetics, a physician
does not need to resort to a crude drug such as marijuana.
Dr. Laszlo concluded that marijuana does not have a currently accepted medical use in the United States for treat-

ment of nausea and vomiting resulting from cancer chemotherapy.

The American Cancer Society provided DEA with its policy statements regarding medical use of marijuana. The administrative law judge refused to admit this document into evidence in this proceeding, relegating it to the "public comment" section of the record. The Administrator, however, considered this document to be extremely relevant and, indeed, of substantial importance in this matter. The American Cancer Society has, and continues to support research with substances which may provide relief to cancer patients, including marijuana. It states, however, that the results of clinical investigations are insufficient to warrant the decontrol of marijuana for medical use. The American Medical Association has expressed a similar option.

The Food and Drug Administration has provided DEA with a scientific and medical evaluation of marijuana as well as testimony from one of its leading pharmacologists. Evaluating marijuana against its criteria for safety and effectiveness, FDA has concluded that there is inadequate scientific evidence to support a finding that marijuana is safe and effective for treating nausea and vomiting experienced by patients undergoing chemotherapy.

The pro-marijuana parties presented cases in which courts did not convict individuals of a crime associated with possession and use of marijuana based upon a legal defense of "medical necessity." These cases have no relevance to this proceeding which relates to marijuana's possible medical use. The courts found only that these individuals, who were seriously ill and believed that marijuana would help them, did not have criminal intent in possessing or using marijuana. The judges and juries in these proceedings were not deciding medical and scientific facts, but legal issues. These decisions do not provide scientific evidence that marijuana has a medical use.

The pro-marijuana parties also presented evidence that 34 states passed laws permitting marijuana's use for medical purposes in those states. These laws provided that marijuana should be available for medical research. The term "research" is essential to a reading of these statutes. These laws made marijuana available for research and, in some states, set up research programs to study marijuana's safety and effectiveness as a medicine. These statutes are read for what they are, encouraging research involving marijuana. They are not an endorsement by state legislatures that marijuana has an accepted medical use in treatment.

The numerous testimonials and opinions of law persons which were presented in this proceeding by the pro-marijuana parties are not useful in determining whether marijuana has a medical use. While experiences of individuals with medical conditions who use marijuana may provide a basis for research, they cannot be substituted for reliable scientific evidence. For the many reasons stated in the previous discussion of scientific evidence, these statements can be given little weight. Similarly, endorsements by such organizations as the National Association of Attorneys General, that marijuana has a medical use as an antiemetic, are of little persuasive value when compared with statements from the American Cancer Society and the American Medical Association.

Glaucoma

The pro-marijuana parties presented several studies to support their contention that marijuana has a medical use for treatment of glaucoma. In order for a drug to be effective in treating glaucoma it must lower the pressure within the eye for prolonged periods of time and actually preserve sight or visual fields. The studies relied upon by the pro-marijuana parties do not scientifically support a finding that marijuana has a medical use for treatment of glaucoma. Five of the studies presented by the pro-marijuana parties are pure THC studies. As previously noted, THC is only one constituent among hundreds found in marijuana. Therefore, the consequences of an individual ingesting pure THC as compared to smoking marijuana are vastly different. A few of the studies presented do document that heavy doses of marijuana over a short time period reduce the eye pressure in most individuals. However, there are no studies which document that marijuana can sustain reduced eye pressure for extended time periods. The acute, or short-term studies also show various side effects from marijuana use, including lowered blood pressure, rapid heart beat, and heart palpitations. In a 1979 study conducted by Drs. Merritt, Crawford, Alexander, Anduze, and Gelbart, the conclusions included a statement: "It is because of the frequency and severity with which untoward events occurred that marijuana inhalation is not an ideal therapeutic modality for glaucoma patients."

The pro-marijuana parties presented testimonials of individuals who suffer from glaucoma and believe their condition has benefited from the use of marijuana. Most of these individuals used marijuana recreationally prior to discovery of their illness. Chief among the individuals presenting statements was Robert Randall. Mr. Randall is president of ACT, and has been on NORML's Board of Directors since 1976. He has been a strong advocate for medical use of marijuana. Mr. Randall also has glaucoma. Mr. Randall began smoking marijuana as a college student in 1967, long before he was diagnosed in 1972 as having glaucoma. At that time, Mr. Randall was treated with standard glaucoma mediations. In the mid 1970's Mr. Randall was involved in a preliminary research study conducted by Dr. Robert Hepler. Dr. Hepler conducted some of the first published short-term marijuana studies relating to glaucoma. Dr. Hepler told Mr. Randall that he believed that marijuana in combination with other standard glaucoma medications would be helpful in reducing his eye pressure. In 1975, Mr. Randall was arrested for growing and possessing marijuana. His defense was medical necessity. He then began receiving marijuana under an Investigational New Drug [IND] protocol sponsored by his physician. He also continued to receive standard glaucoma medications. Since 1978, he has been treated by Dr. Richard D. North. Mr. Randall receives marijuana from the Federal Government and continues to take standard glaucoma medications. Two physicians who treated Mr. Randall, including Dr. North, testified that Mr. Randall's eye pressure appears to have been controlled and his vision kept stable for the last several years.

Mr. Randall smokes approximately 8 to 10 marijuana cigarettes a day. Since Mr. Randall continued to take other glaucoma medications, his controlled eye pressure cannot be attributable solely to marijuana use. In fact, Dr. North testified that Mr. Randall needs the standard medications as well as marijuana, and that the marijuana itself is not totally effective in decreasing Mr. Randall's eye pressure. Mr. Randall's experience with marijuana, although utilized under a physician's directions, is not scientific evidence that marijuana has an accepted medical use in treatment of glaucoma. Dr. John C. Merritt, one of Mr. Randall's physicians, responded to the question of why he did not publish the results of Mr. Randall's treatment by saying: "A single isolated incident of one person smoking marijuana is not evidence for other ophthalmologists who may want to use the drug."

Dr. Hepler, the physician who conducted preliminary studies with marijuana and initially advised Mr. Randall to use marijuana with his other medications, now states that there is insufficient scientific evidence to conclude that marijuana is effective in treating glaucoma. The pro-marijuana parties rely primarily on the opinions of two of Mr. Randall's physicians, Drs. North and Merritt, in supporting their contention that marijuana has a medical use in treatment of glaucoma. Dr. North indicated that his conclusion that marijuana has a medical use in treatment of glaucoma is based solely on his observations of Mr. Randall. Dr. Merritt is a board certified ophthalmologist and researcher who has authored many articles on the use of marijuana and cannabinoids to reduce eye pressure. Dr. Merritt based his opinion that marijuana has a medical use in treatment of glaucoma on published scientific studies, treatment of Mr. Randall, and treatment of other glaucoma patients. As previously stated, all the available studies concern high doses of marijuana taken over short periods of time. Even Dr. Merritt admitted that there are no studies to show that marijuana repeatedly lowers eye pressure over long time periods. The maintenance of lowered eye pressure is crucial in treating individuals with glaucoma. On cross-examination, Dr. Merritt was unable to provide either the specific number of individual patients he had observed or any scientific data relating to those patients. Although Dr. Merritt is a well-known ophthalmologist, the basis for his opinion that marijuana has a medical use in the treatment of glaucoma is not scientifically sound.

The agency presented several experts who testified that there is insufficient scientific evidence to support the conclusion that marijuana has a medical use in treatment of glaucoma. In addition to Dr. Hepler, they include Dr. George Spaeth, Professor of Ophthalmology, Director of the Glaucoma Service at Will's Eye Hospital in Philadelphia and President of the American Glaucoma Society and Dr. Keith Green, Professor of Ophthalmology, pharmacologist and researcher who had conducted research with both marijuana and THC. Perhaps the most persuasive evidence concerning the use of marijuana in treating glaucoma is the opinion of the American Academy of Ophthalmology, an organization representing 12,000 physician members and 6,000 other medical professionals who specialize in ophthalmology. The Academy has concluded that insufficient data exists to demonstrate the safety and efficacy of using smoked marijuana in the treatment of glaucoma. FDA has also determined that there is insufficient evidence to conclude that marijuana has a medical use in treatment of glaucoma.

Spasticity

In support of their contention that marijuana has a medical use in treatment of spasticity, in amputees and those with multiple sclerosis, the pro-marijuana parties presented three studies involving THC, testimonials of individuals with spasticity who use marijuana, medical opinions, and state court decisions on the medical necessity defense. The three studies presented by the pro-marijuana parties were very small studies. All three totalled 17 patients, and used THC, not marijuana, to treat spasticity. There are no studies using marijuana to treat spasticity. These studies to not provide a scientific basis to conclude that marijuana has a medical use in treating spasticity.

Dr. Denis Petro, a board certified neurologist, testified on behalf of the pro-marijuana parties that he believes that marijuana has a currently accepted medical use in treating spasticity. He testified that his opinion is based on the THC studies, experiences and observations of patients, and historical accounts of marijuana use. Dr. Petro knew of no studies in which marijuana was used to treat spasticity. He testified that his information from patients consisted of them telling him how the street marijuana these patients used at home affected their spasticity. He did not conduct any clinical studies or make objective measurements. Dr. Petro's opinion is not based upon any reliable scientific evidence. The same psychiatrists and general practitioners who reported marijuana had a medical use in treating nausea and vomiting and glaucoma also stated that marijuana had a medical use in treating spasticity. None of these physicians based their opinions on reliable scientific evidence.

The agency presented the testimony of national experts in multiple sclerosis and spasticity. Dr. Kenneth Johnson is Chairman of the Dept. of Neurology at the Univ. of Maryland School of Medicine and manages the Maryland Center for Multiple Sclerosis [MS]. He is the author of over 100 scientific and medical articles on MS and has spent most of his medical career researching MS and has diagnosed and treated more than 6,900 patients with the disease. He testified that he is unaware of any legitimate research involving marijuana to treat symptoms of MS. He also stated that, "to conclude that marijuana is therapeutically effective without

conducting rigorous testing would be professionally irresponsible." Dr. Donald Silverberg, Chairman of the Dept. of
Neurology at the University of Pennsylvania School of Medicine and Chief of Neurology Service at the Hospital of
Pennsylvania, has been actively researching and treating
MS for most of his career. He has written over 130 medical
articles on MS. He concluded that not only is there no
legitimate medical or scientific evidence to support a conclusion that marijuana is effective in treating MS or spasticity,
but that long-term treatment of MS patients with marijuana
could be worse than the original disease. Dr. Silverberg
placed no value on the reports of patients who claimed relief
of their symptoms with marijuana because of the sporadic
and episodic nature of MS attacks.

The National Multiple Sclerosis Society has concluded
that marijuana is not an accepted medical treatment for
spasticity. Dr. Stephen Reingold, Assistant Vice President
for Research of the National Multiple Sclerosis Society, indicated in his testimony that because there are no well-designed, well-controlled research studies using marijuana to
treat spasticity, the society does not endorse or advocate the
use of marijuana for such a purpose. The evidence presented
by the pro-marijuana parties regarding use of marijuana to
treat various other ailments such as pain, decreased appetite, alcohol and drug addiction, epilepsy, atopic neuroder-
matitis, scleroderma and asthma was limited to testimony
of individuals who had used marijuana for those conditions
and the testimony of the psychiatrists or general practitioners mentioned earlier. There is not a shred of credible
scientific evidence to support any of their claims.

With regard to marijuana's safety for use under medical
supervision, the Administrator must again rely on the scientific evidence. While the pro-marijuana parties argue that
no one has died from marijuana use, and the individuals
who use have testified that they have not experienced adverse effects, there is little or no scientific evidence to support these claims. For example, while Robert Randall claims

marijuana smoking has had no adverse effect on his health
or respiratory system, he has not had a physical examination or pulmonary function test in over ten years.

In order to be effective, a drug's therapeutic benefits must
be balanced against and outweigh its negative or adverse
effects. This has not been established with marijuana. As
the previously discussed evidence has demonstrated, there
is as yet no reliable scientific evidence to support marijuana's therapeutic benefit. It is, therefore, impossible to
balance the benefit against the negative effects. The negative effects of marijuana use are well-documented in the
record. Marijuana smoking, the route of administration advocated by many witnesses presented by the pro-marijuana
parties, causes many well-known side effects. These include
decreased blood pressure, rapid heart rate, drowsiness, euphoria, dysphoria and impairment of motor function, not to
mention various negative effects on the respiratory and
pulmonary systems. Therefore, the only conclusion is that
marijuana is not safe for use under medical supervision,
because its safety has not been established by reliable, scientific evidence.

In summary, the Administrator finds that there is insufficient, and in many instances no reliable, credible, scientific
evidence supported by properly conducted scientific research to support a conclusion that marijuana has a medical
use to treat any ailment or disease. In addition, there is a
lack of scientific evidence to support a conclusion that marijuana is safe for use under medical supervision. This agency,
and the Government as a whole, would be doing the public a
disservice by concluding that this complex psychoactive
drug with serious adverse effects has a medical use based
upon anecdotal and unreliable evidence. The evidence presented by the pro-marijuana parties in this proceeding consisted of a few published scientific studies involving marijuana and THC, testimony of general practice physicians
and psychiatrists, and testimony of individuals who have
used marijuana for various medical conditions. The majority
of these individuals did not use marijuana under medical

supervision and used "street" marijuana. In contrast, recognized, credentialed specialists in the fields of oncology, glaucoma and multiple sclerosis, and organizations involved in medical research in these areas, have concluded that marijuana does not have an accepted medical use in treatment in the United States. The Administrator would be abdicating his responsibility to the public if he concluded that marijuana has a medical use and is safe for use under medical supervision.

The preceding discussion is based upon the Administrator's review of the entire record in this matter. This record contains volumes of documents and testimony. The procedural history of this scheduling has extended for many years. The procedural history and the findings of fact and conclusions of law upon which the Administrator's decision is based as set forth below.

Procedure

This rulemaking proceeding was originally initiated by a petition filed by NORML on May 19, 1972, with the Bureau of Narcotics and Dangerous Drugs [BNDD]. This petition requested that marijuana be removed from the Controlled Substances Act, or in the alternative, be moved to Schedule V of the Act. After a series of proceedings, including hearings before BNDD and DEA and remands by the United States Court of Appeals for the District of Columbia Circuit, the matter was again the subject of a DEA hearing. This hearing followed a 1980 remand by the United States Court of Appeals for the District of Columbia Circuit, *NORML v. DEA and HEW,* No. 79-1660 [D.C. Cir. Oct. 16, 1980], in which the Court ordered DEA to refer all matters to the Department of Health and Human Services [HHS] for a scientific and medical evaluation and recommendation for scheduling. The matter was forwarded to HSS by DEA, and the Food and Drug Administration [FDA] published "Proposed Recommendations to the Drug Enforcement Administration Regarding the Scheduling Status of Marijuana and

Its Components and Notice of Public Hearing," in the **Federal Register, 47 FR**28141 [1982]. On September 16, 1982, FDA conducted a legislative-type hearing at which it received written and oral testimony. On May 13, 1983, the Assistant Secretary for Health forwarded his department's scientific and medical findings and scheduling recommendation regarding marijuana plant material to the Administrator of DEA. In this document the Assistant Secretary recommended that marijuana plant material continue to be controlled in Schedule I. On July 2, 1987, the Assistant Secretary for Health submitted a letter to the DEA Deputy Administrator in which he stated that it continued to be the position of the Department of Health and Human Services that marijuana continue to be controlled in Schedule I based upon its lack of accepted medical use in treatment in the U.S.

This current proceeding was initiated by publication of a notice of hearing in the **Federal Register** on June 24, 1986, which advised any individual interested in participating in the proceedings to file a written notice of such intent. Seven organizations or individuals participated in the proceeding. Four prehearing conferences were held in late 1986 and 1987. Direct and rebuttal testimony were filed in written affidavit form. Fourteen days of hearings, for the purpose of cross-examination of witnesses, were held in three cities. All parties were permitted to file proposed findings of fact, conclusions of law and argument with Administrative Law Judge Francis L. Young. The pro-marijuana parties, as petitioners, filed their proposed findings on April 15, 1988. The Government filed its proposed findings on May 16, 1988. The pro-marijuana parties then filed rebuttal on June 3, 1988. The administrative law judge issued his opinion and recommended ruling, findings of fact, conclusions of law and decision on September 6, 1988. Exceptions to the administrative law judge's recommended decision were filed by NORML, ACT and the Government. By letter dated December 9, 1988, the administrative law judge forwarded the entire record to the Administrator of DEA.

The Administrator has carefully reviewed the entire record in this matter and hereby issues this final order as prescribed by 21 CFR 1316.67. The Administrator does not accept the recommendation of the administrative law judge that marijuana has an accepted medical use in treatment of some medical conditions, that marijuana has accepted safety for use under medical supervision, and that marijuana should be rescheduled into Schedule II of the Controlled Substances Act. The Administrator finds that marijuana must remain in Schedule I of the Controlled Substances Act because it has no accepted medical use in treatment of any condition in the United States and it is not safe for use under medical supervision. The Administrator has reviewed the proposed findings of fact submitted by all parties and those formulated by the administrative law judge. The Administrator adopts the findings of fact submitted by the Government as his own and in their entirety. They are as follows:

Findings of Fact

1. The cannabis plant [*Cannabis sativa L.*] is an annual weed which belongs to the plant family Cannabaceae. This family has only one genus, the genus *Cannabis* which consists of one highly variable species, *sativa.* Many varieties of this species are known to exist.

2. Over 400 different chemicals have been identified in the extracts of the plant *Cannabis sativa.* They belong to 18 chemical classes of organic compounds. There are at least 61 different cannabinoids. The proportions and concentrations of these cannabinoids, including THC, differ from plant to plant depending on growing conditions, age of the plant, and factors surrounding harvest. Cannabis THC levels in cannabis may vary from less than 0.2% to greater than 10% in high quality plants.

3. Cannabis or marijuana cannot be defined chemically, nor can it be easily standardized. No totally reliable classification system based on a single chemical analysis exists.

Twenty-one [21] cannabinoids have been clinically evaluated. Most of this testing centered on the psychotropic effects of the compounds, and only eight or nine of the cannabinoids have been tested for therapeutic utility. These studies have only been cursory except for the testing of synthetic THC. Cannabigerol [CBG] cannabinoids show antibacterial activity against gram positive bacteria, and have been shown to effect basic cell metabolism. Cannabinol [CBN] type compounds have exhibited anticonvulsant, antiinflammatory, immunological, and behavioral effects. CBN has also exhibited possible potentiation of THC effects in man. Cannabidiol [CBD] has exhibited anticonvulsant activity.

4. As well as significant variations in naturally occurring active substances in natural cannabis, there are variations in the active substances based on conditions under which the plant material has been maintained or stored. THC is liable to air oxidation forming cannabinol [CBN]. Cannabidiol [CBD], in the presence of oxygen and light and upon heating, is converted to cannabielsoic acids.

5. It is not known how smoking or burning marijuana plant material affects the chemical composition of cannabinoids and their products. A large number of pyrolytic products is produced by burning that have not been identified for most of the constituents in *Cannabis*. Smoking as a dosage form to deliver marijuana to the human body is unsuitable for medical treatment due to: [1] Lack of standardization of the marijuana, [2] lack of knowledge of the amounts of each constituent available, [3] lack of knowledge of the activity of the chemicals while burning, [4] amount of product ingested being dependent on the individuals' smoking technique, and [5] possible carcinogenic effect of smoking. There are no drugs delivered by smoking which are medically used in the U.S.

6. *Cannabis sativa L.* was one of the first plants to be used by man for fiber, food, medicine, and in social and religious rituals. There were approximately 20 traditional medicinal uses of cannabis preparations in the 19th century. These

included those recognized in 19th century medicine as well as folkloric use. These used were based upon tradition and experience rather than scientific proof. Early literature is replete with reports of the inconsistent or contradictory effects of marijuana preparations. The cannabis used for medical purposes in the United States and in Western medicine from the mid-19th to the early 20th century was cannabis extract which was orally administered as tinctures and pills. By 1938, marijuana preparations were seldom used in medical practice, and the American Medical Association sated that, "Cannabis at the present time is slightly used for medicinal purposes***" In 1941, marijuana passed out of the *National Formulatory* and *The U.S. Pharmacopeia.*

7. Historically, man used natural plants to treat various ailments. With the advent of science, man began to use plant extracts to determine their effects. These extracts were crude drugs. Fifty years ago *The United State Pharmacopeia* listed many crude drugs. In recent times, scientists discovered that crude extracts owed their activity to chemical compounds from the plants and their extracts. Current technology emphasizes the development of synthetics of natural drugs by using the natural drugs as models.

8. Currently, there are only four plants used in their natural states specifically for medical purposes in the United States. Three other plants are utilized in crude extract form. These include the ipecac and opium extracts, which must meet standards for potency and purity established in *The U.S. Pharmacopeia* before they can be used for medical purposes. In contrast to variations in cannabinoid content evident in cannabis, naturally occurring opium derivatives remain quantitatively stable and the potency can be chemically standardized.

9. Modern drug research is based on the use of well-defined preparations of pure compounds which, when administered, allow reproducible results. The problems associated with using natural substances as drugs include the inability to regulate the doses of active constituents, and the interaction

of the active constituents with other potentially active compounds in the natural substance. The presence of active constituents in most natural drugs may very based on genetic factors, country of origin and growing conditions. As a result, most natural drugs cannot meet established quality control standards in the U.S. Before a drug substance can be used in the practice of medicine, it must have a composition of active ingredients that has been established and accepted as standard. Such standardization, which includes identity, purity, potency, and quality, is specified in either a New Drug Application [NDA] or an official compendium such as *The U.S. Pharmacopeia* or *National Formulatory*.

10. There is no difference in the pharmacological effect between the THC isolated from cannabis and the synthetically produced THC which is now marketed in the United States.

11. In the late '60's, the Dept. of Health, Education and Welfare [DHEW] initiated a process to facilitate FDA reviewed Investigational New Drug [IND] applications for marijuana and THC, assisted researchers and physicians in preparing IND protocols, and sent out information packets and model protocols.

12. The IND procedure is in the process by which drugs are introduced into man and their safety and effectiveness is evaluated over a period of years. The stated objectives of the FDA in regulating the clinical testing of new drugs are to "protect the rights and safety of human subjects of such testing while, facilitating the development and marketing of beneficial drug therapies. "The Food, Drug, and Cosmetic Act emphasizes the need to carry out scientifically valid studies as well as the need to control the investigational drug supply and obtain informed consent of the subject or patient. The drug used in the study must be able to be traced to the patient, and the investigator must submit annual reports to FDA and report adverse reactions.

13. The protocols for the INDs with marijuana, especially the state protocols and those for individual patients did not describe controlled studies. Controlled studies are necessary

as the basis of a New Drug Application [NDA]. No NDA for marijuana has been submitted to FDA for approval. Thus, marijuana remains an investigational drug subject to IND requirements. Due to the lack of an approved NDA, marijuana is not available by prescription in the United States.

14. As of January 6, 1987, there were 30 active INDs for marijuana; 82 INDs for marijuana have been discontinued.

15. The National Institute on Drug Abuse [NIDA] has shipped a total of 160,700 marijuana cigarettes for human studies from 1976 to 1986. Fifty-nine thousand [59,000] cigarettes were shipped to eight sponsors for human use outside state-sponsored programs. More than half of those 30,900 cigarettes, were shipped to one sponsor during that period.

16. Thirty-four states have passed legislation concerning the use of cannabis [marijuana] and THC by physicians. Of these states, at least 24 define this use of marijuana and THC as research. Of these 34 states, only 17 states [New Mexico, Illinois, Louisiana, Washington, Florida, Michigan, Oregon, Colorado, California, Nevada, Ohio, West Virginia, Georgia, Arizona, New York, Vermont and Tennessee] had approved INDs for marijuana or marijuana/THC as of March 1, 1984. Ten state-sponsored programs received marijuana cigarettes from the NIDA during the period 1978 to 1986. During this period 101,700 cigarettes were distributed to those states; California received 38,700 cigarettes, the most of any state. New Mexico received 8,700 cigarettes in the period from 1978 to 1986. In 1986, four state programs received a total of 1,860 cigarettes. In March, 1982, a National Conference on the Therapeutic Application of Cannabinoids was held. The report of that conference indicates that "state programs in general had a small volume of participation and a high loss of data." The report also concluded that the designs of the state programs varied widely.

17. The California Research Advisory Panel, a California government agency, sponsored the California Cannabis Therapeutic Research Program. After six years of operation, from 1979 to 1986, the Research Advisory Panel found that only 101 patients received 210 treatments with marijuana

cigarettes. Slightly more than one-third of the patients received a second treatment of marijuana cigarettes. Approximately 20 percent of the patients stopped using the cigarettes either because the cigarettes were ineffective, or the side effects were too severe.

18. Approximately 250 individuals received marijuana and/or THC capsules under the New Mexico Controlled Substances Therapeutic Research Program from February 1979 to June 1986 for control of nausea and vomiting associated with cancer chemotherapy. For admission to the program, patients must have experienced nausea and vomiting in previous chemotherapy. An average of four to six individuals a month participated in the program. Approximately 20 New Mexico physicians participated in the state-wide program. There was no randomization in the study; the patients themselves chose to use either marijuana or THC. They were also free to switch from one drug to the other once they began treatment. Under the program, 16 individuals switched from one drug to the other; 13 switched from cigarettes to capsules, the others from capsules to cigarettes. Of the patients selected for evaluation, 94 used THC capsules and 75 used marijuana cigarettes. There was no objective measurement of success or failure. The patients evaluated themselves based upon the degree of chemotherapy sessions as compared with the degree of nausea and vomiting when marijuana or THC was used.

19. One hundred-five patients enrolled in the State of Georgia marijuana and THC research study which was designed to evaluate the efficacy and toxicity of marijuana and THC as an antiemetic in cancer patients undergoing chemotherapy treatment. Emory University enrolled 85 patients in their marijuana and THC research study. Thirty-eight patients from the State of Georgia study, and 81 patients from the Emory University study were evaluated. Of the 119 patients evaluated in the combined studies, 44 smoked marijuana; the other 75 used THC capsules. The success rate for use of THC capsules was 76 percent, and the success rate for smoking marijuana was 68.2 percent. Success was

measured by patient self-assessment or satisfaction. The primary reason for marijuana's failure as a treatment was the patients' intolerance of the cigarettes, or its failure to improve nausea and vomiting.

20. Of the 165 individuals evaluated in the Michigan Therapeutic Research Project for the years 1980–1982, 83 receive marijuana after receiving Toracan (a phenothiazine in the same family as Compazine) during the same trial. The purpose of the trial [Trial A] was to evaluate the efficacy of marijuana to control nausea and vomiting induced by cancer chemotherapeutic agents. Thirty-four [34] of the patients discontinued the study because they did not like smoking marijuana. Twenty-one[21] patients reported the adverse effect of sleepiness/fatigue, 13 reported sore throat, 7 reported headache, and 4 reported being light-headed after smoking marijuana. Of 93 individuals who smoke marijuana at the first patient session, 14 reported no nausea, 31 reported mild nausea, 22 reported moderate nausea, and 19 reported severe nausea. Of the 93 patients who smoked marijuana in the initial session, 63 percent reported they felt "high," and 58 percent reported no increased appetite stimulation.

21. The State of New York Controlled Substances Therapeutic Research Program Report for 1982 indicates that by the end of July 1982, 840 marijuana cigarettes had been distributed to 45 patients under the New York program. These 45 patients had 99 treatment episodes. The treatment of 18 patients was evaluated, and 15 found that they benefited from smoked marijuana in some manner. For the period from November 1981 to May 1986, 199 patients received marijuana cigarettes under the New York program. During that period, 6,044 marijuana cigarettes were distributed. Of the 199 patients who received marijuana, only 90 were evaluated. The evaluations were based solely on patient self-assessments of nausea and vomiting, appetite, physical status, mood, "high" feeling, and a record of the amount of drug taken. The program was also plagued by lack of compliance with reporting procedures. The results of

the evaluations indicated that large percentage of the individuals who received chemotherapeutic agents which are known to produce moderate to severe emesis failed to respond to the smoked marijuana. The New York Summary Report concluded that while preliminary results of the "Inhalation Marijuana Research Project" were encouraging, further analysis, more data, and more research are needed.

22. The July 1983 Report of the State of Tennessee program to evaluate marijuana and THC in treatment of nausea and/or vomiting associated with cancer therapy indicates that 43 patients have been enrolled in the program. Of these, 27 were evaluated. The patients enrolled in the program self-evaluated their nausea and vomiting, appetite and food intake, physical state, mood, high, and dosages of the drugs they received. Twenty-one [21] of the 278 patients used marijuana cigarettes. Nineteen [19] of the 21 evaluated the cigarettes as successful, success being defined as partially, moderately or very effective. The major reason for failure of marijuana cigarettes was smoking intolerance.

23. Nausea and vomiting (emesis) are common side effects of cancer chemotherapy. Vomiting is controlled by two distinct areas in the brain, the vomiting center and the chemoreceptor trigger zone [CTZ]. Various cancer chemotherapeutic agents can trigger the vomiting center and the CTZ, thus causing nausea and vomiting. The incidence of emesis resulting from cancer chemotherapy often depends upon the type of agent used for the chemotherapy treatment. Chemotherapeutic agents most often associated with emesis also induce emesis of the greatest severity. Cisplatin causes the highest incidences of emesis, whereas methotrexate causes only a moderate incidence of emesis. Other factors not specifically related to chemotherapy can also influence a patient's emesis, such as emotional status, alcohol consumption, age, and past chemotherapy experience.

24. Prior to 1980, little research was conducted regarding antiemetics used to treat nausea and vomiting related to cancer chemotherapy. At that time, the most commonly used antiemetic was Compazine [prochlorperzine]. Com-

pazine was largely ineffective in treating emesis caused by most cancer chemotherapy regimens. Since 1980, research with new antiemetics has proliferated. As a result of this additional research, several new and highly effective antiemetics and their combinations are now available including: metoclopramide, thiethylperazine malate, haloperidol, droperidol, fluphenazine hydrochloride, perphenazine, lorazepam, dronabinol [synthetic THC] in sesame oil in a soft gelatin capsule, and nabilone [a synthetic substance chemically and pharmacologically similar to THC].

25. To properly evaluate the effectiveness of a new antiemetic drug, researchers must perform carefully conducted randomized, double-blind testing of the drug against either a placebo or an established antiemetic, using a statistically significant patient population. Several factors are important when planning or evaluating an antiemetic study: [a] Standardization of the emetic stimulus, [b] accuracy in data collection, with the use of objective parameters, such as the number of emetic episodes and the volume and duration of emesis, [c] standardization of patient population, with an indication of whether or not patients had previously received chemotherapy, and [d] proper selection of route of administration, and drug schedule and dosage, based upon proper trials with the agent. It is important to determine quantitatively the efficacy of antiemetic agents used singularly, so that results can be compared and further trials, including combination studies, can be planned appropriately.

26. For a new antiemetic drug to be considered effective, it must be as effective or more effective in controlling emesis than the currently-available antiemetics.

27. Relatively few scientific or medical studies have been conducted to evaluate marijuana's effectiveness as an antiemetic. Information concerning marijuana's antiemetic properties is primarily anecdotal. The research that has been conducted with marijuana has been primarily in the form of loose, uncontrolled studies which provide little valuable information as to the drug's effectiveness. Most re-

search with marijuana has been conducted under state protocols. The state sponsored research conducted thus far has not employed carefully controlled double-blind, randomized testing of marijuana, nor has it involved large patient populations. As a result, little reliable information can be gleaned from these types of studies.

28. Based upon the lack of quality testing, marijuana's antiemetic activity is not as established as that of THC or other available antiemetics. There are no double-blind randomized studies that conclude that marijuana is as effective or more effective than synthetic THC, or any of the other currently available antiemetics. In fact, in 1984, the only controlled, randomized, double-blind, crossover study comparing the antiemetic effectiveness of smoked marijuana to orally ingested synthetic THC involved 20 patients and concluded that orally ingested THC was superior to smoked marijuana.

29. Although THC is usually a constituent present in marijuana, since marijuana also contains at least 60 other active cannabinoids in varying quantities, the results of antiemetic trials using THC cannot be extrapolated in evaluating marijuana's antiemetic properties. For example, cannadibiol, a constituent present in marijuana, can potentiate some effects of THC, while suppressing other effects, including the antiemetic effect.

30. No formal, well-controlled studies have been conducted which compare marijuana's effectiveness as an antiemetic against any of the currently available antiemetics such as metoclopramide, haloperidol, dexamethasone, prochlorperazine, nabilone, lorazepam, or any of the highly effective combinations of available antiemetics.

31. The only studies which have been conducted using marijuana as an antiemetic include the following: [1] The state programs [discussed previously]; [2] the study mentioned above which compared smoked marijuana to oral synthetic THC and concluded that THC was more effective; [3] a "compassionate" study conducted by Thomas J. Ungerleider involving 16 bone marrow transplant patients. In

that study, the efficacy of the drug was measured only by subjective testing techniques; and [4] a study conducted by Alfred E. Chang which involved 15 patients receiving methotrexate chemotherapy.

32. The purpose of the Chang study was to compare the antiemetic effectiveness of THC to a placebo. Initially in the study, patients randomly received either an oral THC capsule or placebo capsule prior to chemotherapy. Neither the patients nor the researchers were aware of which drug they received. Three separate chemotherapy trials were conducted during the study. Only if the patient vomited during a trial would he or she receive a marijuana cigarette for the remaining doses of that chemotherapy trial. All patients who received marijuana cigarettes were experienced smokers. The study does not indicate how many patients resorted to smoking marijuana during each trial. Since six patients did not vomit at all on the THC, they did not receive marijuana cigarettes. The purpose of the study was not to compare the effectiveness of oral THC to marijuana but, rather, to compare THC's effectiveness against a placebo. Dr. Chang concluded that the combination of oral THC and smoked marijuana is a highly effective antiemetic in patients receiving methotrexate chemotherapy. Although Dr. Chang found that smoked marijuana was more reliable than oral THC in achieving therapeutic blood levels, he also found that it had drawbacks in patient acceptability; patients complained of its adverse taste, which induced nausea and vomiting in some instances. He also surmised that patients who are nonsmokers may not be willing and/or able to smoke marijuana. Based upon these drawbacks, Dr. Chang concluded that "an alternative parenteral drug route needs to be established if THC [or marijuana] is to have wide clinical acceptability." In addition, he determined that additional studies relating to drug tolerance, effectiveness against nausea and vomiting produced by other chemotherapy regimens, and comparisons with conventional antiemetics needed to be conducted.

33. A study conducted by Stephen E. Sallan, M.D., which

is cited by NORML and ACT, involved a double-blind, randomized evaluation of the antiemetic effect of synthetic THC capsules in 16 patients receiving chemotherapy [although 22 patients participated in the study, only 16 received oral THC]. There is no indication as to what types of chemotherapeutic agents were administered to the patients during the study. Dr. Sallan concluded that THC had antiemetic effects. Further, he made "preliminary observations" comparing the antiemetic effect of smoked marijuana and oral THC capsules, based upon some patients' illicit marijuana use which was neither qualitatively nor quantitatively controlled. He found that "[f]or most patients, both smoked and oral routes had identical effects." This study was not a scientific comparative study of smoked marijuana and oral THC, but a formal comparison between oral synthetic THC and placebo.

34. Even in its limited use, marijuana has not been shown to be very effective in reducing nausea and vomiting when used with chemotherapeutic agents which produce severe emesis.

35. In contrast to marijuana, synthetic oral THC [dronabinol], nabilone, metoclopramide, and other currently available antiemetics have been tested extensively through well-designed, controlled double-blind studies for both safety and efficacy. For example, more than 1,300 patients were tested with synthetic THC before it was made available as a Schedule II drug. Marijuana, on the other hand, has only been tested in 20 patients in a formal comparative study, and roughly less than 500 patients in loosely controlled state studies.

36. Neither marijuana nor oral THC has been demonstrated to be an effective antiemetic for patients receiving radiation therapy. In a THC study conducted at UCLA, Dr. Ungerleider concluded that oral THC was only slightly more effective than Compazine in controlling emesis caused by radiation therapy. No studies evaluating marijuana's effectiveness in this area were introduced during this proceeding.

37. Since the advent of the new, highly effective antiemetics, few cancer chemotherapy patients discontinue treatment as a result of nausea and vomiting.

38. Although the newer antiemetics and their combinations have been shown to be highly effective in treating emesis, even in conjunction with chemotherapy treatments known to produce severe nausea and vomiting in most patients, a small number of patients are refractory to all antiemetic treatment. There is no scientific or medical reason to believe that patients who do not respond well to currently-available antiemetics would respond any better after smoking marijuana. The only method to determine marijuana's effectiveness for that purpose would be to conduct controlled double-blind trials with the drug in that group of patients.

39. There is neither any scientific or medical support for the hypothesis that either marijuana or any of the cannabinoids are effective in treating emesis in children receiving chemotherapy treatments. Again, only controlled trials comparing marijuana to other available antiemetics could support that contention. No such trials have been conducted as of this time.

40. Smoking as a route of administration for antiemetics has not been demonstrated to be more advantageous than intravenous or oral administration. The claimed advantage of self-titration through smoking is only a hypothesis and has not been scientifically proven. In fact, oral administration of antiemetics is highly effective if effective antiemetics are given. Intravenous administration also is highly effective, especially since most chemotherapy agents are intravenously administered as well.

41. Currently available antiemetics are also highly effective in outpatient care. Most patients can receive the newer antiemetics on an outpatient basis. There is no scientific or medical reason to conclude that marijuana is better-suited than currently available antiemetics in the treatment of emesis of outpatients. Carefully conducted clinical trials would be needed to demonstrate otherwise.

42. In addition to not being as effective or more effective

than currently-available antiemetics, the use of smoked marijuana in the treatment of emesis in cancer patients has significant drawbacks. As a psychoactive substance, marijuana causes anxiety and panic in inexperienced users. Marijuana smoking also caused nausea and vomiting in some patients, and left an unpleasant residual taste. Because tachycardia and orthostatic hypotension are negative side effects of marijuana smoking, it should not be administered to patients with heart disease and angina. Marijuana smoking can also lead to pulmonary problems including bronchitis and emphysema. Marijuana is a crude plant material which contains pathogenic bacteria that could prove harmful to immuno-comprised patients with various cancers or leukemias. The cannabinoids present in marijuana can further suppress the immune functions of individuals whose immune systems are already severely compromised by chemotherapeutic agents. Also, few patients can tolerate marijuana smoking. In fact, in the state programs employing marijuana, significant numbers of patients either switched from smoking to oral THC capsules or withdrew from research because they could not tolerate smoking marijuana. In Dr. Ungerleider's study involving 16 bone marrow transplant patients, three dropped out of the study because they found marijuana smoking to be undesirable, even though at the time of the study, no other antiemetics were available to them. In addition, because of the lack of standardization of the drug and varying smoking techniques, there is a problem with bioavailability and reproductibility of an administered dose of the drug. If the dose is not constant from treatment to treatment, the patient may go unprotected.

43. The combination of currently available antiemetics produce less side effects than do each of the drugs given individually. These combinations produce less side effects than the cannabinoids, including marijuana. There is no scientific or medical evidence which demonstrates that marijuana produces fewer and less severe side effects than the currently-available antiemetics.

44. Patient satisfaction with combination antiemetic therapy is greater than that seen with marijuana.

45. Interest in research using marijuana to treat emesis in cancer chemotherapy patients has waned as the availability of new, highly-effective antiemetics has increased.

46. Patient interest in using marijuana to treat emesis due to chemotherapy has declined recently.

47. The oncological community does not consider marijuana to have currently accepted medical use in the United States for the treatment of emesis caused by cancer chemotherapy. In addition, David Ettinger, M.D., Richard Grall, M.D., and John Laszlo, M.D., each a highly respected oncologist and antiemetic researcher who has treated numerous patients and conducted extensive research with various cannabinoids and highly effective antiemetics, have concluded that based upon their research and knowledge of the field, marijuana does not have a currently accepted medical use in the United States for the treatment of emesis caused by cancer chemotherapy, nor has it been proven safe for use under medical supervision.

48. The American Cancer Society has concluded that insufficient research has been conducted to advocate that marijuana be used as an antiemetic for chemotherapy patients.

49. In its 1984 report, the National Academy of Sciences did not make any conclusions regarding marijuana's accepted medical use in the treatment of emesis in cancer chemotherapy patients. the only conclusion made in the report was that marijuana's antiemetic properties were less established than those of synthetic THC.

50. The American Medical Association has concluded that marijuana does not have a currently accepted medical use in the United States for the treatment of emesis caused by cancer chemotherapy, nor has it been proven to be safe for use under medical supervision.

51. Glaucoma is a term which describes a group of chronic ocular diseases which cause an increase in intraocular pressure that damages the retina and optic nerve and can lead to

eventual loss of vision. The most common form of glaucoma is primary open-angle glaucoma [POAG]. This form of glaucoma is caused by an obstruction in the pathways for fluid exit from the eye while fluid inflow continues unabated. As a result, the pressure within the eye [intraocular pressure] increases beyond a level tolerated by the eye and can cause damage to the retina and optic nerve.

52. Persons suffering from glaucoma have intraocular pressures which are higher than their eyes can tolerate. Traditionally, glaucoma was measured by a statistical measure of intraocular pressure [a norm], meaning that if an individual's pressure was higher than the average, he was thought to have glaucoma; if the pressure was below the norm, he was thought not to have glaucoma. It is now known that this is not the proper method for diagnosing glaucoma. Ninety-five percent of individuals with statistically-elevated intraocular pressure are never afflicted with glaucoma, while one-third of glaucomatose individuals have intraocular pressure in the statistically normal range.

53. Effective treatment for glaucoma involves the use of pharmaceutical agents or surgical procedures that prevent progressive optic nerve damage. If intraocular pressure can be lowered sufficiently, it can usually alter the course of the glaucoma. But, merely reducing intraocular pressure is not necessarily beneficial to the eye, and pressure reduction does not necessarily prevent glaucomatose optic nerve damage. For a treatment to be effective, it must lower intraocular pressure sufficiently to prevent additional damage to the optic nerve and retina and also not cause unacceptable damage to the eye or to other parts of the body. In addition, it must be able to sustain the lowered pressure and preserve visual function for the patient's lifetime.

54. When new glaucoma treatments are tested for efficacy, they are evaluated for their ability to sufficiently lower intraocular pressure and to maintain visual fields. To properly measure the treatment's effect on both, it must be used in long-term testing. Timolol, a drug currently used to treat glaucoma, has been tested in this manner. Before it was

approved for use in treating glaucoma, timolol was rigorously tested in 300 to 400 persons through controlled, double-masked clinical trials. These studies involved treating patients with the drug for a minimum of three months, with a majority of the studies lasting for six months or more, during which time, the patients' visual fields were measured to determine whether there had been any progression of the disease. In addition, other conventional glaucoma medications have proven their efficacy through years of clinical experience. The miotics, apinephrine compounds and carbonic anhydrase inhibitors have been proven effective in lowering intraocular pressure and preserving visual function.

55. The most efficacious way of delivering any drug to the eye is through a topical drop, rather than by systemic application. Topical application reduces the possibility of systemic adverse effects from a drug since the total amount of the drug being delivered to the body is considerably less.

56. In 1971, Robert S. Hepler, M.D. and Ira R. Frank, M.D. published preliminary results of one of the first experiments which measured the effect of smoked marijuana on intraocular pressures of normal, healthy males. The study involved acute administration of smoked marijuana through an ice-cooled water pipe to eleven youthful men who did not suffer from glaucoma. After the one-time administration of the marijuana, nine subjects experienced decreases in intraocular pressure which ranged from 16 percent to 45 percent, one subject experienced a 4 percent increase in intraocular pressure, and one subject experienced no change following smoking. These results were later published in 1974 as part of a larger study in which Thomas J. Ungerleider, M.D. participated, aimed at measuring pupillary constriction, intraocular pressure, tear production, and conjunctival hyperemia [redness and irritation of the eye]. The overall study involved 21 healthy subjects who smoked marijuana in an ice-cooled water pipe. Only the 11 subjects described in the earlier publication were tested for change in intraocular pressures. In addition to the results of changes in intraocu-

lar pressures, the authors also noted that smoking marijuana was associated with minor decreases in pupillary size,
decrease in tear production, and conjunctival hyperemia.
Central visual acuity, refraction, peripheral visual fields,
binocular fusion and color vision were not altered by the
single-dose administration of the marijuana. In addition,
the authors noted that fatigue and sleepiness occurred several hours following the marijuana-induced "high."

57. There are no published scientific reports or studies
which demonstrate marijuana's ability to lower intraocular
pressures in long-term chronic testing of glaucomatose research subjects. The only long-term study reported was one
conducted by Dr. Hepler at U.C.L.A. The study evaluated
response of 19 normal, non-glaucomatose patients for a period of 94 days. The results of the 94-day study were not
available at the time Dr. Hepler's paper was published. The
only conclusions made were that in the normal research
subjects, intraocular pressure showed a prompt drop as soon
as the subjects began to smoke, and that there were no
indications of cumulative effects upon the intraocular pressure response.

58. There are few published scientific reports or studies
which evaluate marijuana's effect on lowering intraocular
pressure in glaucomatose individuals. All of the studies
involve acute administration of the drug and each involve
relatively small numbers of research subjects. In 1976, Drs.
Hepler and Petrus reported the results of their study which
involved 12 research subjects who suffered from glaucoma.
Each subject was seen on four occasions. On one occasion,
the subjects were given a placebo in a smokable form; on the
other occasions, the subjects were either given oral [syn-
thetic] THC or smoke marijuana. Some of the research subjects continued their usual course of medication during the
testing. The published study only reported the results of
four of the research subjects. Two subjects failed to achieve a
reduction in intraocular pressure. Also, the study did not
indicate which of the four subjects, if any, had continued
their conventional medication during the study. The study

did not differentiate between the effectiveness of marijuana or oral THC. The researchers concluded that "patients with proven glaucoma frequently, although not invariable, demonstrate substantial decrease in intraocular pressure following smoking of marijuana or ingestion of THC." In 1976, Drs. Hepler, Frank and Petrus reported on the results of another small study involving 11 glaucomatose individuals who were observed after acute administration of marijuana. Of the 11 patients studied, seven demonstrated drops in intraocular pressure averaging 30 percent. The remaining four did not experience any drop in intraocular pressure.

In 1979, Drs. Merritt and Crawford published results of an acute study of the effects of marijuana and placebo on 16 glaucomatose research subjects. They concluded that "inhaled tetrahydrocannabinol [delta-9-tetrahydrocannabinol] lowers blood pressure and intraocular pressure, commensurately with tachycardia [rapid heart rate], in systemic normotensive and hypertensive glaucoma patients." In 1980, Drs. Merritt, Crawford, Alexander, Anduze, and Gelbart reported the results of a study which observed the effect of acute administration of marijuana and placebo to 18 glaucoma patients. They concluded that acute administration of marijuana lowered both intraocular pressure and blood pressure in a heterogeneous glaucoma population. They also noted that eight of the patients suffered from anxiety with tachycardia and palpitations; five suffered from postural hypotension [reduction in blood pressure upon standing]; 18 suffered from sensory alterations including hunger, thirst, euphoria, drowsiness and chills; and nine suffered from conjunctival hyperemia and ptosis [dropping upper eyelid]. Based on the side effects the researchers concluded that "it is because of the frequency and severity with which untoward events occurred that marijuana inhalation is not an ideal therapeutic modality for glaucoma patients." A total of no more than 50 glaucomatose individuals have been administered smoked marijuana in a research setting.

Approximately 40 of these individuals received marijuana during limited acute trials of the drug. The progress of the other individuals, who included Robert Randall and those who used the drug together with their conventional glaucoma medications, were never published since they only involved anecdotal observations, providing insufficient data to report which would be useful for ophthalmologists in treating glaucoma patients.

59. In 1976, Dr. Mario Perez-Reyes reported the results of his preliminary study of acute intravenous administration of various cannabinoids on intraocular pressure. Twelve normal, nonglaucomatose patients were injected with a variety of cannabinoids which are present in marijuana; the cannabinoids were administered individually so that the effects could be evaluated separately. He concluded that several of the cannabinoids had intraocular pressure lowering qualities, including delta-8-tetrahydrocannabinol, which is less psychoactive than THC. THC appears to be the most effective cannabinoid for acutely reducing intraocular pressure, but it is also the most psychoactive. Although marijuana, which consists of various cannabinoids, would have a different effect on eye pressure than one of its single constituents, the literature indicates that the effect would either be the same or less.

60. There are no published scientific or medical reports which evaluate marijuana's ability to preserve the visual function of glaucomatose individuals.

61. None of the IND reports or studies submitted in this processing have compared marijuana's effectiveness in lowering intraocular pressure and preserving visual function to any of the currently accepted glaucoma medications. Although not proven through comparative studies, it is accepted that reductions in intraocular pressure continue for longer periods of time following administration of either timolol, pilocarpine, or phospholine iodide, than following administration of smoked marijuana.

62. No evidence was introduced in this proceeding from states which have scientific protocols for researching marijuana's effect in the treatment of glaucoma. In 1986, the California Research Advisory Committee reported the re-

sults of its research protocol in this area which covered only the use of THC. Only one individual received marijuana cigarettes for glaucoma. This was after the Research Advisory Panel mailed information about the program to ophthalmologists throughout the State of California. Rhode Island reported that 28 ophthalmologists in that state were contacted to determine if they had any interest in conducting research with marijuana. None of the ophthalmologists contacted responded affirmatively. Those who responded to the inquiry claimed that the drugs which were currently available sufficiently controlled glaucoma.

63. Acute marijuana administration has demonstrated unacceptable negative side effects in research subjects participating in glaucoma studies. They include orthostatic hypotension, tachycardia, conjunctival hyperemia, euphoria, dysphoria, drowsiness, depersonalization, difficulty in concentrating and thinking, motor coordination impairment. Since the drop in intraocular pressure after smoking marijuana noted in acute studies lasts for approximately 4 to 5 hours, with the maximal fall occurring about 1 to 2 hours after administration, to be considered in treating glaucoma, marijuana would have to be administered 6 to 8 times per day for the duration of the disease. Such use constitutes chronic administration of the drug. The negative effects of chronic administration of marijuana have not been adequately tested. Yet, specific unacceptable negative effects can be attributed to chronic administration of marijuana. These include: possible brain damage, sore throat, rhinitis, bronchitis and emphysema; suppression of luteinizing hormone secretion in women [which affects the production of progesterone]; abnormalities in DNA synthesis, mitosis and growth; carcinogenicity; and genetic mutations.

64. While marijuana plant material and some cannabinoids have been shown to lower intraocular pressure in acutely-treated normal human volunteers and glaucoma patients, it may lower intraocular pressure without preventing visual impairment in glaucoma patients. As noted above, there has been no documentation that marijuana use

preserves the visual function of glaucomatose individuals. Because acute studies have shown that marijuana appears to act by lowering intraocular pressure and blood pressure concomitantly, there is some concern that lowering the blood pressure limits the blood supply to the optic nerve. Since the optic nerve relies on a constant supply of blood to function adequately, there is a concern that by reducing its blood supply by lowering systemic blood pressure, visual function will be further impaired in glaucomatose individuals.

65. Based on the lack of documented evidence showing its utility in lowering intraocular pressure in the long-term and maintaining visual function, coupled with the adverse side effects associated with its use, most experts agree that smoked marijuana has not been proven to be a viable drug for the treatment of glaucoma. These medical and scientific experts include: Mario Perez-Reyes, M.D. [a source often cited by NORML and ACT]; Robert Hepler, M.D.; Keith Green, Ph.D.; George Spaeth, M.D.; Leo Hollister, M.D.; Reese Jones, M.D. and Raphael Mechoulam, Ph.D. In addition, in previously published articles, John Merritt, M.D., a witness for ACT, has taken the position that glaucoma's use in treating glaucoma is unacceptable because of the frequent and untoward side effects associated with its use. Also, the American Academy of Ophthalmology, an organization which represents more than 12,000 physician members and approximately 6,000 other medical professionals who specialize in the field of ophthalmology, has taken the position that insufficient data exists to demonstrate the safety and efficacy of using smoked marijuana in the treatment of glaucoma. The National Academy of Sciences, another source frequently cited by NORML and ACT, also concluded that smoking marijuana is not suitable for the treatment of glaucoma.

66. Multiple Sclerosis [MS] is the major cause of neurological disability among young and middle-aged adults. It is a life-long disease which attacks the myelin sheath [the coating surrounding the message-carrying nerve fibers in the

brain and spinal cord]. Once the myelin sheath is destroyed, it is replaced by plaques of hardened tissue known as sclerosis. The plaques can obstruct impulses along the nerve systems which will produce malfunctions in the body parts affected by the damaged nervous system. The symptoms can include one or a combination of the following: weakness, tingling, impaired sensation, lack of coordination, disturbances in equilibrium, double vision, loss of vision, involuntary rapid eye movement, slurred speech, tremors, stiffness, spasticity [involuntary and abnormal contractions of muscle or muscle fibers], weakness of limbs, sexual dysfunction, paralysis, and impaired bladder and blower functions. Spasticity can also result from serious injuries to the spinal cord, not related to MS. The effects of MS are sporadic in most individuals and the symptoms occur episodically, either triggered by the malfunction of the nerve impulses or by external factors. Because of the variability of symptoms of the disease, MS is difficult to detect and diagnose. There is no known prevention or cure for MS; instead, there are only treatments for the symptoms.

67. There are no published scientific reports or studies which evaluate marijuana's effectiveness in treating spasticity. The only existing information regarding the use of marijuana to treat the effects of MS or spasticity is primarily anecdotal. Anecdotal information is only useful for providing a basis for conducting controlled research with the drug to evaluate its effectiveness. In order to sufficiently verify that a drug is effective for treating MS or spasticity, double-blind, controlled studies must be conducted on large groups of persons.

68. The only studies evaluating the effect of cannabinoids on MS and spasticity employed synthetic THC or cannabidiol. These studies have been uniformly small, and the data presented are insufficient to evaluate the nature and quality of controls used. In 1981, Drs. Denis J. Petro and Carl Ellenberger published the results of a limited acute study using synthetic THC. That study involved the acute administration of oral synthetic THC to nine MS patients.

The researchers noted that the spasticity scores of four of the nine patients improved significantly after the administration of the synthetic THC; one patient improved after receiving the placebo; only two of three patients who felt improved actually demonstrated improvement by objective criteria. The EMG index of spasticity [electromyography – a method of measuring reflex responses, neuromuscular function and condition, and extent of nerve lesion] was impractical in five of the nine patients. The researchers concluded that further study should be conducted to determine the effectiveness of THC or one of its derivatives in treating spasticity. In a 1986 abstract, W.C. Hanigan, R. Destree, and X.T. Troung reported the results of a 20-day study in which they administered oral synthetic THC to five spastic patients. They concluded that two patients experienced significant reductions in stretch resistance and reflex activity; and one patient withdrew from the study because of negative emotional side effects. In another abstract, R. Sandyk, P. Consroe, L. Stern and S.R. Snider, evaluated the effects of cannabidiol [a major nonpsychoactive cannabinoid of marijuana] on three patients suffering from Huntington's Disease [a progressive central nervous system disease characterized by muscular twitching of the limbs or facial muscles]. The first week they noted mild improvement in choreic movements. Improvement was noted the second week and remained stable for another two weeks. The only side effects observed were cases of transient, mild hypotension.

69. There are no reported scientific or medical studies which have compared the effectiveness of marijuana or its derivatives, with conventional treatments for MS and spasticity. There is no indication that marijuana would be more effective or safer than currently available treatments. In addition, conventional drugs may reduce spasticity with fewer side effects than marijuana.

70. No long-term clinical studies employing marijuana, or any of its derivatives, have been conducted with respect to treating MS or spasticity.

71. The long-term safety of using marijuana to treat MS and spasticity has yet to be established. Marijuana's long-term effects on memory and intellect, its pulmonary effects, risks in pregnancy, and tolerance to the drug, are unresolved. Since marijuana may have undesirable side effects at doses necessary to reduce spasticity, the use of marijuana for long-term treatment such as is needed to treat MS and spasticity would be worse than the disease itself.

72. None of the state reports submitted in this proceeding indicate that any state research with marijuana was conducted with respect to spasticity. The National Multiple Sclerosis Society does not advocate the use of marijuana to treat spasticity associated with MS. In addition, the International Federation of Multiple Sclerosis Societies does not recommend marijuana's use in treating spasticity. Also, noted neurologists who specialize in treating and conducting spasticity research, including Drs. Silberberg and Johnson, concluded that marijuana has not been proven to have an accepted medical use in the treatment of spasticity, nor has it been proven to be safe under medical supervision. Dr. Denis Petro, a witness for ACT, concluded in his synthetic THC study that "research needs to cover a larger and better controlled sample before any definitive statement would be possible."

73. Epilepsy involves the progressive recruitment of normal brain neurons into rhythmic and then high frequency bursting. With the overwhelming of inhibitory restraints, the pauses between bursts disappear and are replaced by tonic high frequency firing and the seizure appears. A prominent feature of epilepsy is its episodic nature.

74. There are no studies of the effects of crude marijuana on existing epileptic symptoms in man. Only survey and case report data are available. In 1976, Dennis M. Feenely reported the results of his survey among young epileptics in the Journal of the American Medical Association. In that survey, young epileptics were questioned about their illicit use of marijuana, amphetamine, LSD, barbiturate, cocaine and heroin. Most of the subjects reported that marijuana

had no effect on their seizures. In addition, one subject reported that his marijuana use reduced the frequency of seizures, while another subject claimed that marijuana caused him to have seizures. Also, published case reports indicate marijuana's conflicting properties of both reducing and causing seizures. Although case reports and surveys of this type are not highly reliable sources of scientific information, they follow the conflicting pattern suggested in animal studies employing synthetic THC.

75. Smoked marijuana has only been tested on experimental epilepsy in 1 study which evaluated marijuana's effect on seizures in 5 mongrel dogs. After chronic administration of marijuana smoke, 2 of the 5 dogs exhibited grand mal convulsions. In a study involving the administration of marijuana smoke to normal rats, "popcorn convulsions" [involuntary vertical jumping] were observed in 50% of the animals after 6 to 9 exposures to the drug.

76. Because of its potential to induce convulsant seizures, marijuana should not be used by epileptics.

77. Cannabidiol [CBD] has also been studied for its anticonvulsant effects in animals. CBD is neither psychoactive nor convulsant. Conclusions drawn from animal testing of this drug suggest that CBD shows promise to an anticonvulsant, and that its use should be clinically investigated in human epilepsy to determine its therapeutic utility.

78. Marijuana has not been proven to be an effective appetite stimulant, or antianorectic drug. Most studies have involved oral THC rather than marijuana. In a double-blind study employing smoked marijuana, normal patients using marijuana increased their caloric intake more than those using the placebo, but the variability was too great to draw any conclusions. Studies employing THC have failed to demonstrate an appreciable appetite stimulating or antianorectic effect. State reports of cancer chemotherapy patients receiving either synthetic THC or marijuana have failed to support any claims of marijuana's appetite stimulating properties. Several of the currently available antiemetics have appetite-stimulating properties. With patients under-

going cancer chemotherapy, controlling emesis generally eliminates problems with anorexia or appetite loss. Marijuana has not been compared with currently available anti-emetics to evaluate its appetite stimulating properties.

79. There is no scientific or medical indication that marijuana is effective in the treatment of alcoholism or drug addiction. Recent studies now demonstrate that abuse of marijuana and alcohol are frequently combined. In addition, animal studies present no evidence that marijuana is more effective than currently available treatments for opiate withdrawal.

80. Marijuana has not been demonstrated to be an effective analgesic. Studies have demonstrated that marijuana and THC both increase and decrease pain. In addition, there is no indication that marijuana or synthetic THC are as effective or more effective than currently available analgesics.

81. Marijuana has not been shown to be effective in the treatment of asthma and bronchial spasms. Although smoked marijuana and THC were found to have bronchodilating effects following acute and short-term administration, smoke, even if it provides relief, is not desirable for asthmatics. Also, long-term smoking of marijuana reduces bronchodilation and causes significant airway obstruction.

82. Although marijuana has also been suggested for several other medical problems, there is insufficient scientific data to support its use for these purposes. Although marijuana and some of the cannabinoids have sedative or hypnotic effects, their activity is not constant, nor is there any indication that marijuana is even comparable to currently-available antianxiety and insomnia medications. There also is no support for marijuana's use as an antidepressant drug. Nor is there sufficient indication that marijuana, or its constituents, would be a useful medical alternative in the treatment of hypertension, neoplasms [tumors], infections, or migraine headaches.

83. A primary method for determining whether a particular drug is safe for use under medical supervision is to weigh

actual therapeutic benefit against negative or unintended side effects. A side effect is a pharmacologic activity other than the desired effect. If the measurable therapeutic benefits of the drug outweigh its negative effects, the drug is generally considered safe for use; if the negative effects outweigh the therapeutic benefits, the drug is not considered safe for its intended use.

84. In evaluating the negative side effects of a drug, several factors are taken into consideration. Generally, initial animal studies are conducted to determine the drug's toxicity. An LD–50 is established [the dose which causes death in 50 percent of the animals tested]. Factors other than the LD–50 are also considered in determining safety and toxicity. Additional pharmacological data is also needed, including the drug's bioavailability, metabolic pathways and pharmacokinetics. Acute and chronic testing must be conducted; first in animals, then in humans.

85. Most pharmacological research with cannabis or its constituents has been conducted with orally ingested THC, not smoked marijuana. Although the pharmacologic effects are presumed to be similar, the studies with oral THC do not provide a complete picture of marijuana's effects. Few of the other cannabinoids have been pharmacologically evaluated. The health consequences from smoking marijuana are likely to be quite different from those or orally ingested THC. Yet most of the chronic animal studies have been conducted with oral or intravenous THC.

86. There is a need for more information about the metabolism of the various marijuana constituents and their biologic effects. This requires many more animal studies. Then the pharmacologic information obtained from the animal studies must be tested in clinical studies involving humans. The pharmacologic testing of cannabinoids in animals thus far has shown that while they do not appear to be highly toxic, they exert some alteration in almost every biological system that has been studied.

87. Well-designed studies on the health effects of marijuana are relatively few. This is especially true with respect

to chronic studies. Field studies in this area are deficient. Most are too small to detect unusual or rare consequences which could be of great importance. In addition, only modest research has been conducted using healthy male volunteers; very limited studies have been conducted using females, older individuals, or persons in poor health. The studies using marijuana on healthy male volunteers lead to a biased conclusions that the drug is safe without properly evaluating the populations at risk. To eliminate any such bias and to expand our knowledge of the chronic, long-term effects of marijuana use, sophisticated epidemiological studies of large populations, similar to those conducted for alcohol and tobacco use, must be done. It may take years of extensive research before all of marijuana's deleterious effects become apparent.

88. The acute effects of marijuana use are fairly well established. Marijuana smoking usually causes acute changes in the heart and circulation which are characteristic of stress, including rapid heart rate [tachycardia], orthostatic hypotension, and increased blood concentrations of carboxyhemoglobin [hemoglobin combined with carbon monoxide]. The drug is not indicated for persons who suffer from cardiovascular problems including angina, congestive heart failure, and arteriosclerosis. In addition, acute marijuana use also causes euphoria; dysphoria; anxiety, confusion; psychosis; drowsiness; convulsions; and impairment of motor coordination, tracking ability and sensory and perceptual functions. Based upon these effects, marijuana should not be used by anxious or depressed, or unrecognized psychotic individuals, or epileptics.

89. Many persons who have smoked marijuana in a research setting could not tolerate its harshness and complained of throat soreness and other problems associated with smoking as a route of administration. In addition, many patients cannot, and will not, smoke a substance like marijuana for therapeutic purposes.

90. Even though inadequate studies have been conducted concerning the effects of long-term chronic use of marijuana,

certain detrimental effects on respiratory and pulmonary functions are well-established. Marijuana smoke inhibits pulmonary antibacterial defense systems, possibly making marijuana users more susceptible to bacterial infections of the lung. One chronic smoking experiment tested pulmonary functions of healthy volunteer subjects before and after 47 to 59 days of daily smoking of approximately five cigarettes per day. The study concluded that very heavy smoking for only six to eight weeks caused mild but significant airway obstruction. In addition, a study of heavy hashish [a crude smokable preparation of cannabis resin] users revealed a high incidence of bronchopulmonary consequences, including chronic bronchitis, chronic cough, and mucosal changes of squamous metaplasia [a precancerous change]. Chronic smoking can also result in emphysema.

91. Regular and frequent marijuana smoking causes preneoplastic changes in airways similar to those produced by smoking tobacco. Marijuana smoke does not contain nicotine; but like tobacco, it does have an equally complex aerosol of particles in a vapor phase that form a tar mixture. The mixture contains many of the same hydrocarbons contained in tobacco tars which are thought to be associated with cancer causation. Marijuana also contains more tar than tobacco cigarettes. Animal studies using smoked marijuana have documented the growth of precancerous cells after 30 months. Dr. C. Leuchtenberger, a professor at the Swiss Institute for Experimental Cancer Research, noted that exposure of human lung explants to fresh marijuana or tobacco cigarette smoke evoked abnormalities in DNA synthesis, mitosis, and growth with consequent genetic disturbances that may lead to malignant transformation. The abnormalities were more pronounced following exposure to marijuana than to tobacco smoke. These findings were later confirmed in a similar study. Marijuana smoke also contains benzene, a substance associated with leukemia, and 2-aminonapthalene, which causes bladder cancer.

92. Recent evidence also indicates that marijuana can depress an individual's immune function. The immune sys-

tem's sensitivity to marijuana depends on the cannabinoid compound and varies among immune cell types. In addition to the various cannabinoids, bacteria present in the plant material can further affect the immune function. A number of microbial contaminants have been isolated from marijuana samples, including pathogenic aspergillus, *Klebsiella pneumoniae, Enterbacter agglomerans,* group D streptococcus, *Enterbacter cloace, Bacillus* sp. and salmonella enteritis. The bacteria were found in licit and illicit supplies of marijuana. At the Memorial Sloan-Kettering Cancer Center, it is estimated that 60 patients die each year from invasive aspergillus. Aspergillus was cultured from samples of marijuana from patients who developed invasive pulmonary and allergic bronchopulmonary aspergillus. The data supports the theory that marijuana smoking during periods of immunosuppression [as during cancer chemotherapy], may lead to infection. Therefore, because of its own immunosuppression properties, and its propensity for causing infections in immunosuppressed individuals, marijuana smoking may be contraindicated in chemotherapy patients.

93. Studies conducted with respect to passive inhalation of heavy marijuana smoke demonstrate that passive inhalation of a substantial amount of sidestream marijuana can produce subjective effects, plasma levels of THC and urinary cannabinoid metabolites, in subjects similar to those found after the smoking of marijuana. The researchers concluded that with sufficient time and high marijuana smoke conditions, it becomes difficult to distinguish between active smoking and passive inhalation.

94. Marijuana has also produced genetic and nongenetic birth defects in many animal species. Pure THC is not thought to produce permanent alterations of genes in cells studied to date, but other components of cannabis smoke can cause such mutations. When animals of one generation were exposed to cannabis smoke during pregnancy, birth defects were found in the third generation, suggesting that a gene change had been transmitted through second generation animals which were only exposed to cannabis smoke prior to

birth. Cannabis smoke has been related to the increased
numbers of early fetal deaths, decreased fetal weight, and
an increased death rate at birth in study animals. Although
there have been some cases reported of deformed babies
being born to marijuana smoking mothers, no causal links
can be made based upon the limited evidence. Further human research is necessary to establish or rule out such
effects. Based upon the insufficient and inconclusive research in this area, pregnant women and those with marginal fertility may be at risk in smoking marijuana, even at
moderate levels.

95. Chronic marijuana use may also have a toxic effect on
the human brain. Preliminary studies indicate that THC
changes the way sensory information gets into and is acted
on by the hippocampus. Chronic exposure damages and de-
stroys nerve cells and causes other changes which are identical to normal aging and may be additive to the aging
process. Therefore, chronic marijuana use could result in
serious or premature memory disorders. The results of these
studies are now being confirmed.

96. Animal studies and some human studies have found
that in males, sperm count and motility are decreased during cannabis use. In female animals, THC suppresses the
secretion of luteinizing hormone. Prolonged suppression
would eventually lower gonadal steroid levels. Whether
these changes have any effect on human sexual function and
fertility is not yet known.

97. In addition to the known and suspected health risks
associated with marijuana use, there is also evidence to
suggest that tolerance to its therapeutic effects also develops.

98. The National Academy of Sciences found that the dose
of marijuana necessary to produce a therapeutic benefit is
often close to one that produces an unacceptable frequency
of toxic side effects.

99. The severity and frequency of negative side effects
experienced from marijuana smoking exceed those caused

by accepted medications used to treat glaucoma, emesis and Multiple Sclerosis and spasticity.

100. Because of its unacceptable side effects and undetermined therapeutic utility, smoked marijuana is not recommended for the treatment of glaucoma, emesis, Multiple Sclerosis and spasticity, epileptic seizures and convulsions, asthma, appetite loss or anorexia, alcoholism and drug abuse, pain and inflammation, anxiety, insomnia, migraine headaches, hypertension, depression, infections or tumors.

Conclusion

The Administrator finds that the administrative law judge failed to act as an impartial judge in this matter. He appears to have ignored the scientific evidence, ignored the testimony of highly-credible and recognized medical experts and, instead, relied on the testimony of psychiatrists and individuals who used marijuana. The administrative law judge relied heavily on anecdotal accounts of marijuana use by both physicians and seriously ill persons. The administrative law judge's findings of fact ignored any evidence presented by the Government. For example, in his findings regarding marijuana and nausea and vomiting associated with chemotherapy, judge Young cites many of the physicians presented by the pro-marijuana parties by name as accepting marijuana as "medically useful." Not once in his findings or discussion does the judge acknowledge or mention the Government's experts. Not once does the judge mention why he chose to find the pro-marijuana parties' evidence more credible. The administrative law judge failed to acknowledge the position of a major organization of physicians, the American Medical Association; and those of organizations whose existence is dedicated to the treatment and study of the diseases at issue such as the American Cancer Society, the National Academy of Ophthalmology and the National Multiple Sclerosis Society. He chose instead to rely on the testimony of a very small number of physicians. Most significantly, the administrative law judge did not follow the standard for "accepted medical use in treatment in the United States," and "accepted safety for use * * * under medical supervision" established by the Administrator in previous scheduling proceedings. The administrative law judge chose instead, to develop his own standard for both accepted medical use and accepted safety; standards which were specifically rejected by the Administrator in the scheduling of 3,4-methylenedioxymethamphetamine [MDMA].

The administrative law judge did not apply his own standard consistently. While the administrative law judge found that marijuana had an accepted medical use in treatment of nausea and vomiting associated with chemotherapy; of spasticity associated with multiple sclerosis and amputation; and of pain associated with hyperparathyroidism; he concluded that it did not have accepted medical use in treatment of glaucoma. His rationale was that in applying his standard of accepted medical use, which is that a "significant minority" of physicians accept marijuana as medically useful, there were not enough physicians to establish such a "significant minority" with respect to glaucoma. He found that one physician's opinion was sufficient to establish an accepted medical use of marijuana regarding hyperparathyroidism, because it was a rare disease.

The Administrator rejects the administrative law judge's findings and conclusions. They were erroneous; they were not based upon credible evidence; nor were they based upon evidence in the record as a whole. Therefore, in this case, they carry no weight and do not represent the position of the agency or its Administrator. The inadequacy of Judge Young's analysis of the case is exemplified by his acceptance of, and reliance upon, irresponsible and irrational statements propounded by the pro-marijuana parties. Such statements include the following: "marijuana is far safer than many of the foods we commonly consume. For example, eating ten raw potatoes can result in a toxic response. By comparison, it is physically impossible to eat enough marijuana to induce death." That such a statement would come from the proponents of marijuana is understandable. To give it the weight of an administrative law judge's finding is appalling.

The Administrator has accepted the agency's findings of fact as his own. In order to conclude that these facts support a conclusion that marijuana remain in Schedule I, they must be applied to the criteria set forth in the Controlled Substances Act for substances in Schedule I.

The three criteria are found at 21 U.S.C. 812[b][1] and are as follows:

[a] The drug or other substance has a high potential for abuse,

[b] The drug or other substance has no currently accepted medical use in treatment in the United States,

[c] There is a lack of accepted safety for use of the drug or other substance under medial supervision.

For purposes of this proceeding, the parties stipulated that marijuana has a high potential for abuse. The criteria for substances listed in Schedule II also includes that the drug has a high potential for abuse.

The issue of what "currently accepted medical use in treatment in the United States," and "accepted safety for use * * * under medical supervision" mean, has been the subject of a previous scheduling proceeding involving the drug MDMA. In that proceeding, the Administrator did not adopt Judge Young's recommendation and defined both phrases to mean approved for marketing as safe and effective pursuant to the Food, Drug, and Cosmetic Act. 51 FR 36552, October 8, 1986. The Administrator's decision was reviewed by the United States Court of Appeals for the First Circuit in *Grinspoon v. DEA,* 828 F.2d 881 [1987]. The Court remanded the matter to the Administrator finding that his standard was too restrictive. The Court did not suggest a standard to be adopted and, instead, stated that "Congress has implicitly delegated to the Administrator the authority to interpret these portions of the CSA * * *" *Grinspoon,*

p. 892. The Administrator then published a reviewed final rule in which he listed several characteristics of a drug or other substance which has an "accepted medical use in treatment in the United States." 53 FR 5156, February 22, 1988. These characteristics are:

1. Scientifically determined and accepted knowledge of its chemistry;

2. The toxicology and pharmacology of the substance in animals;

3. Establishment of its effectiveness in humans through scientifically designed clinical trials;

4. General availability of the substance and information regarding the substance and its use;

5. Recognition of its clinical use in generally accepted pharmacopeia, medical references, journals or textbooks;

6. Specific indications for the treatment of recognized disorders;

7. Recognition of the use of the substance by organizations or associations of physicians; and

8. Recognition and use of the substance by a substantial segment of the medical practitioners in the United States.

These characteristics rely heavily on verifiable scientific data and acceptance by the medical community. These two areas go hand-in-hand, as aptly demonstrated by the record in this proceeding. Most physicians and organizations of physicians rely on scientific data in formulating their opinions regarding the safety and effectiveness of a drug and whether they will provide it for their patients. Many of the experts and organizations who concluded that marijuana did not have an "accepted medical use in treatment in the United States," stated that they reached this conclusion because of the lack of adequate scientific data to support the safety and efficacy of marijuana. The Administrator also notes that the Controlled Substances Act and its legislative history require him to consider scientific evidence in determining the schedule in which a drug should be placed. For example, the Controlled Substances Act at 21 U.S.C. 811[c] lists eight factors to be considered in evaluating the three scheduling criteria. Included among those factors are "scientific evidence of its pharmacological effect, if known" and "the state of current scientific knowledge regarding the drug or other substance." In addition, the Controlled Substances Act requires the Administrator to request a scientific and medical evaluation from the Secretary of Health and Human Services. The Administrator is then bound by the Secretary's recommendation as to scientific and medical matters. 21 U.S.C. 811[b]. In this proceeding, the Assistant Secretary for Health has provided the Administrator with an extensive scientific and medical evaluation in which it was recommended that marijuana remain in Schedule I because there is insufficient scientific and medical evidence to conclude that marijuana is a safe and effective drug.

It is clear from the evidence presented in this proceeding that marijuana does not have the characteristics of a drug which has an "accepted medical use in treatment in the United States." Because of the complex composition of marijuana, containing over 400 separate constituents [many of which have not been tested] varying from plant to plant, the chemistry, toxicology and pharmacology of marijuana is not established. As discussed previously, the effectiveness of marijuana has not been documented in humans with scientifically-designed clinical trials. While many individuals have used marijuana and claim that it is effective in treating their ailments, these testimonials do not rise to the level of scientific evidence. Marijuana is available from the Federal Government to those researchers who obtain proper licensure. However, the evidence suggests that only small numbers of researchers and physicians have obtained marijuana for this purpose, and that some research programs sponsored by states had trouble getting physicians to participate. The vast majority of physicians do not accept marijuana as having a medical use. Marijuana is not recognized as medicine in generally accepted pharmacopeia, medical references, journals or textbooks. As evidenced by expert physician testimony and the statements of many professional medical and research organizations, marijuana is not accepted by organized medicine or a substantial segment of the physician population. The administrative law judge's conclusion that a "respectable minority" of physicians is all that is necessary to establish accepted medical use in treatment in the United States is preposterous. By placing a substance in Schedule II, the Administrator, and through him, the Federal Government, establishes a national standard for drug use. Using the same criteria as medical malpractice cases to determine a national standard of medical acceptance is untenable. It must be recognized that in every profession, including the medical and scientific community, there are those that deviate from the accepted practices of the profession. These deviations may be the beginning of new revolutionary treatments or they may be rejected as quackery. The opinions of those few physicians and scientists are not sufficient to create a finding of national acceptance. The Administrator feels that, in light of the potential risks of declaring a drug has an accepted medical use in treatment in the United States, he must adhere to the strict standard that was established in the MDMA proceeding. It is clear that the evidence conclusively demonstrates that marijuana does not have an accepted medical use in treatment in the United States or an accepted medical use with severe restrictions.

The Administrator's standard for "accepted safety for use * * * under medical supervision" was also stated in the second MDMA final rule published on February 22, 1988, 53 FR 5156. The tests for determining accepted safety of a drug were stated as follows:

The first requirement in determining safety of a substance is that the chemistry of the substance must be known and reproducible. The next step is to conduct animal toxicity studies to show that the substance will not produce irreversible harm to organs at proposed human doses. Limited clinical trials may then be initiated, but they must be carefully controlled so that adverse effects can be monitored and studies terminated if necessary * * * safety in humans is evaluated as a risk/benefit ratio for a specific use. 53 FR 5158.

It is clear that marijuana cannot meet the criteria set forth above for safety under medical supervision. The chemistry of marijuana is not known and reproducible. The record supports a finding that marijuana plant material is variable from plant to plant. The quantities of the active constituents, the cannabinoids, vary considerably, In addition, the actions and potential risks of several of the cannabinoids have not been studies. Animal toxicity studies with marijuana show several potential risks or hazards of marijuana use, especially when the marijuana is smoked. These hazards have not been evaluated against the benefit or effectiveness of the drug. This is due, in great part, to the fact that marijuana's effectiveness in treating specific medical conditions has not been established by reliable scientific studies. Since a prior risk/benefit ratio cannot be made, the safety of marijuana for medical use cannot be demonstrated. Such lack of information is the basis for the majority of the medical and scientific community, and the Food and Drug Administration, concluding that marijuana does not have "accepted safety for use * * * under medical supervision." The Administrator, therefore, concludes that marijuana lacks "accepted safety for use * * * under medical supervision."

As a final note, the Administrator expresses his displeasure at the misleading accusations and conclusions leveled at the Government and communicated to the public by the pro-marijuana parties, specifically, NORML and ACT. These two organizations have falsely raised the expectations of many seriously ill persons by claiming that marijuana has medical usefulness in treating emesis, glaucoma, spasticity and other illnesses. These statements have probably caused many people with serious diseases to experiment with marijuana to the detriment of their own health, without proper medical supervision, and without knowledge about the serious side effects which smoking or ingesting marijuana may cause. These are not the Dark Ages. The Congress, as well as the medical community, has accepted that drugs should not be available to the public unless they are found by scientific studies to be effective and safe. To do otherwise is to jeopardize the American public, and take advantage of desperately ill people who will try anything to alleviate their suffering. The Administrator strongly urges the American public not to experiment with a potentially dangerous, mind-altering drug such as marijuana in an attempt to treat a serious illness or condition. Scientific and medical researchers are working tirelessly to develop treatments and drugs to treat these diseases and conditions. As expressed in the record, treatments for emesis [nausea and vomiting] associated with cancer chemotherapy have advanced significantly in the last ten years. Recent studies have shown an over 90 percent rate of effectiveness for the new antiemetic drugs and therapies. NORML and ACT have attempted to perpetrate a dangerous and cruel hoax on the American public by claiming marijuana has currently accepted medical uses. The Administrator again emphasizes that there is insufficient medical and scientific evidence to support a conclusion that marijuana has an accepted medical use for treatment of any condition, or that it is safe for use, even under medical supervision.

Based upon the evidence in the record and the conclusions discussed previously, the Administrator, under the authority vested in the Attorney General by section 201[a] of the Controlled Substances Act [21 U.S.C. 811[a]] and delegated to the Administrator of the Drug Enforcement Administration by regulations of the Department of Justice, 28 CFR 0.100[b], hereby orders that marijuana remain a Schedule I controlled substance as listed in 21 CFR 1308.11[d][14].

This order is effective December 29, 1989.

WHERE TO GET HELP AND INFORMATION

There are many local, state and national organizations, both public and private, that help families deal with drug dependence. Following is a list of some of the resources available nationally.

ACTION
Drug Prevention Program
Room M–606
806 Connecticut Ave., N.W.
Washington, D.C. 20525

Committees of Correspondence
Connie and Otto Moulton
57 Conant Street, Rm 113
Danvers, MA 01923
(508) 774-2641

National Parents Resource Institute for Drug Education (PRIDE)
1-800-241-7946
Information on signs and symptoms of drug abuse; prevention programs; referrals for treatment; free written information.

Drug Abuse Resistance Education (DARE)
1-800-223-DARE
Information for educators and parents for teaching children how to resist peer pressure to use drugs and alcohol.

National Institute of Drug Abuse
1-800-662-HELP
Information on drug/alcohol treatment programs.

The National Institute on Drug Abuse Workplace Helpline
1-800-843-4971
For employers who would like to establish drug-abuse programs.

Cocaine Hotline
1-800-COCAINE
24-hour information on cocaine/crack treatment programs.

National Clearinghouse for Alcohol and Drug Information
1-301-468-2600
P.O. Box 2345
Rockville, MD 20852

Campuses Without Drugs
2350 Holly Drive
Pittsburgh, PA 15235
412-731-8019

US Dept. of Education Alcohol and Drug Abuse Education
Program
1-202-732-3030
400 Maryland Avenue, S.W.
Room 4145/MS 6411
Washington, D.C. 20202
Information to help schools reduce alcohol and drug use.

SELECTED BIBLIOGRAPHY

Agurell, S., W.L. Dewey, R.E. Willette. *The Cannabinoids.* New York: Academic Press, 1984.

Bejerot, N. *Addiction and Society.* Springfield, Ill.: Charles C. Thomas, 1970.

Braude, M., and Szara, S., eds. *The Pharmacology of Marijuana.* New York: Raven Press, 1976.

Brecher, E.M., and Editors of Consumer Reports. *Licit and Illicit Drugs.* Boston: Little, Brown, 1972.

"Chronic Cannabis Use." *Annals of the New York Academy of Sciences.* 282 (1976): 1–430.

de Felice, P. *Poisons Sacrés, Ivresses Divines.* Paris: Editions Albin Michel, 1936.

Dupont, R.L. Jr. *Getting Tough on Gateway Drugs.* American Psychiatric Press. Washington D.C., 1984.

Grinspoon, L. *Marihuana Reconsidered.* Cambridge, Mass.: Harvard University Press, 1971, 1977.

Harvey, D., Paton, W.D.M. and Nahas, G.G., eds. *Marihuana 1984.* Oxford: I.R.L. Press, 1985.

Hollister, L.E. Health Aspects of Cannabis. *Pharmacological Reviews* 38 (1986):2–20.

Lindesmith, A.R. *The Addict and the Law.* Bloomington, IN: Indiana University Press, 1965.

MacDonald, D.I. *Drugs, Drinking, and Adolescents.* Yearbook Medical Publishers. Chicago, 1984.

Mann, P., *Marihuana Alert.* New York: McGraw Hill, 1984.

"Marihuana: Chemistry, Pharmacology, and Patterns of Social Use." *Annals of the New York Academy of Sciences* 191 (1971):1–269.

Marijuana and Health: An Institute of Medicine, National Academy of Sciences Report, Washington, DC, 1982.

Maugh, T.H. "Marihuana: New Support for Immune and Reproductive Hazards." *Science.* 190 (1975):865–867.

Mendelson, J.H., Rossi, A.M., Meyer, R.E., *The use of marihuana*. New York, Plenum Press, 1974.

Miller, L.L. *Marijuana: Effects on Human Behavior*. New York: Academic Press, 1974.

Moreau, J.J. *Hashish and Mental Illness*. Edited by H. Peters and G. Nahas, New York: Raven Press, 1973.

Nahas, G.G. *Marihuana, Deceptive Weed*. New York: Raven Press, 1973, 1975.

Nahas, G.G., *Physiopathology of Illicit Drugs (Cannabis, Opiates, Cocaine)*. Pergamon-Macmillan, 1991.

Nahas, G.G., and H.C. Frick. *Drug Abuse in the Modern World*. New York: Pergamon Press, 1981.

Nahas, G.G., with D. Harvey, M. Paris and H. Brill. *Marihuana in Science and Medicine*. New York: Raven Press, 1984.

Nahas, G.G., Paton, W.D.M. *Marihuana, Biological effects*. Oxford: Pergamon Press, 1979.

Nahas, G.G., Paton, W.D.M., and Idanpaan-Heikkila, J., eds. *Marihuana: Chemistry, Biochemistry, and Cellular Effects*. New York: Springer-Verlag, 1976.

Olds, J. *Drives and reinforcements*. New York. Raven Press, 1977.

Rosenthal, F. *The Herb Hashish versus medieval Muslim Society*. Leiden: E.J. Brill, 1971.

Rubin, V. and Comitas, L. *Ganja in Jamaica*. The Hague: Mouton, 1975.

Stefanis, C., Dornbush, R., Fink, M. *Hashish: Studies of long term use*. New York, Raven Press, 1977.

Tinklenberg, J.R., ed. *Marijuana and Health Hazards: Methodological Issues in Current Research*. New York: Academic Press, 1975.

U.S. Congress, Senate Subcommittee on Internal Security. *Marihuana-Hashish Epidemic and Its Impact on United States Security*. 93 Congress, 2d session, 1974.

U.S. National Commission on Marihuana and Drug Abuse. *Marijuana: A Signal of Misunderstanding*. First Report, Washington, D.C.: U.S. Government Printing Office, 1972.

Wilson, C.W.M. *Adolescent Drug Dependence.* Oxford: Pergamon Press, 1968.

Wittenborn, J.R., Brill, H., Smith, J.P., and Wittenborn, S.A. *Drugs and Youth.* Springfield, IL: Charles C. Thomas, 1969.

World Health Organisation Addiction Research Foundation (Toronto). Health Hazards of Cannabis. Toronto, 1983.

Index